CORPORATE COMMUNICATION

CORPORATE COMMUNICATION

Paul A. Argenti
The Amos Tuck School of Business Administration
Dartmouth College

IRWIN

Burr Ridge, Illinois
Boston, Massachusetts
Sydney, Australia

Senior sponsoring editor:	Craig Beytien
Marketing manager:	Kurt Messersmith
Project editor:	Rebecca Dodson
Production manager:	Jon Christopher
Art coordinator:	Heather Burbridge
Art studio:	Jay Benson Studios
Compositor:	TCSystems, Inc.
Typeface:	10/12 Times Roman
Printer:	Malloy Lithographing, Inc.

Library of Congress Cataloging-in-Publication Data

Argenti, Paul A.
    Corporate communication / Paul A. Argenti.
       p.   cm.
    Includes index.
    ISBN 0-256-05705-2
    1. Communication in management. 2. Communication in
organizations. I. Title.
    HD30.3.A73 1994
    658.4'5—dc20   93–1310

Printed in the United States of America
  4 5 6 7 8 9 0 ML 0 9 8 7 6 5

To Mary, Julia, and Lauren.

This book grows out of more than 10 years of work in developing a new field of study that I will refer to in this book as *corporate communication*. While the term itself is not new, the notion of it as a functional area of management equal in importance to finance, marketing, and production is very new. In the last decade, more and more companies have come to realize the importance of a unified communication function, and senior managers tend to realize it more than anyone else.

In this introduction, I would like to talk a bit more about my expertise, what the book is all about, and why I think everyone involved in organizations today needs to know about this emerging discipline.

Author's Expertise

For the last 12 years, I have been a professor of management communication at the Tuck School of Business at Dartmouth College. Prior to that, I taught at the Columbia and Harvard Business Schools.

The tradition of teaching communication has been a long one at Tuck, but as at most schools, the focus was always on skills development, including primarily speaking and writing. The first development in the evolution of this new field was an interest among businesspeople about how to deal with the media. Since this mostly involved applying oral presentation skills in another setting, the faculty teaching communication were a logical choice for taking on this new task. So, when I began teaching the first management communication course in 1981 at Tuck, I was asked to include a component on dealing with the media. I became interested in this through my study of marketing and had already written my first case on the subject, Hooker Chemical, which appears in Chapter 1.

Over the years, my interest in the subject grew beyond how companies deal with the media to how they deal with all communication problems. As I began to write more case studies on the subject and to work with managers inside companies, I saw the need for a more integrated function. The reason for this is that I found most companies, and, indeed, all organizations, conducting communication activities in a highly decentralized way.

For example, the employee communication function at Hewlett-Packard in the mid-1980s was in the personnel department, where it had always been, when I wrote a case on how HP dealt with voluntary severance and early retirement programs. As I looked at other companies I found basically the same structure everywhere. Yet the people in those various personnel departments were doing exactly the same thing internally that a communication specialist in the public relations department was doing for the external audience—sending a specific company message to a specific audience.

The same was true in terms of investor-relations functions, which were typically found in the treasury department in most companies until very recently. Why? Because the chief financial officer or the treasurer was the one who knew the most about the company's financial performance and traditionally had been responsible for developing the annual report. Communication was seen as a vehicle for getting that information out rather than as a function in itself.

Again as I worked with companies on developing new identities and images, I tended to find marketing people involved because they had traditionally dealt with image in terms of products and services and were often the most quotable personalities. Yet those marketing folks didn't always know what was being communicated to the press or to securities analysts by their counterparts in other functional areas.

All of these experiences led me to believe that companies and other organizations, from universities to churches to law firms, could do a much better job of communicating with everyone if they lumped all of their communication activities under one umbrella. That was the theory at least, but I could find precious little evidence in practice.

Then, in 1990, I was fortunate enough to be given a consulting assignment that allowed me to put into practice what I had been talking about in theory for many years. I received a call from the chairman and chief executive officer of a major corporation after my picture appeared on the front page of the *New York Times* Sunday business section in an article about how professors were teaching business students about dealing with the media.

Ostensibly, the chairman's call was about how his company could get more credit for the great things it was doing. Specifically, he wanted to know if I had a "silver bullet." My "silver bullet," as it turned out, was the development of a new corporate communication function for the company.

As with most companies, they had let communication functions decentralize into a variety of other functional areas over the years with the predictable result: no integration. The public relations people were saying one thing, the investor relations folks were saying another; the marketing folks were developing communication strategies for the outside and the personnel department for inside.

But no one except the chairman, who sat at the top of this $30 billion behemoth, could see the big picture, and none of those intimately involved with the various activities had an inside track on the overall strategy for the firm. Over the next year and a half, the chairman and I came up with the first integrated communication function that had all of the different subsets I had tried unsuccessfully to bring together at other companies and even at my own university.

This manager had the courage to try, and as a result he was able to change the impression people have about his business. We changed everything—from the company's image to its relationship with securities analysts on Wall Street. Today this company has one of the very few totally integrated communication functions anywhere in the world. This book will explain what all of the component parts of this new function are all about.

What Is This Book About?

In Chapter 1, "It's a New World," I describe the changes that have taken place over the last half century that led inexorably to the development of the new, totally integrated corporate communication function. While attitudes about business have never been totally positive at any time in history, they have reached an all-time low in the last 20 years.

Hooker Chemical serves as a case in point at the end of this chapter. This company faced the worst environmental problem any company had ever seen until the late 1970s. Were they really responsible for what happened at Love Canal, or was it a much more complicated situation?

In Chapter 2, "Reinventing Communications," I talk about how companies should use a more strategic approach to communications. In the past, most communication activities were dealt with reactively as organizations responded to events in the world around them. When Morton Thiokol was blamed for a crack in the space shuttle that led to the disastrous explosion several years ago, they had to react to the allegations with little information to go on. Wouldn't it have been much easier if they had planned on dealing with crises before, rather than after something so horrible happened?

In the Brown & Sharpe case, we find an example of a company that knew exactly what it was about and was thus able to deal with a labor crisis by using a coherent communication strategy rather than simply reacting to the crisis for the short term.

In Chapter 3, "An Overview of the Corporate Communication Function," I go into detail about the evolution of the corporate communication function. I also describe each of the subfunctions that should be included in the ideal corporate communication department.

The fictional Deltoid Corporation presents a hypothetical situation in which a company is struggling with developing the communication function.

In Chapter 4, "Image and Identity," I describe the first, and probably the most important, function of a corporate communication department—to reflect the actual reality of the firm itself through visual images and the right choice of words. The study of image and identity has blossomed in the last decades as graphic designers have worked with companies to develop the right look for a particular approach to the marketplace.

The General Electric Corporation serves as an example of how one company deals with image and identity.

Organizations also reflect their image and identity through advertising. In Chapter 5, "The Corporation is the Message," we take a look at how companies use mass advertising to sell the organization as a whole as opposed to just the products or services they offer to the public. Sometimes companies do this because they have so many different components as a result of the merger-and-acquisition-crazed 1980s. Companies also use corporate, as opposed to product, advertising to present a point of view on a topic of importance to the corporation or organization.

The exercise at the end of Chapter 5 represents some recent campaigns.

Next, in Chapter 6, "No More Press Releases," we look at how today's corporate communications function has evolved away from the public relations function of old. In the old days, companies would hire a former journalist to put out one press release after another for a less-than-eager media. Today we use more sophisticated methods that rely on building relationships with journalists before you have a specific story to sell them.

The Adolph Coors Company serves as a case in point for this chapter. In the case, we see how this company dealt with the formidable "60 Minutes" as it came to rake the company over the coals.

The finance function has been affected by corporate communications as well. In Chapter 7, "A Random Walk Down Wall Street," we see how companies are using communication strategies to deal with analysts, shareholders, and other important constituencies. In the past, this corporate communication subfunction would be dealt with by managers with excellent financial skills and mediocre communication skills. Yet these financial experts would also have to produce a slick annual report to compete with other firms in the industry.

Our case in point this time is Jewett Bank (disguised), which had to convince Wall Street that it was worth investing in despite some minor crises and management turnover.

Perhaps the most important function of all, however, deals with an internal rather than an external, constituency. In Chapter 8, "Communicating Internally," we look at employee communication's migration away from the human resources area.

Hanover Software (disguised) shows one company's attempt to deal with voluntary severance and outplacement issues related to downsizing.

No matter how well an organization plans or develops strategies, it inevitably will have to deal with some kind of crisis. In Chapter 9, "What to Do When It Hits the Fan," we look at how companies should prepare for the inevitable. Many authors have lauded Johnson & Johnson for its exemplary handling of the Tylenol crisis in the 1970s. But, it's a lot easier to deal with a crisis that was not really your fault, as in this case, than when you are really the one to blame.

Our case in point at the end of this chapter is Exxon's *Valdez* crisis. No external force created this problem; it was a case of someone's negligence within the company. How did the company respond to this incredible environmental disaster? Could they have prepared for this in a different way?

Why Is CorpComm So Important Today?

Every functional area at one time or another was the newest and most important one of all. But as we look toward the 21st century, the importance of communication is obvious to virtually everyone. Why is that more true today than when other functional areas developed?

First, we live in a more sophisticated era in terms of communication. Information travels with lightning speed from one side of the world to another as a result of technological developments that we could only have dreamed about at the beginning of this century.

Second, the general public is more sophisticated in its approach to organizations than before. People tend to be more skeptical and more educated. Thus, companies cannot get by on statements like, "What's good for General Motors is good for everyone," or, "If we build a better mouse trap, customers will beat a path to our door." Maybe not, if they don't know who you are.

Third, information comes to us in more beautiful packages than it did before. We now expect to see a glossy annual report from a major corporation. We don't want to walk into grimy-looking stores even for our discount shopping. Gas stations are modern looking and totally designed from top to bottom by fancy New York design firms.

Fourth, organizations are more complex today. In earlier times, and even for very small organizations today, companies were small enough that they could get by with much less sophisticated communications activities. Often, one person could do many different functions at one time. But in organizations with thousands, even hundreds of thousands, of people, it is much more difficult to keep track of all the different pieces that make up a coherent communication strategy.

This same development is taking place in Japan, which until very recently, has been able to keep communications very personal. All of the employees in a department still sit in one huge room rather than different offices. As companies get larger, they need to allow communication between different departments. But how do you maintain the same level of quality in communications when the company is spread throughout the world with people from many different cultures, as is the case with Toyota?

This book describes not only what's happening in a new era of advanced communications but what you can do to keep your company one step ahead of the competition. By creating a coordinated, coherent corporate communication system, your organization will be able to face the new century with the strategies and tools that few companies in the world have at their fingertips.

I hope you enjoy reading about this exciting new field as much as I have enjoyed discovering it hidden among the different departments. I am sure that 20 years from now, when another functional area develops that we cannot even imagine right now, much will have been written about this field and most complex organizations will have a corporate communication department with many of the subsets described in this book. Until then, however, join me in exploring what to many is still the great unknown.

Throughout this book you will find cases or examples of company situations that typically relate to material covered in each of the chapters.

What Are Cases?

Cases are much like short stories in that they present a slice of life. Unlike their fictional counterpart, however, cases are usually about real people, organizations, and problems (even though the names may be disguised for proprietary reasons from time to time). Thus, a reader has an opportunity to participate through this method in decisions that managers had to make on a variety of problems.

The technique of using actual business situations as an educational and analytical instrument began at Harvard in the 1920s, but the use of a case as a method of educating students began much earlier. Centuries earlier students learned law by studying past legal cases and medicine through the use of clinical work.

Unlike textbooks and lectures, the case method of instruction does not present a structured body of knowledge. This often proves frustrating to students who may be used to more traditional teaching methods. For example, cases are frequently ambiguous and imprecise, which can easily confuse a neophyte. This complexity, however, represents what practitioners usually face when making decisions.

In cases, as in life, problems can be solved in a variety of ways. Sometimes one way seems better than others. Even if a perfect solution exists, however, the company may have difficulty implementing it. You may also find that you have a completely different solution to the problem than another student. Try to forget the notion of an "answer" to the problem. The goal in using this method is not to develop a set of correct approaches or right answers, but rather to involve you in the active process of recognizing and solving managerial problems.

In class you will represent the decision maker (usually a manager) in a discussion that is guided by the professor (or facilitator). While the professor may suggest ideas from time to time or provide structure to ensure that students cover major issues, each student's insight and analytical prowess is displayed in this context. Often a professor will play devil's advocate or pursue an unusual line of reasoning to get students to see the complexities of a particular situation. As a teaching device, the case method relies on participation rather than passive learning.

Although cases come in all shapes and sizes, two categories define the scope of most: evaluative and problematic. An evaluative case presents the reader with a description of a company's actions. The purpose of an analysis is thus to evaluate what management has done and then to determine whether the actions were well founded. (See Jewett Bank, Chapter 7.)

On the other hand, problem cases, which are far more common, describe a specific problem a manager faces, such as whether to launch a new corporate advertising program, to choose one method of handling the media over another, or even whether to choose one form of communication rather than another. Such problems call for development of alternative strategies leading to a specific recommendation. (See Adolph Coors Company, Chapter 6.)

Case Preparation

No matter what type of case you're dealing with, a common approach will help you to prepare cases before you have time to develop what will eventually become your own style. In time, you will no doubt find a method that works well and proves more suitable to you. Regardless of the approach, a thorough analysis requires a great deal of effort.

Begin, however, with a quick reading of the case. This gives you a sense of the whole rather than what can often appear as a dazzling array of parts if you start by analyzing each section in detail. You should extract a *sense* of the organization, some impressions of what *could be* the problem, and a working knowledge of the amount and importance of information presented in the case.

A more careful, second reading of the case will allow you to begin the critical process of analyzing business problems and solving them. What you should hope to cull from this analysis follows.

Problem Definition

First, you must establish a specific definition of the problem(s). While this may be clearly stated in the case, usually problem definition is a crucial first step in the analysis. You need to go beyond simple problem definition and look for symptoms as well. For example, as part of the analysis you might wonder why or how the defined problem has developed in the company. Avoid, however, a repetition of case facts or an historical perspective. Assume that your reader has all the facts you do and choose reasoning that will serve to strengthen, rather than bloat, your problem definition.

Company Objectives

Once you have defined the problem, place it within the context of management's objectives. How does the problem look in this light? Do the objectives make sense given the problems facing management?

In some cases objectives are defined explicitly, such as "increase stock price by 10 percent this year." If the problem in the case proves to be that the company's investor-relations function is a disaster, this objective is probably overly optimistic. Goals can be more general as well: "Change from a centralized to a decentralized communication organization in five years." In this instance, a centralized department with independent managers at the divisional level has a good chance of meeting its objectives.

Data Analysis

You next need to analyze information presented in the case as a way of establishing its significance. Often this material appears in exhibits, but you will also find it stated within the case as fact or opinion. Remember to avoid blind acceptance of the data, no matter where they appear. As in the real world, information presented in the case may not be reliable or relevant. But you may find that by manipulating or combining the data, they ultimately will prove valuable to your analysis. Given the time constraints you will always be under in case analysis and in business, you should avoid a natural tendency to spend more time than you can really afford analyzing data. Try to find a compromise between little or no data analysis and endless number crunching.

Alternative Strategies and Recommendations

After you have defined the problem, identified company objectives, and analyzed relevant data, you are ready to present viable alternative strategies. Be sure the alternatives are realistic for the company under discussion given management's objectives. In addition, you must consider the implications of each alternative for the company and management.

Once you have developed two or three viable alternative solutions, you are ready to make a recommendation for future action. Naturally, you will want to support the recommendation with relevant information from your analysis. This final step completes your case analysis, but you must then take the next step and explore ways to communicate all the information to your reader or listener.

Cases in the Real World

A few final words to distinguish the case from a real situation. Despite the hours of research time and reams of information amassed by the case writer, he or she must ultimately choose which information to present. Thus, you end up with a package of information in writing. Obviously, information does not come to you in one piece in business. A manager may have garnered the information through discussions, memos, reports, magazines, and so on. The timing will also be spread out over a longer period than in a case.

Also, given the necessary selectivity of the case writer, you can be sure a specific teaching objective helped focus the selection of information. In reality, the "case" may have implications for several different areas of a business, not just the corporate communication function.

Since a case takes place within a particular period of time, it differs in another important way from management problems. These tend to go on and change as new information comes to light. A manager can solve some of the problems now, search for more information, and decide more carefully later on what is best for a given situation. You, on the other hand, must take one stand now and forever.

Finally, case analyses differ from the realities of management in that students do not have responsibility for implementing decisions. Nor do they suffer the consequences if their decision proves untenable. But you should not assume that this absolves you from any responsibility. On the contrary, the class (in a discussion) or your professor will be searching for the kind of critical analysis that makes for excellence in management.

A C K N O W L E D G M E N T S

I could not have completed this book without the help and support of the Tuck School at Dartmouth College. Over the last 12 years, I have been given funds to write cases and conduct research as well as time to work on the material in this book. I am particularly grateful to Dick West for investing in my career here at Tuck initially and encouraging me to develop a new area of study.

More recently, I must thank my friends and colleagues, John Shank, Vijay Govindarajan, and Mary Munter for making me sit down and finally produce a text after years of collecting materials and thoughts in files and boxes. The International University of Japan also deserves credit for providing me with the contemplative setting I needed to write the first draft.

So many clients helped me to test the ideas I have developed over the last decade, but I am particularly indebted to Joseph Antonini, Chairman and Chief Executive Officer of Kmart for allowing me to think creatively about the possibilities for a unified corporate communication function.

I am also indebted to the students I have taught here at Tuck, at the International University of Japan, the Helsinki School of Economics, Columbia Business School, and Harvard Business School. They have tested these ideas in their fertile minds and given me inspiration for coming up with new ways of thinking about communications.

Many research assistants helped me with this project over the years, but I am particularly grateful to Christine Keen and Patricia Gordon. I also want to thank my administrative assistants, Linda Hartson and Mary Hill for all of their help with the manuscript. The reviewers who looked over various editions of the book deserve special thanks for their helpful comments and advice:

Carter A. Daniel
Rutgers University

Jerry Dibble
Georgia State University

Chris Kelly
New York University

Margo Northey
University of Western Ontario

Charlotte Rosen
Cornell University

Irv Schenkler
New York University

Sherron B. Kenton
Emory University

Mary E. Vielhaber
Eastern Michigan University

Joan M. Lally
University of Utah

JoAnne Yates
Massachusetts Institute of Technology

Otto Lerbinger
Boston University

My thanks also go to the staff at Irwin especially my editor, Craig Beytein, and Bevan O'Callaghan, who signed the book initially. Their patience allowed me the freedom to develop this material over a much longer period of time than I would have guessed it would take initially.

And finally, I would like to thank my parents for giving me the raw material initially and the education later on that allowed me to become an academic.

                                                            Paul A. Argenti

The author would like any comments or questions as well as corrections to the text. Please write to Professor Paul A. Argenti, The Amos Tuck School, Dartmouth College, Hanover, New Hampshire, 03755.

C O N T E N T S

1   IT'S A NEW WORLD

Most of the people in positions of power in American business today grew up in an era different from the one they find themselves in now. A top executive, typically a white male in his 50s, grew up during one of the most prosperous and optimistic periods in American history. The difference between the world these people grew up in and the one their grandchildren will face at the beginning of the 21st century is staggering.

Americans growing up in the 1940s became aware at the time when our country fought and won World War II against the Germans and Japanese. They were the first generation to live in an America that was truly the best and most prosperous nation on earth. They were the first to expect that they would own their own home, buy a new car from the best auto makers in the world, and to assume that they would be able to send their children to college. Many of these notions had been impossible just a generation earlier as their parents and grandparents lived through the Great Depression.

These expectations and the environment they grew up in explain a lot about how senior executives look at the world and why many of them have failed to keep up with the rapid change taking place in today's high technology, borderless world.

Many of these same executives never imagined that the Germans and Japanese would again seize power through economic, not military, superiority. They never imagined that Detroit would come to symbolize decline, poverty, and an aging auto industry that was attacked and beaten, this time by the Japanese.

These changes are just some that have taken place in the last half century—changes that lead me to believe that it really is a different world from the one our parents and grandparents lived in. In this chapter, we will look at the changing environment of business and how it has led inexorably to the need for a new functional area called corporate communication.

We begin by looking at the growth in negative attitudes toward American business, then at the reflection of these negative attitudes in popular culture. Next we turn to the international environment as a source of change in the business environment. And finally, I offer some advice about how to compete in a new world through better communications.

Changing Attitudes toward American Business

Business has never had the completely positive image in the United States that it has in a country like Japan. Part of the reason for this is that, throughout our history, businessmen (given that women entered the work-

1

force only in the last 20 years as managers, it is right to use this term) have been involved in some of the worst scandals we have known.

Americans in the mid-19th century were horrified at what southern businessmen were doing about slavery. Slaves were forced to work from sunup until after sundown, if there was a full moon, to pick cotton for the growing export market in Europe. The development of Eli Whitney's cotton gin created further demand for cotton and made working conditions even worse for slaves.

The development of rail systems and the concomitant need for steel created similar horrifying working conditions that we would cringe at today. Coal mines were also places that one associated with the worst working conditions imaginable. The "robber barons" as they came to be known, who created all of this, were seen as corrupt businessmen looking out for their own interests rather than the good of all citizens.

Ironically, these negative attitudes toward the first modern businessmen were coupled with a deep admiration for them. Most Americans wanted the lifestyle these wealthy businessmen had and came to see this pursuit as part of the American dream.

Yet, more-educated citizens and those with aristocratic pretensions have always seen business and the pursuit of the American dream as something rather shallow. The tension between old money, for instance, and new money or the bourgeoisie, has existed for decades in this country. Old money, long removed from the world of commerce, was a good thing to have, while new money, taken from the corrupt practices of modern business, was seen as bad. The Carnegies, Mellons, Rockefellers, and Morgans did little at the beginning of this century to enhance attitudes toward American business. The incredible wealth these men amassed at the expense of other Americans led to the crash of the stock market in 1929 and the first real trough in attitudes toward American business.

Prior to this time, most of the common folk who dabbled in the stock market knew that the really wealthy investors were rigging the market and making a fortune, but that was fine as long as they too could get a piece of the action. As the public became aware of what really went on in the 1920s, their euphoria over what they had made in the stock market turned sour as the Great Depression spread over the land.

This connection between American attitudes toward business and the economy has continued throughout the century. When things have gone well, typically, the general public has positive feelings toward business. When they have gone less well, however, more negative attitudes have prevailed.

Just think of the metaphors such as "the rat race" and "dog eat dog" that are typically used to describe American business. These terms hardly conjure up positive impressions in our minds. Historically, business has not been renown for its charitableness, and this creates a great dichotomy for us as citizens in a capitalistic society. Most of us want to have our cake and to eat it too, as the expression goes, which explains the fascination among the middle class in winning the lottery and other statistically impossible contests like the Publisher's Clearing House sweepstakes.

This dichotomy surfaces again in the inconsistency between our love for mavericks and individual entrepreneurs and our scorn for the very institutions that reflect their greatest success. Look at how positive citizens in small towns across America were to the great retailing entrepreneur, Sam Walton, who built Wal-Mart from nothing to the largest retailing enterprise in the country during his career. Yet the same Americans who loved Walton and all that he stood for despised what his stores did to the small enterprises on main street in virtually every town a Wal-Mart store was built. Even though he was one of the richest Americans at the time of his death in 1992, what prevailed and caught the imagination of Americans was the vision of him riding in a beat-up, old pick-up truck to go to one of his thousands of stores rather than the reality of what he did to eliminate thousands of small-town businesses across the country.

Tom Peters said in *In Search of Excellence* that virtually anyone could have succeeded in the business environment after World War II and achieved what a Walton did. Businesses started rebounding during the war as companies geared up for the war effort. The steel industry, the automotive industry, the military-industrial complex— all of which made the prosperity of the 1950s and 60s a reality—got their start during World War II.

With much of Europe and Asia in ruins by the mid-1940s and America physically untouched, our country was ready to invest in infrastructure at home and rebuild the rest of the world in its own image abroad. This is a time in American history that most of us who are old enough to remember now look back on as the golden years.

Perhaps the apotheosis of this era came during the Camelot years of the Kennedy administration. The economy was booming, a handsome young man of ethnic ancestry from new money was in charge of the Western world, and we were able to stave off the onslaught of communism in the aftermath of the Cuban missile crisis. Even after Kennedy's death, which marks the first shift toward decline in American attitudes towards all institutions, prosperity continued, and with economic growth, public attitudes toward business soared. Over a period of 20 years, the Roper organization asked the question of American citizens, "Does business strike a balance between profit and the public interest?" In 1968, 70 percent of the population answered "yes" to that question.

By this time, Richard Nixon, not his young handsome nemesis, John F. Kennedy, was on his way to the White House. The nation was torn apart by civil unrest, due in part to the sweeping changes brought about by the Civil Rights movement and also due to demonstrations against U.S. involvement in the Vietnam war. A split between Americans for and against the war marked another deterioration in attitudes toward all institutions. For those who were against the war, the executive branch of government came to stand for all that was wrong with America.

American business shared in this negative shift in attitudes toward institutions as it helped make the war possible. Dow Chemical's ability to manufacture napalm and agent orange, which would then be used to defoliate a seemingly innocent and poor Southeast Asian nation, led to student protests on campuses throughout America. Other companies involved in the manufacture of products for the war received similar welcomes on college campuses. Young Americans came to distrust the institutions involved in the war, whether government agencies or businesses. This represented a huge change from the attitudes Americans had during World War II. Those in power failed to see that this time it was a different war with people ambivalent about what we were actually fighting for.

The end of the 1960s and a rise in radicalism in America marked the beginning of a long decline in positive attitudes toward business and other institutions. The events of the early 1970s did little to help this shift. For example, the Watergate break-in affirmed what most young Americans had believed all along about the Nixon administration. We found out that the reality was worse than our imaginations had conjured up during protest marches in the 1960s.

Similarly, the war that had claimed so much of our nation's emotional energy, not to mention the lives of so many innocent victims on both sides, seemingly was fought in vain as America pulled out of Vietnam. In other public events, Gulf Oil was involved in bribes in Italy, and the first oil embargo coupled with huge profits for oil companies led many to distrust all large organizations once again.

With Watergate, Vietnam, and the oil embargo behind us, by the mid-1970s American attitudes toward business reached an all-time low. In answer to the same question ''Does business strike a fair balance between profit and the public interest?'' those answering ''yes'' in the Roper poll dropped to 15 percent in 1976 when Jimmy Carter took office. This drop of 55 points in just eight years says more about the changing attitudes toward business than a thousand anecdotes could.

Confidence in all large institutions fell at an alarming rate in the 1970s. An opinion research poll that asked the general public to rate their confidence in a number of institutions showed declines in all areas, as shown in Table 1–1. Although figures don't exist for other institutions, we can imagine similar dips in attitudes toward the police, the armed forces, and even organized religion based on how people felt about large institutions in the 1970s.

These numbers reflect changes in social attitudes and behavior that go far beyond the scope of this book. But let's stop to think about how far reaching the negative attitudes have been in changing American society over the last 20 years. In a society where public confidence toward institu-

TABLE 1-1

	1966	1971
How much confidence do you have in these institutions?*		
Large companies	55%	27%
U.S. Congress	42%	19%
Executive Branch	41%	23%
Supreme Court	51%	23%

* Answers reflect those answering most positively.

tions runs high, we would expect that the optimism necessary for success in business would be quite high as well. People would be more willing to sacrifice for the greater good of society if their confidence in authority were high. They would also be willing to surrender control to those in charge if their confidence were high. And obviously, the reverse is also true.

As you read this, you may be asking yourself whether the 1980s, which was perhaps the final economic boom in the 20th century, changed attitudes back to where they had been in the 1960s. The answer is, unfortunately, no. In answer to the question about whether business strikes a fair balance between profit and the public interest, the percentages climbed back to a high of only 30 percent answering "yes" in 1984.

In terms of confidence in major institutions, the news is even worse. Only 14 percent had a lot of confidence in large companies in 1989 (from 27 percent in 1971). And even the executive branch of government, which Reagan and Bush seemed to rescue from the depths of the Carter administration, climbed only four points to 27 percent in 1989 from its all-time low of 23 percent in 1971 during the Nixon administration.

When people were asked to rate the moral and ethical practices of different professions in the mid-1980s in a Yankelovich survey, corporate executives ranked dead last after doctors, university professors, the president of the United States, lawyers, and members of Congress. In the "good to excellent" category, doctors received affirmative responses from 70 percent of those surveyed, corporate executives only 29 percent.

When I go through these numbers with senior executives across the United States, many of them are shocked at the tremendous decline in positive attitudes toward American business over the last 25 years. Some of this can be explained by the environment they grew up in, but much of their surprise reflects a lack of knowledge about the world around them. It also reflects an unwillingness to accept the changes that are here to stay.

Several times during the century, American business was given an opportunity to demonstrate its ability to lead the nation toward prosperity and away from government, and each time it failed. From the 1920s, when American business boomed, until its failure with the beginning of the Great Depression; to the 1950s and 60s following World War II, when America and the rest of the world were hungry for consumer goods at a rate we are unlikely to see again; to the Reagan era of the 1980s, when the service sector seemed to be the great savior for an economy that limped through the latter half of the 1970s; we have seen business given the opportunity to provide leadership, and each time it has failed to solve societal problems.

Each time this failure occurs, attitudes toward business become more negative. And each negative movement requires managers to work that much harder with external constituencies. The problem is that often business people have the opposite response. When public attitudes turn negative, they "tend to business" rather than trying to change public opinion. Managers are taught to focus on the marketplace, and that's good, but today's managers must also realize that external forces can have a tremendous effect on the marketplace as well. Nowhere are the attitudes that prevail in the external environment more clearly defined than in the popular arts.

How Hollywood Hurts Main Street and Wall Street

Throughout history, literature and the arts have commented on and had a profound effect on perceptions about public institutions like business. Greek attitudes about government and religion were affected by theater; Shakespeare shaped notions about English history for generations; and for the United States in the 20th century, cinema and television have helped foster negative attitudes about business.

For many Americans today, what they see in fictional or "factional" accounts in films and on television helps shape their attitudes even more than educational institutions. In fact, Americans spend far more time in front of the television set than they do in the classroom. According to research undertaken by a number of different organizations, the average American household spends approximately 40–50 hours per week in front of the television set. Many have written about what this has done to our society in a broader context over the last 25 years. But in this book, I would like to focus on the relationship between the popular arts and business.

The Media Institute, a research organization funded by corporations, has been tracking media coverage of business for over a decade. Each time it issues a report, the results are the same: businesspeople are portrayed negatively in almost two thirds of all television programs. In a report issued by the institute in the 1980s, researchers concluded that half of the time, businesspeople portrayed on television were involved in criminal activities.

On a consulting trip to Nigeria in the early 1980s, I was repeatedly asked if all American businessmen were really like J.R. Ewing of *Dallas*. Larry Hagman's portrayal of the sleazy businessman stands as one of the clearest reminders about how television portrays business. Obviously, most of us involved in business are nothing like J.R. Ewing, but the perception that years of watching such programs leaves with the ordinary viewer is that businesspeople are downright evil.

In addition, most Americans get their news from television. So, the negative portrayals viewers see in fictional programming get blurred into the negative news they watch. In fact, one of the most popular programs in the history of television, CBS's *60 Minutes,* often portrays business in a very negative light. The viewer might, for example, see someone like J.R. Ewing doing all manner of horrible deeds in the oil industry one night, watch an account of an oil company doing something awful on the news the next night—say Exxon's *Valdez* disaster, and then see an oil executive making a fool of himself on *60 Minutes* the third night. All of the information comes from the same source, all of it is bad, and viewers have a difficult time sorting out what was real and what was not from the various programming. Thus, it is not so surprising that the American public holds negative views about business that are based partially on reality and partially on fiction.

Films add insult to injury. One of the most successful films of the late 1970s was called *The China Syndrome,* a movie about problems at a nuclear reactor. Soon after the release of the film, a real nuclear accident occurred at Three Mile Island in 1979. While everyone would agree that Metropolitan Edison did a poor job of communicating about this accident, few would say that the company was as bad as the one we saw in the movie. Yet many Americans lumped the two events together in their mind, which made matters much worse than they really were.

It's often eerie how Hollywood has been able to pick up on things that are going on in business exactly at the right time as in the case mentioned above. The movie *Wall Street* is another example of the same sort. Oliver Stone's movie came out just ahead of the great scandals that racked the real Wall Street. Yet reality and fiction intertwined within the film itself.

Gordon Gekko, the evil financial genius meant to represent someone like the notorious arbitrageur, Ivan Boesky, makes a speech in the film about greed. "Greed is good, greed purifies," Gekko says in a passionate speech at an annual meeting. Months earlier, the real Ivan Boesky had made a similar speech to a group of graduates at the University of California's Berkeley campus.

The books *Barbarians at the Gate* and *Den of Thieves,* which came out in the early 1990s, were journalistic accounts of what happened on Wall Street in the 1980s, and they said approximately the same thing that Oliver Stone had said in his fictional account a few years earlier. Similarly, Tom Wolfe's *Bonfire of the Vanities* captured the crazed 1980s on Wall Street better than either of the two actual accounts.

But can we really blame the general public for holding negative impressions about business when we learn that Drexel, Burnham's Michael Milken had an annual bonus of $550 million in his last year with the firm, which exceeded the entire yearly budget of the Securities and Exchange Commission that was trying to investigate him? Even after he was found guilty and convicted, Milken made the cover of *Forbes* magazine in 1992 for an interview from prison that tried to position him as an American hero wronged by a ridiculous system.

One of the few television programs that tried to capture accurately what life is really like in business, the groundbreaking *Thirysomething,* was canceled just as we were starting to see characters with real depth and feeling in business situations. ABC's *Viewpoint,* which tried to give businesspeople who felt wronged by biased coverage a chance to respond, similarly got canceled. In fact, the only successful program I can think of that deals with business issues accurately week after week is Louis Rukeyser's *Wall Street Week,* which has to rank as one of the most boring television programs in the history of the medium.

Of course, business's response, which is to continue to sponsor programs that regularly depict businesspeople as evil and fight with the networks and producers over the amount of sex we see each night, is another example of how far removed businesspeople have become from their environment. In the meantime, Hollywood will continue to characterize businesspeople as it sees fit, and as a result another generation, not to mention millions abroad, will form negative opinions about business.

The Borderless World

As I mentioned earlier, senior executives in their 50s and 60s today, could hardly have imagined the revolution that has taken place in terms of globalization over the last 20 years. How does this affect the environment for business, and what are the implications in terms of corporate communication?

One of the biggest changes in the business environment has been written about endlessly over the last decade. It is the growth of Japan as a world economic power. What has not been written about enough, however, is what this means for companies trying to do business with the Japanese both at home and abroad.

Again, company executives seem to have missed the mark in preparing for this changed environment. Don't forget that most of these executives saw Japan destroyed in their lifetime, only to see this small country, devastated by war just half a century ago, turn out to be one of the main competitors for American business in both the domestic and international markets.

Companies trying to compete in Japan have, in general, had little success, due in part to problems of communication. Yes, Japan is more difficult to do business in because of the strong ties between government and business, but this is usually not the main impediment to success for American companies. What is the problem, then?

First, Americans are ill equipped to deal with the Japanese and other international competitors because of our incredible chauvinism toward things American and the belief, until just a few years ago, that the rest of the world would have to bend to our ways if they wanted to be successful. Think about how ridiculous that attitude looks today in a global business environment. Americans are now trying to catch up with international competitors who usually have a command of our language, some understanding of our culture (if only through the filter of our television programs and films), and more of a willingness to learn how to communicate across cultures.

I am amazed at how naive many people in the United States are about doing business in Japan. Since I have taught for part of each of the last four years in Japan, I am often asked questions about what it is like and what possibilities exist for foreigners in Japan. Just recently, someone asked me whether I thought that they could succeed in Japan selling blue jeans. This person's understanding was that jeans were still unavailable in Japan and that she could make a killing in the market by being the first to sell them! Such naiveté about what is happening abroad, and particularly in far-off Japan, comes up in conversations with businesspeople all the time.

Part of the problem for bigger, more established companies has been a lack of understanding about how to communicate with the Japanese as individuals and as a corporation. Two examples, one positive and one negative, should help to clarify what I mean.

IBM and Kmart are two of America's most successful companies by any measure. Even though they operate in totally different fields, both companies came to Japan trying to continue the success they had found in the United States. Today, IBM is so successful that most Japanese do not even realize that it is not a Japanese company. Mostly through patient communication with Japanese bureaucrats, suppliers, and employees, IBM has succeeded in Japan. The company did not try to present itself as an extension of American culture or as a major competitor trying to beat the Japanese system. By communicating through the strength of its products and showing the Japanese how willing the company was to adapt itself to the new environment, IBM succeeded in Japan.

Kmart's experience was very different from that of IBM. This company came to Japan just as IBM did with the goal of extending its franchise abroad. Unlike IBM, however, the managers sent to deal with the Japanese were unwilling to wait patiently for the wheels of the Japanese bureaucracy to grind away for months and possibly years as the company sat by to get its chance in Japan. The result? Kmart ended up selling the rights to its name in Japan to a Japanese firm.

Similar examples occur again and again. Look at General Motors's and Chrysler's experience, for example, as compared to that of Toys "R" Us. The giant auto companies can hardly sell a few thousand cars a year in one of the largest and most affluent markets on earth, while Toys "R" Us is able to establish a foothold in an equally competitive industry (and one very similar to the one given up by Kmart).

The American companies that succeed in Japan and in other parts of the world were able to recognize that the environment and the rules had changed and that they needed to adapt to the market as quickly as they could. Most important of all for these companies, however, was their ability to communicate across cultures and meet the competition, sometimes at an initial disadvantage.

How to Compete in a New World

Sloan Wilson's novel, *Man in the Gray Flannel Suit,* summed up his generation's new attitude about business in the 1950s. The protagonist's attitude was essentially that, rather than be a faceless, gray, drone in the business world, he wanted to be closer to his family and try to latch on to the American dream of a nice home and a good job. Tom Wolfe's antihero in *Bonfire of the Vanities* summed up his generation's attitude as well. This attitude was to try to win at any price. You might lose your family and home in the process, but who cares?

These two works of fiction show the different attitudes between businessmen in the 1950s and businesspeople today. The period after the war was an optimistic time in America, filled with hope and prosperity. The 1990s are a much less optimistic time filled with irony and a lack of the family values that this country was built on.

How can today's managers meet changes in the environment and adapt to the new world? This book focuses on one aspect of this problem as it relates to communication and business, but some of the lessons learned here have broader implications as well.

First, managers need to recognize that the environment is different. The short-term orientation of today's managers hardly gives them an opportunity to look at the big picture to see how the environment is likely to affect the way a company should or could present itself to a variety of audiences. Many managers, particularly older ones, seem so set in their ways that they have difficulty trying to see the forest for the trees.

Second, adapt to the changing environment without changing what the company stands for or compromising your own principles. If GM had tried to adapt itself to the reality of its environment, it would never have allowed itself to get blindsided by the Japanese. Nor would it have allowed a small, independent film maker, like Michael Moore, to produce a successful documentary like *Roger and Me* without trying to influence the end product.

Third, keep the company's communications on the cutting edge. Even if the mission statement is just hot off the press, get the message out to the world quickly. Since few managers recognize the importance of the communication function, they are reluctant to hire the quality staff necessary to succeed in today's environment. As a result, they tend to keep the communication people "out of the loop," or as one vice president of communication put it to me: "They treat us like mushrooms; keep 'em in the dark and they can't do us any harm."

Fourth, avoid trying to cut corners. Many of the cases you will read in this book are about companies that tried to respond to change and problems only when they really had no other alternative. Often the decision was based on short-term, financially oriented thinking. It costs a lot more to fix a battered image after, rather than before, a problem arises. Pay up front with clear communication.

Fifth, avoid the *gnat theory*. This theory says that eventually the problem will go away. Assume things will only get worse rather than better and you will be better off in today's complex environment. Hooker Chemical executives had no way of knowing that the Love Canal story would run as long as it did. Most managers assume that the American public gets bored fast and will forget about problems companies get into.

Some companies seem to be getting it right, but most are still getting it wrong. A look at today's news will show two illustrative examples. Caterpillar Inc., the world's largest manufacturer of construction equipment, allowed itself to get into a battle with one of the strongest unions in the United States, the United Automobile Workers. Despite all that is now known about negotiation and how you should never argue over positions, the company decided to replace 12,600 workers over issues of wages and health benefits.

USX, on the other hand (the former U.S. Steel corporation) seems to be taking a different approach. The day after reading about Caterpillar's antediluvian approach to labor relations, we read that the new president of the vast steel operation, Thomas J. Usher, unexpectedly strolled into the offices of the United Steelworkers local to listen to what union leaders might have on their minds about the company's largest mill. The president of the local union said this kind of behavior was very unusual: "Other heads of U.S. Steel would never have dreamed of being in the same room with the union people. He is bringing in a breath of fresh air."

I don't know how well either of these companies will fare in the years to come, but if I had to wager, I would put my money on USX's approach. Recognizing that the union's interests are essentially the same as management's is a stretch for managers mired in old fashioned thinking. The autocratic managers at U.S. Steel that President Kennedy once referred to as ''a bunch of S.O.B.'s'' would have never been able to step up to the changes in the environment the way Mr. Usher has.

It's a new world for everyone in business today, whether at a huge corporation with a national union to deal with or a small business looking to make its mark in the international arena. The way these companies and other organizations adapt and modify their behavior as manifested through their communication will determine the success of American business as a whole for the next century.

CASE
HOOKER CHEMICAL COMPANY

Sandie Kroeger, communications coordinator for Hooker Chemical Company, sat at her desk in Houston, staring out the window at the humid sunset. It was the summer of 1978. Sandie had just hung up the phone after speaking with Don McNeil from *The New York Times*. The *Times* was going to break the following day with McNeil's front-page piece on an old chemical dump at the Love Canal site that had once belonged to the company (see Exhibit 1–1).

McNeil wanted a comment from Donald Baeder, Hooker's president. The reporter's deadline for filing the story was fast approaching. Sandie, however, knew she would be unable to contact Baeder because he was in a meeting. McNeil asked to be put through to Baeder anyway, but Sandie told him this was impossible.

As she sat thinking about how the next day's news would be received, she remembered her introduction to the company. She had been hired by the vice-president of employee relations to work on internal communications, and as she put it: "Oh, maybe I'd have to get out a couple of press releases a month." In the months that were to follow McNeil's ominous call, she would do far more than that.

History of the Love Canal

The story began in 1892 when an enterprising young man named William Love decided to build a canal connecting two lakes. It was the era of direct current: the canal was designed to bring hydroelectric power from the nearby falls to local industry. A model city would be built, having ready access to cheap electricity and to markets via the canal. Two years later, however, alternating current made the canal obsolete. In addition, a recession made funding scarce for the canal as a transit route. So the partially dug canal was left unfinished until Hooker Chemical Company thought to use the land as a waste disposal site.

The company used the site for 10 years beginning in 1942 when it received a license to dump. (Due to title problems, Hooker did not actually acquire the land until 1947.) During the same period, the U.S. Army also dumped an undetermined amount of toxic chemicals in the canal. In addition, the city used the canal for general refuse. The generally accepted procedure at the time was to make a dam of clay to isolate the newly used portions of the dump and then to cover it with a four-foot cap of clay.

In 1952 the Niagara Board of Education needed a site for a new school but was short of cash. The board asked Hooker for the now vacant land at Love Canal. One year before, the board had drawn up plans for a school and threatened to condemn the property if the land was not deeded over to them. Had the city condemned and taken the land, Hooker would have had no voice over the use of the land. On the advice of the firm's attorney, the company insisted on transferring the deed and receiving $1 for the land. This deed included provisions stating the former use of the land, limiting any future liability for the company, and ensuring that any future owners were given the same provisions (see Exhibit 1–2).

The school was built, but in the process the construction contractor dug into the chemical zone. He suggested that the chemicals might hurt the concrete foundation. The architect moved the site 30 feet east and construction continued.

Exhibit 1–1

Upstate Waste Site May Endanger Lives: Abandoned Dump in Niagara Falls Leaks Possible Carcinogens

Donald G. McNeil, Jr.

Niagara Falls, NY, August 1—Twenty-five years after the Hooker Chemical Company stopped using the Love Canal here as an industrial dump, 82 different compounds, 11 of them suspected carcinogens, have begun percolating upward through the soil, their drum containers rotting and leeching their contents into the backyards and basements of 100 homes and a public school built on the banks of the canal.

Children and dogs have received chemical burns playing on the canal site and large numbers of miscarriages and birth defects have been found among residents of the homes along the site.

Tomorrow, the State Health Department is scheduled to recommend whether the Governor should declare a health emergency and evacuate the area's families with small children.

The canal, dug in the 1890s to provide power and water for a model-city scheme, was used as a toxic-waste dump by the Hooker Chemical Company from 1947 to 1952. Thousands of drums were dropped directly into the receding water or buried in its banks.

In 1953, Hooker sold the land to the city's Board of Education for $1. The school was built on it, and lots were sold to developers of "raised ranch" and box houses, which sold for $20,000 and $30,000 a few years ago.

In 1976, after six years of abnormally heavy rains, the canal "overflowed its underground banks," residents say, and the stuff began surfacing—an incredible mixture of 82 industrial chemicals so far, 11 of them suspected carcinogens, according to the Federal Environmental Protection Agency.

Children and dogs have been burned playing in the fields, visitors have had the soles of their shoes corroded through, and some backyard trees have been completely gnawed away by chemical action.

It has also begun seeping through basement walls, and air monitors placed by the Federal Agency have counted levels of from 250 to 5,000 times as high as is safe for some chemicals in some homes.

The State Health Department ran blood tests and epidemiological histories on residents of 97th and 99th Street between Frontier Avenue and Colvin Boulevard—about 100 families.

Preliminary figures counted four children with birth defects among 24 in the southern block of the stretch, all of them mentally retarded, one mother said. It also showed a miscarriage rate of 29.4 percent. Thus far the department has refused to draw conclusions from these figures because the statistical sample is very small.

A Case in Point

Residents say many in the neighborhood have died of rectal, breast, and blood cancers, and the Health Department has said it plans to make a study going as far back as 20 years to test the truth of this. Many residents said their dogs had died of tumors or distemper before they reached the age of 3.

Karen Schroeder, one of whose four children was born with a cleft palate, an extra row of teeth, and slight retardation, grew up at 476 99th Street, and now lives at 480. Her protest to *The Niagara Falls Gazette* and Rep-

Exhibit 1–1 continued

resentative John LaFalce, Democrat of Tonawanda, first raised the official concern for the neighborhood.

Her backyard seems to be the lowest draining point for the waters leeching out of the fill. Her swimming pool was popped out of the ground by the rising water table, her whole garden killed. The redwood posts of her backyard fence eaten away, and local authorities pumped 17,500 gallons of chemical-filled water out of her yard in two days this year, water than even Chemtrol, the country's biggest waste disposal company, refused to handle, she said. So it was trucked to Ohio and poured down a deep-well disposal site.

Her dog died young and now her husband, Timothy, jokes that their daughter's Easter rabbit has become their miner's canary. "If it dies, we'll know to move away."

Asked to Repeat Tests

She and 40 other neighbors have been asked to repeat their state blood tests because of "abnormalities" that were found. A State Health Department spokesman identified them as liver abnormalities, but said it might be a laboratory problem.

Mrs. Schroeder said she had heard they found a high white blood count in her and in her mother, Aileen Voorhees, who is the neighborhood record-holder for chemicals detected in basement air: 12,835 micrograms per cubic meter.

"Do you want to see the paper of what's coming through my wall?" Mrs. Voorhees asked yesterday, handing over a sheet sent her by the EPA to translate blips that had come over on the air monitoring machine installed on a big basement workbench. The elements included chloroform, benzine, trichlorethane, toluene, petrachloroethene, 1,3,5 trichlorobenzene—high amounts of 9 of the 11 it could test or—at least two of them carcinogens.

The homeowners who bought land next to the canal did so because they had been told it would be turned into a park and be near the school, Mrs. Voorhees said.

"Ticking Time Bombs"

"They didn't let anybody know it was dangerous," she said. "They didn't know how far the stupid chemicals were going to run."

The Love Canal site is one of 38 known industrial waste landfills in Niagara County, and probably the most serious health hazard of the thousands in the nation, Eckhardt C. Beck, regional director for the EPA said.

"We've been burying these things like ticking time bombs—they'll all leech out in 100 or 100,000 years," he said. "We're mortgaging our future if we don't control them more carefully. And the bottom line is who's going to pay to clean this thing up?

The Hooker Company, which has offered to share the cleanup costs of a tentative city plan to dig tiled drainage ditches along the sides of the canal, has had no comment throughout the controversy.

A spokesman at the company's Houston headquarters, Sandie Kroeger, said the president, Donald Baeder, could not be reached yesterday. No lawsuits have yet been filed by any party to the dispute, and no culpability has been acknowledged by anyone.

The city appears to have been uncooperative with neighborhood requests for help and with state and Federal agencies. Commissioner Robert P. Whalen ordered the county to fence off and decontaminate the area, cover or remove all the exposed pesticides, and ventilate the homes.

Tax Abatements Denied

The County Health Commissioner, Francis J. Clay, installed $15 supermarket fans in two homes, and put up a fence children still walk through without knocking down.

Exhibit 1–1 continued

The city's tax assessor has refused to grant any tax abatement on the homes, even though banks now refuse to mortgage them, or lawyers to title them, Mrs. Schroeder said. And she must still pay $1,200 taxes on a home whose market value she says has fallen to zero.

The City Council voted last Thursday to acquiesce to the opinion of its bond counsel they ought not spend any public money on the land since some of the canal site is owned privately, by a schoolteacher in Pennsylvania who, according to a local reporter, has stopped paying his taxes.

Federal involvement and liability is also an issue. Representative LaFalce's office is investigating whether the Army dumped chemical warfare material into the canal. A retired city bulldozer operator, Frank Ventry, said that he had helped backfill about 18 barrels the Army trucked to the area from what he called a chemical warfare site. The Army has denied any files on such a dumping, but told Mr. Lafalce's assistants it was still checking.

"If the Army dumped, we should get Federal aid, damn it," Mrs. Schroeder said. "If they dumped, let them get their fanny in here and clean it up, too."

A young man who asked not to be identified who used to swim in the canal as a child, said he had seen the Army dump material there three times. Over the years, as dumping continued, the canal's water began to sting like battery acid and boils appeared "the size of silver dollars," he said. "Every kid I knew had them. The Army has talked to lots of them."

He is 34, and totally disabled with Hodgkin's disease, a lymph cancer. "Two of my friends from then have the same thing—but not the bleeding as much," he said. "My brother has nerve disease. But I got Social Security. I don't want trouble. I don't want help. I don't want nothing from the Army, from Hooker, from the city, from nobody."

Reprinted courtesy of *The New York Times,* August 1, 1978.

In 1957 the school board tried to sell unused portions of the 32,000-foot-long canal to residential developers. Hooker protested to the board, and a split decision by the board prevented the sale this time. But in 1958 the first of a few storm sewers was put through the canal area, puncturing the clay walls. Developments in succeeding years further disturbed the cover when more sewers and then roads were built across the canal.

The current controversy started up in the late 1970s after a period of heavy snow and rainfall. Starting in October of 1976, the local press reported that chemicals from the former dump site had seeped into some basements of homes along the boundaries of the canal. The *Niagara Gazette* reported that analyses of residues near the dump site at Love Canal indicated the presence of 15 inorganic chemicals, including three chemicals known to be toxic (see Exhibit 1–3). There were reports of illnesses and injuries among local residents and damage to animals and plants.

In 1977 a task force composed of the city of Niagara Falls, the Niagara County Health Department, and Hooker Chemical Company was formed to study the situation. In addition, the Calspan Corporation was commissioned to prepare an abatement plan. The study, completed and presented to the city in August, was not approved.

In March of 1978, the city commissioned Conestoga-Rovers, a private engineering firm, to design a remedial plan. In June the company

EXHIBIT 1–2

Letter from Hooker to School Board, 1952.

HOOKER ELECTROCHEMICAL COMPANY
NIAGARA FALLS, N. Y.
FORM 1076

October 16, 1952

Mr. William J. Small, Superintendent
Board of Education
Administration Building
Sixth Street and Walnut Avenue
Niagara Falls   New York

Dear Mr. Small:

Reference is made to our recent conversations during which you advised us that the Board of Education was desirous of acquiring a site in the 97th Street area for the purpose of constructing a new elementary school. You have stated that as a result of a survey made by the board it had been determined that a portion of the premises owned by this Company, commonly known as the Love Canal, appeared to be the best location, and you have asked whether this Company would be willing to sell the same for this purpose. We understand that your plans call for the erection of a school on a portion of the property between Wheatfield Avenue and Read Avenue. This location is approximately in the center of the strip of land owned by us between Colvin Boulevard and Frontier Avenue.

Our officers have carefully considered your request. We are very conscious of the need for new elementary schools and realize that the sites must be carefully selected so that they will best serve the area involved. We feel that the Board of Education has done a fine job in meeting the expanding demand for additional facilities and we are anxious to cooperate in any proper way. We have, therefore, come to the conclusion that since this location is the most desirable one for this purpose, we will be willing to donate the entire strip of property which we own between Colvin Boulevard and Frontier Avenue to be used for the erection of a school at a location to be determined between Wheatfield Avenue and Read Avenue and the balance of the property maintained as a park. With the increasing growth of this area and its present lack of any park facilities, we understand that there is a need for areas devoted to this purpose.

As explained to you at our conferences, <u>in view of the nature of the property and the purposes for which it has been used, it will be necessary for us to have special provisions incorporated into the deed with respect to the use of the property and other pertinent matters</u>. If this proposal is acceptable to the Board of Education, we will be glad to have our attorneys prepare a proposed form of deed containing the necessary conditions which we will submit to you for approval.

Very truly yours,

B. Klaussen
Executive Vice President

presented a plan recommending a system to contain wastes migrating from the canal. It was expected to cost $840,000, and Hooker offered to pay one third. By June, however, the school board wanted to drop its share of the costs. State health officials and the U.S. Environmental Protection Agency were studying the situation, including the complaints of health problems among residents. These studies, which spanned April–July, led to the declaration of a state of emergency by New York Health Commissioner Robert Whalen on August 2. Love Canal hit national news that day with McNeil's article.

Exhibit 1–3

Dangerous Chemicals Found Leaking from Hooker Dump

David L. Russell and David Pollak

NIAGARA FALLS—Dangerous chemicals are oozing out of the ground at an old Hooker Chemicals & Plastics Corp. waste dump site in LaSalle, and the presence of the toxic materials may be a health hazard to residents and others in the vicinity.

Chemical analysis of ground residues near the old Love Canal dump site between 97th and 99th streets indicate the presence of heavy concentrations of about 15 organic chemicals, including three toxic chlorinated hydrocarbons.

The analysis of ground residues, taken from the basement of a 97th Street home, was performed for the Niagara Gazette by private chemists. The analysis found concentrations of orthochlorotoluene, parachlorbenzotriflouride, and hexachlorocyclopentadiene.

The three hydrocarbon compounds are described in an authoritative chemical text as "toxic by inhalation," and "flammable and toxic by ingestion or inhalation," and "highly toxic by ingestion, inhalation and skin absorption," respectively.

The toxicity of the three chlorinated hydrocarbons, which are listed in the Condensed Chemical Dictionary, 8th Edition, depends on the extent of exposure, the number of exposures and the concentration of the chemicals.

The samples used in the chemical analysis for the Gazette were taken from a sump pump in the home of Peter P. Bukla Jr. of 753 97th St.

The sump pump was in the Bukla basement, about 100 feet from the edge of [the] Hooker former chemical dump site which has not been used for more than 20 years.

One chemist who analyzed the ground residues said all three of the hydrocarbon compounds found are "an environmental concern" and "certainly are a health hazard" in the concentrations indicated by the analysis.

"Those chemicals should be removed (from the ground) if they are not entirely isolated from the human exposure," he said.

Hooker officials have refused comment on the contents of the company's former dump, located in a 224-foot wide strip in an abandoned landfill between 97th and 99th streets, between the Niagara River and Colvin Avenue.

The 99th Street School is built partly over the landfill, and there are rows of single-family homes on either side of the strip.

A spokesman for the state Department of Environmental Conservation said there is "no new word" on Hooker's response in a DEC request last month for information on the location and contents of all of the company's former dump sites in the Niagara area.

Besides the Love Canal site, Hooker used at least two other areas as private chemical waste dumps in the late 1940s and 1950s.

The dump sites are believed to contain a combination of caustics, alkalis, fatty acids, and chlorinated hydrocarbons, probably buried as limestone sludge and in metal barrels.

The dump site between the Niagara River and Colvin Avenue in LaSalle was known as Love Canal for decades before Hooker acquired the property.

In 1894 the Niagara Power and Development Corp. began an ill-fated canal that was designed to connect the upper and lower Niagara River. The canal was never finished.

Exhibit 1–3 continued

Hooker bought the land in 1947 and, according to the DEC used it as the company's first solid waste disposal site. In 1953, the Board of Education expressed an interest in acquiring the land as elementary enrollment boomed in the LaSalle area.

Hooker transferred the property to the board, but disclaimed any responsibility for future injuries related to chemicals stored underground.

Portions of the property are now owned by the city and by a private speculator. The Federal Housing Administration about six years ago sponsored construction of a number of FHA-235 low-cost homes along the old dump site.

Mrs. Bukla said her family has put up with "horrible smells" and a "black, oily substance" oozing through their cellar walls during the entire 11 years the family has lived on 97th street.

She said they are on their fourth sump pump, the first three having been destroyed by the slime in the groundwater.

Neighbors tell of the time a boy ran barefoot in the unmarked, open field between the rows of homes and came home with minor burns on both feet.

Others in the area have reported similar incidents in recent years, and health department officials have investigated numerous odor complaints.

The three hydrocarbon compounds identified in the samples taken from the Bukla home were used by Hooker as solvents and as intermediary chemicals for production of various insecticides, dyes, resins, and other organic products.

Reprinted courtesy of the *Niagara Gazette*, from November 2, 1976.

Hooker Chemical Company

In 1968 Occidental Petroleum Company (Oxy), owned by Armand Hammer and based in Los Angeles, acquired Hooker Chemical. Oxy took the Hooker name for its chemical division, and future chemical-related businesses were merged into the Hooker Chemical Company.

By 1976 these businesses had combined sales of over $1 billion and included electroplating, metal finishing, plastics, fertilizers, and the original specialty and industrial chemicals. In the early 1970s these were profitable businesses, providing 27–35 percent of Oxy's sales, yet contributing 30–57 percent of operating income (see Exhibit 1–4).

Growth and Expansion in the 1970s. Most of these profits went to develop Oxy's oil and gas operations. In 1972, however, Hammer went to the USSR as Nixon's emissary to develop trade. Two years later, Hammer signed an agreement called the "Russian Project" — a 20-year fertilizer agreement to sell superphosphoric acid to Russia in return for Russian urea, ammonia, and potash.

The Russian Project was a mammoth undertaking. Major capital investments were made in Hooker, in fertilizer facilities, phosphoric acid processing facilities, phosphate mine development, port facilities, and, in another major portion of the portfolio, the Niagara Industrial Chemicals Group. That same year, a $60 million project for converting Niagara's city wastes into electrical energy began.

Strategic Planning at Hooker. In the late 1970s, Hooker had a "bottom up, top down" planning process that resulted in optimistic plans from

EXHIBIT 1–4

1980 Occidental Petroleum Annual Report

Industry Segments and Foreign Operations

	Revenues			Operating Profit	
	Year ended December 31,			Year ended December	
	1980	1979	1978	1980	1979
Industry Segments			(in millions)		
Oil and gas operations:					
Exploration and production	$ 5,008.5	$ 3,943.2	$ 1,958.0	$ 1,806.7(1)	$ 1,255.7(1)
Marketing and transportation	4,326.7	2,931.6	2,211.4	53.9	70.2(2)
Chemical operations:					
Chemical products	1,359.4	1,259.3	1,123.3	79.0	69.4
Agricultural products	1,081.8	718.9	526.7	43.3	15.7
Coal	721.3	693.1	456.1	2.4	48.1
Other	265.8(6)	138.9	90.8	93.7(6)	(28.4)
	12,763.5	9,685.0	6,366.3	2,079.0	1,430.7
Unconsolidated affiliates	15.6	7.7	1.5	15.6	7.7
Corporate	—	—	—	(107.2)	(80.8)
Interest expense	—	—	—	(129.4)	(137.8)
Other revenue and expense	22.0	3.0	1.5	(1.2)	(22.7)
Income taxes	—	—	—	(1,144.8)	(634.4)
Elimination (4)	(74.8)	(57.5)	(53.7)	(1.2)	(1.1)
	$12,726.3	$ 9,638.2	$ 6,315.6	$ 710.8	$ 561.6
Geographic Locations					
United States	$ 7,062.4(5,6)	$ 5,090.1(5)	$ 3,726.0(5)	$ 142.3(6)	$ 37.4
Canada	123.6	98.7	80.4	34.1	27.3
European Economic Community	1,710.1	1,256.5	948.5	1,060.6	721.6(2)
Africa	2,691.0	2,400.7	1,110.6	314.1(1)	311.4(1)
Latin America	1,031.2	733.1	391.8	542.6	335.7
Other areas	130.9	84.3	91.4	(14.7)	(3.8)
	12,749.2	9,663.4	6,348.7	2,079.0	1,429.6
Unconsolidated affiliates	15.6	7.7	1.5	15.6	7.7
Corporate	—	—	—	(107.2)	(80.8)
Interest expense	—	—	—	(129.4)	(137.8)
Other revenue and expense	22.0	3.0	1.5	(1.2)	(22.7)
Income taxes	—	—	—	(1,144.8)	(634.4)
Elimination (4)	(60.5)	(35.9)	(36.1)	(1.2)	—
	$12,726.3	$ 9,638.2	$ 6,315.6	$ 710.8	$ 561.6

(1) After Libyan taxes.
(2) Includes a $31.4 million gain related to the sale of Occidental's Belgian refinery.
(3) Includes a $122.1 million charge related to Occidental's European refining investments (consisting of a $95.6 million write-down of book value and a $26.5 million reserve for possible future obligations).
(4) Elimination of intersegment sales relates to various sales between certain segments and were immaterial to any single segment.

EXHIBIT 1–4

(*continued*)

(7) 31, 1978	Identifiable Assets			Depreciation, Depletion and Amortization			Capital Expenditures		
	December 31,			Year ended December 31,			Year ended December 31,		
	1980	1979	1978	1980	1979	1978	1980	1979	1978
				(in millions)					
$ 516.7(1)	$ 2,333.6	$ 2,146.6	$ 1,695.4	$ 287.2	$ 250.9	$ 158.7	$ 500.5	$ 483.1	$ 434.8
(120.6)(3)	716.2	705.1	481.7	7.0	15.9	8.1	14.8	16.3	11.6
120.0	1,204.7	878.5	805.2	44.9	55.8	36.8	129.2	81.6	79.2
(29.8)	668.6	538.8	439.8	24.0	23.9	15.2	42.9	70.7	72.4
5.6	1,107.9	993.0	793.4	40.5	34.6	29.2	153.4	158.6	152.3
(14.2)	200.0	111.8	104.9	14.9	16.8	8.8	70.7	43.5	13.7
477.7	6,231.0	5,373.8	4,320.4	418.5	397.9	256.8	911.5	853.8	764.0
1.5	98.0	113.2	118.8	—	—	—	—	—	—
(58.9)	300.9	73.3	169.3	19.6	5.1	2.5	13.9	4.6	2.0
(112.7)	—	—	—	—	—	—	—	—	—
(24.3)	—	—	—	—	—	—	—	—	—
(274.6)	—	—	—	—	—	—	—	—	—
(2.0)	—	—	—	—	—	—	—	—	—
$ 6.7	$ 6,629.9	$ 5,560.3	$ 4,608.5	$ 438.1	$ 403.0	$ 259.3	$ 925.4	$ 858.4	$ 766.0
$ 66.3	$ 3,868.3	$ 3,179.7	$ 2,456.2						
22.8	101.4	69.3	64.0						
231.0(3)	831.7	963.4	857.1						
40.9(1)	332.3	307.0	363.7						
120.7	1,042.2	824.3	556.2						
(6.0)	55.1	30.1	23.2						
475.7	6,231.0	5,373.8	4,320.4						
1.5	98.0	113.2	118.8						
(58.9)	300.9	73.3	169.3						
(112.7)	—	—	—						
(24.3)	—	—	—						
(274.6)	—	—	—						
—	—	—	—						
$ 6.7	$ 6,629.9	$ 5,560.3	$ 4,608.5						

(5) Includes export sales, consisting principally of agricultural chemical products and coal, of approximately $651 million in 1980, $499 million in 1979 and $442 million in 1978.

(6) Includes $123.6 million trading profits from forward sales of silver and gold.

(7) Research and development costs were $63.5, $46.5 and $35.5 million in 1980, 1979 and 1978, respectively.

EXHIBIT 1–4

(continued)

1979 Occidental Petroleum Annual Report

Summary of Consolidated Operations

offset by lower domestic undeveloped lease and exploration costs.

Depreciation, depletion and amortization of property, plant and equipment increased $80,521,000 (48.7 per cent) in 1978 primarily due to a full year of production in the Claymore field in the North Sea in 1978 as compared to one month in 1977 and to the buildup of production in Peru with related amortization. Payroll, sales, property and other taxes increased $12,405,000 (10.6 per cent) primarily due to increases in the tax base and the related rates. Royalties increased $47,883,000 (23.2 per cent) largely as a result of payments due on North Sea production.

The increase of $8,402,000 (7.1 per cent) in interest and debt expense before capitalized interest resulted primarily from two major Eurodollar borrowings. The decrease in capitalized interest of $8,455,000 (36.6 per cent) resulted from discontinuing the capitalization of construction-period interest relating to the development of the Claymore field in the North Sea following commencement of production at the end of 1977 partially offset by an increase in the capitalization of construction-period interest relating to development of coal reserves.

The provision for domestic taxes decreased by $11,019,000 (58 per cent) in 1978 due to reduced domestic income. The provision for foreign taxes increased by $171,928,000 (26.3 per cent) due to increased production and sales from the United Kingdom and Peru.

	Identifiable Assets		Revenues			
	December 31,			Year ended December 31,		
	1979	1978	1979	1978	1977	1976
				(in millions)		
						(Una
Industry Segments						
Oil and gas operations:						
Exploration and production	$ 2,146.6	$ 1,695.4	$ 3,943.2	$ 1,958.0	$ 1,830.4	$ 1,294.1
Marketing, transportation and refining	705.1	481.7	2,931.6	2,211.4	2,119.3	2,196.1
Chemical operations:						
Industrial chemicals	527.2	469.1	592.0	555.0	538.8	532.9
Plastics	239.0	230.1	376.8	307.5	294.8	297.3
Metal-finishing	112.3	106.0	310.4	278.2	246.5	238.8
Agricultural products	538.8	439.8	718.9	526.7	517.8	468.0
Coal	993.0	793.4	693.1	456.1	569.9	576.8
Other	111.8	104.9	138.9	90.8	65.5	70.1
	5,373.8	4,320.4	9,704.9	6,383.7	6,183.0	5,674.1
Unconsolidated affiliates	113.2	118.8	7.7	1.5	5.5	8.6
Corporate	73.3	169.3	—	—	—	—
Interest expense	—	—	—	—	—	—
Other revenue and expense	—	—	3.0	1.5	1.9	1.6
Income taxes	—	—	—	—	—	—
Elimination (4)	—	—	(77.4)	(71.1)	(110.1)	(74.8)
	$ 5,560.3	$ 4,608.5	$ 9,638.2	$ 6,315.6	$ 6,080.3	$ 5,609.5
Geographic Locations						
United States	$ 3,179.7	$ 2,456.2	$5,090.1(5)	$ 3,726.0(5)	$ 3,737.2(5)	
Canada	69.3	64.0	98.7	80.4	74.5	
European Economic Community	963.4	857.1	1,256.5	948.5	661.4	
Africa	307.0	363.7	2,400.7	1,110.6	1,397.4	
Latin America	824.3	556.2	733.1	391.8	192.7	
Other areas	30.1	23.2	84.3	91.4	129.0	
	5,373.8	4,320.4	9,663.4	6,348.7	6,192.2	
Unconsolidated affiliates	113.2	118.8	7.7	1.5	5.5	
Corporate	73.3	169.3	—	—	—	
Interest expense	—	—	—	—	—	
Other revenue and expense	—	—	3.0	1.5	1.9	
Income taxes	—	—	—	—	—	
Elimination	—	—	(35.9)	(36.1)	(119.3)	
	$ 5,560.3	$ 4,608.5	$ 9,638.2	$ 6,315.6	$ 6,080.3	

(1) After Libyan taxes.
(2) Includes a $31,400,000 gain related to the sale of Occidental's Belgian refinery.
(3) Includes a $122,100,000 charge related to Occidental's European refining investments.

EXHIBIT 1–4

(concluded)

Industry Segments and Foreign Operations

Occidental's business consists of several industry segments. The exploration and production segment is engaged in the exploration and extraction of crude oil, natural gas and natural gas liquids from subterranean reserves and in the development of a process for the extraction of shale oil from oil-bearing shale. The marketing, transportation and refining segment purchases and sells crude oil and natural gas from and to third parties, transports third party crude oil by marine vessels, trucks and pipelines and, through mid-1978, refined and marketed oil purchased from internal and external sources. The industrial chemicals segment develops, produces and sells a variety of industrial chemical products. Similarly, the plastics segment develops, produces and sells a variety of plastic materials, products and resins. The metal-finishing segment develops, manufactures and distributes metal-finishing chemicals, products, equipment and processes. The agricultural products segment mines, produces and sells agricultural chemicals, fertilizers and related products and distributes fertilizer materials. The coal segment mines, processes and sells both metallurgical and steam grades of coal.

The following tables set forth financial information related to Occidental's industry segments and geographic locations. Intersegment sales and transfers between geographic locations were not significant.

1975 (udited)	Operating Profit — Year ended December 31,				1975 (in millions) (Unaudited)	Depreciation, Depletion and Amortization — Year ended December 31,		Capital Expenditures	
	1979	1978	1977	1976		1979	1978	1979	1978
$ 1,108.7	$ 1,255.7(1)	$ 516.7(1)	$ 241.1(1)	$ 19.1(1)	$ (62.0)(1)	$ 250.9	$ 158.7	$ 483.1	$ 434.8
2,203.5	70.2(2)	(120.6)(3)	(8.5)	6.3	36.7	15.9	8.1	16.3	11.6
474.2	22.0	71.9	98.7	97.8	85.1	38.3	24.5	56.4	60.2
242.1	25.6	26.3	36.4	34.7	26.7	9.1	8.1	19.1	15.9
269.6	21.8	21.8	16.9	13.6	(6.8)	8.4	4.2	6.1	3.1
613.5	15.7	(29.8)	4.1	10.5	74.2	23.9	15.2	70.7	72.4
663.3	48.1	5.6	86.1	110.5	170.5	34.6	29.2	158.6	152.3
37.4	(28.4)	(14.2)	.4	8.6	(1.9)	16.8	8.8	43.5	13.7
5,612.3	1,430.7	477.7	475.2	301.1	322.5	397.9	256.8	853.8	764.0
4.4	7.7	1.5	5.5	8.6	4.4	—	—	—	—
—	(80.8)	(58.9)	(39.5)	(30.2)	(40.7)	5.1	2.5	4.6	2.0
—	(137.8)	(112.7)	(95.9)	(81.9)	(73.3)	—	—	—	—
11.1	(22.7)	(24.3)	(10.6)	(11.1)	.5	—	—	—	—
—	(634.4)	(274.6)	(180.5)	(57.4)	(37.1)	—	—	—	—
(230.4)	(1.1)	(2.0)	(.4)	(.2)	—	—	—	—	—
$ 5,397.4	$ 561.6	$ 6.7	$ 153.8	$ 128.9	$ 176.3	$ 403.0	$ 259.3	$ 858.4	$ 766.0

1979	1978	1977
$ 37.4	$ 66.3	$ 176.5
27.3	22.8	23.2
721.6(2)	231.0(3)	195.2
311.4(1)	40.9(1)	37.8(1)
335.7	120.7	26.6
(3.8)	(6.0)	17.4
1,429.6	475.7	476.7
7.7	1.5	5.5
(80.8)	(58.9)	(39.5)
(137.8)	(112.7)	(95.9)
(22.7)	(24.3)	(10.6)
(634.4)	(274.6)	(180.5)
—	—	(1.9)
$ 561.6	$ 6.7	$ 153.8

(4) Elimination of intersegment sales in 1979, 1978, 1977 and 1976 relates to various sales between certain segments and were immaterial to any single segment. Intersegment sales in 1975 consist principally of sales by Occidental's Libyan production operations to its European marketing and refining operations.

(5) Includes export sales, consisting principally of agricultural chemical products and coal, of approximately $499,000,000 in 1979, $442,000,000 in 1978 and $487,000,000 in 1977.

the divisions according to managers in the planning department. Hooker corporate examined capital availability, basing its assessment on past financial performance, market position, product maturity, and so on. Any gap in the projections was filled by a contingency reserve. Risk analysis of the various divisions' plans justified the reserve. Finally, negotiation between divisions and staff settled the final reserve issues and related costs. The plan was then sent off to Oxy corporate.

According to managers involved in strategic planning at Hooker, issues raised through risk analysis were sometimes buried in the financials. The extensive five-year financial plan required by Oxy included the strategic plan boiled down to negotiated issues. At that time Hooker was the only one of Oxy's three (oil and gas, coal, and chemicals) groups that provided a strategic plan along with the five-year financial projections.

Top management in Houston was technology oriented and unused to strategic planning. In addition, with the financial orientation of Oxy, it was difficult for Hooker to gain management attention for an issue like environmental concerns, an area difficult to quantify and with few precedents from which to develop a solution.

In the 1978 strategic plan, two areas of potential environmental concern were raised: the pollution of the river adjoining Hooker's Montague, Michigan, facilities (where the company later settled out of court with Michigan for a $15 million clean-up bill) and a potential Niagara Falls clean up estimated at $5 million. However, the probability for the Niagara Falls contingency was so low that the amount was never included in the final reserve (see Exhibit 1–5).

During the reserve development process, it was suggested that Hooker buy out the first ring of homes around the canal dump site. The legal staff rejected the plan saying Hooker did not want to admit any legal liability. Thus a major strategic issue—in this case Niagara en-

vironmental clean-up—was again buried in the financials. As a member of the strategic group said, "The trouble with trying to do effective strategic planning under such circumstances was that it was like plunking a sophisticated planning system, based on that of General Electric, onto an 'old nag.' "

By April 1978 the HCC 1978–1982 strategic plan had been approved by Oxy management and then by the board of directors in early May—the usual procedure. When the Love Canal crisis hit later that summer, the plan to buy out homes was not an official contingency plan.

That same spring, Hooker announced a major corporate reorganization. The idea was to centralize the staff of the different businesses, creating a unified corporation instead of a number of autonomous holding companies. An international division was put in place to focus on ex-U.S. enterprises and expansion overseas. The business divisions became groups, and all their presidents and staff were relocated to Houston. This had considerable impact on the Niagara Hooker chemicals and plastics division, which was divided into a few groups, its top layer of staff relocated to Houston, and a number of people laid off in Niagara Falls.

Mead Corporation

On August 11, 1978, Occidental Petroleum announced its intent to acquire the Mead Corporation, a forest products company, for $1 billion. Mead tried to prevent the takeover, and Hooker headquarters in Houston was soon overrun with lawyers from both sides collecting information for the ensuing court battle. Nearly every piece of paper in the files was numbered and "hot" files were marked with red stickers for possible future use. The Securities and Exchange Commission (SEC) was demanding more information on the potential riskiness of many of Oxy's businesses, and the company had to satisfy the SEC without

EXHIBIT 1-5

HCC - STRATEGIC PLAN 1978   EXECUTIVE SUMMARY

HCC RISK ANALYSIS (Cont.)
(Millions of Dollars)

Contingency	5-Yr Impact Range	Probability	Included in HCC "Reserve"	Recovery Options
B. Industrial Chemicals Group				
1. Montague environmental clean-up	$ 5 to 25	Low	$ 5	Exit
2. Niagara Falls environmental clean-up	5 to 25	Low	5	Legal action
3. Inability to achieve 2.2% increase in chlorine merchant market share	5 to 15	Med	10	Attempt to get competitor(s) to buy from HCC rather than to produce their own
4. Inability to achieve projected industrial systems technology sales	5 to 15	Med	5	1. More aggressive marketing of related products (phosphate evaporation) 2. Greater technical effort
5. Chlorine caustic prices and volume below forecast	4 to 22	Med	12	More aggressive marketing
6. Chlorate prices below forecast	5 to 15	Med	10	-----------
7. Power cost increase at Taft	16	Med	16	Co-generation
TOTAL INDUSTRIAL CHEMICALS	$45 - $133		$63	

appearing to have withheld information from its shareholders.

Communications were in turmoil. Once they had been provided to the SEC, thousands of internal company documents became publicly available through the Freedom of Information Act. The company lawyers had to approve all public statements by any employee.

Hooker joined the rest of Oxy under the public magnifying glass primarily because of the high-risk Russian Project, which was expected to provide a net loss of $40 million in the next year alone. Moreover, the fertilizer and commodity chemicals businesses (industrial chemicals) were in a cyclical market slump at the same time that the company was racking up multimillion-dollar expenses to get the Russian Project underway.

Occidental's attempted takeover of the Mead Corporation further aggravated Hooker's problems because all of Oxy's files—and thus Hooker's—were open to public scrutiny in the takeover battle. Ultimately Oxy lost Mead, but it still had to suffer the conse-

quences of the unfriendly takeover and the effects of having many of its internal documents become "evidence" against the corporation.

August 2, 1978

Hooker management began to feel the pressure when, by coincidence, Don McNeil's piece on the front page of *The New York Times* (see Exhibit 1–1) coincided with a declaration of a state of emergency by the New York state health commissioner, Robert Whalen.

Sandie Kroeger conferred with top management in Houston that day to decide on a public relations strategy during the crisis. Given the company's previous stance, she wondered whether Hooker should be more aggressive in its relations with the media. Members of the legal staff and management, however, wondered whether a more passive stance would be appropriate. They reasoned that the current attention in the press would die down in a few days.

2   REINVENTING COMMUNICATIONS

In the first chapter, we looked at how the environment that organizations must operate in has changed dramatically over the last half century. What I am calling "the new era of communications," which results from these changes, requires a totally different approach to corporate communications than we have seen in the past.

To begin that approach, we need to return to the basic theory behind all communications, whether an individual or organization is communicating. Much of this theory comes from ideas that were generated thousands of years ago by Aristotle. More recently, communications experts have adapted these same theories for use by individuals as they communicate in writing and speaking.

Few, however, have looked at how these same basic theories apply in the corporate communication context, that is, in the way organizations communicate with various groups of people. In this chapter, then, we will begin to apply these principles for use in organizations. Some of these ideas are just common sense, but it is amazing how often the simplest ideas are the most difficult for us to use in daily practice.

The chapter begins with a discussion of how communication theory developed, then moves to a discussion of how that theory can be used to set communication strategies in organizations. Then we turn to its application for the most important starting point of all—the connection between corporate communication and the mission of the firm itself.

The Ancient Roots of Communication Theory

Most of the theories we think about today in terms of communication are based on notions that are as old as language itself and the beginnings of social and political life. In ancient Greece, the subject we now refer to as communication was known as rhetoric, which meant using language to persuade whoever was listening to do something. Practicing the art of rhetoric was highly regarded by the Greeks. Many examples abound in the ancient literature that we read in college courses on the development of Western civilization.

The reputation of Odysseus as a great speaker bears witness to the notion that rhetoric was highly regarded and justifies the opinion among the ancient Greeks that Homer was the real father of oratory. After the age of Homer and Hesiod and the establishment of democratic institutions, the rapid development of industry and business, as well as the military, forced statesmen to become orators.

The birthplace of rhetoric as an art, however, was not in Greece, but in Sicily. According to Cicero, Aristotle gave an account of its origin in his lost history on the subject. But it is Aristotle himself, who lived and studied under Plato and taught in Athens from 367–347 B.C., who is most often associated with the development of the art of rhetoric. In his major work on the subject, *The Art of Rhetoric,* we can find the roots of modern communication theory.

Early in this seminal text, Aristotle defines the composition of every speech:

> . . . every speech is composed of three parts: the speaker, the subject of which he treats, and the person to whom it is addressed, I mean the hearer, to whom the end or object of the speech refers.

This tripartite system that we find in Aristotle's definition of speech has also been applied to all communication, whether written or oral, by a modern communications expert, Professor Mary Munter, in her *Guide to Managerial Communication.* Munter, however, extends the definition to managerial communication and includes other elements that are relevant for our discussion:

> Effective managerial communication—written or oral—is based on an effective strategy. Therefore, you should analyze the five strategic variables . . . before you start to write or speak: (1) communicator strategy . . . (2) audience strategy . . . (3) message strategy . . . (4) channel choice strategy, including when to write and when to speak; and (5) culture strategy, including how cultural variations affect your strategy.

As you can see, Munter has added the notion of which communication option (or channel) to use and cultural variation to Aristotle's basic theory of communication.

But how can an organization use ideas developed for individual communication to think about the way it communicates? In the next section, we will apply these concepts toward that end.

Developing Corporate Communication Strategies

Whether your organization is trying to develop a coherent image for itself through corporate advertising, to communicate effectively with employees about health benefits, to convince shareholders that the company is worth investing in, or just to get customers to buy products, it pays to use a coherent communication strategy to achieve these ends. And this strategy depends on thinking carefully about the same three parts that Aristotle used to describe the components of speech.

Instead of a speaker, *the organization itself* is the first component. The second component to think about in developing a corporate communication strategy would be what I will refer to throughout this book as *the constituents,* in place of Aristotle's "person to whom the end or object of the speech refers." While the final component, which Aristotle describes as "the subject of which he treats," I will refer to as *the message* (as Munter does in her definition). Figure 2–1 may be useful in thinking about the interaction among these three variables.

As we look at the interaction among the three variables, we see that each is connected to the others in some way and that strategies will develop according to these basic dependencies. In addition, the model is circular rather than linear, which means that it is an ongoing process rather than a system with a beginning and an end. Let's further define each of these variables and apply them to real situations to see how they operate in practice.

Setting an Effective Organization Strategy

Setting an effective organization strategy involves some of the same steps that you would take as an individual to communicate in a particular situation. These steps include determining what the *objectives* are for the particular communication, deciding what *resources* are available for achieving those objectives, and determining the organization's *image credibility* in terms of this task.

Defining Objectives. An organization, like an individual, might have many different reasons for deciding to communicate. For example, a company might want to announce to employees a change in its benefits package for the upcoming year. Let's suppose that the organization has decided to cut back on what it will pay toward each employee's health plan. In this case, its objective is more than just announcing the new package. It must also try to convince employees that there is a good

FIGURE 2–1

Corporate Communication Strategy Model

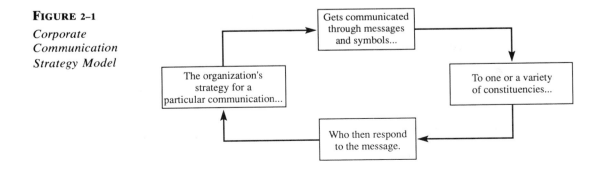

reason for taking something away from them. Thus, the objective here is to get employees to accept the change with a minimal amount of difficulty.

On the other hand, let's suppose that a Japanese sweets manufacturer has decided to enter the U.S. market. To stimulate interest in its confections, the company decides to produce a brochure that will both show and explain what the product is and how it is an extension of Japanese culture. The company's objective, then, is to create a demand among American consumers for something they neither know about currently nor want.

Notice that in both of these cases, the response from the constituency in question is what is most important. What the organization wants doesn't really matter as much as what the constituency in question is going to do. That is the basis for all communication strategy: *What is it that the organization wants in response from a particular constituency?*

Determining What Resources Are Available.   Deciding to communicate about something like an employee health plan or introducing a new product into a market depends to a great extent on what resources are available within the organization. Typically, the most important resource is money. But human resources are equally important, as is the amount of time it will take to accomplish the communication objective as defined above.

Let's go back to our example of the company that has decided to cut back on its health benefits for employees. In terms of money, the company must decide whether it is better just to announce the program as simply as possible, say through the company newspaper, or to hire a benefits consultant who has had a lot of experience with scaling back health benefits at other companies to help sell the new program to employees. The first possibility looks less expensive than the second in the short term, but if the employees revolt because they feel they are losing something for no good reason, the company might end up spending far more than it would have if it had hired the consultant in the first place.

Most of the companies I have worked with, unfortunately, err on the side of short-term, inexpensive solutions to communication problems because they are not looking at the problem from the perspective of the constituency in question. This is similar to the problem individuals have in communicating. They often look at their own needs rather than the needs of their audience and end up having difficulty reaching their own communication objective.

Part of the problem is that people just do not take communications very seriously. Since we all communicate regularly, it's harder to imagine such an all-encompassing activity being a discipline than it is for a function like accounting or a subject like calculus. But it is a discipline with rules and predictable results based on both common sense and some excellent research that has taken place at many universities over the last decade.

I also mentioned that human resources are an important factor in determining the success or failure of a company in achieving its objectives. Typically, too few are assigned to deal with a communication task, and the few involved are usually inexperienced or unqualified.

Imagine a company that has just gone public and has decided to create an investor relations function to deal with shareholder relations and communication with securities analysts. It could assign one person to do all of these things, or it may decide that it really needs three. Obviously, the best approach would depend on the size of the company and its shareholder base. But I have seen a multibillion dollar company turn this function over to one person with weak communication skills rather than devote two or three experts to deal with the different constituencies involved. In this company's case, it wasn't a question of whether they could afford to pay more people to do the job correctly, it was the lack of understanding about how important the communication function really is and the limitations put on the human resources needed to accomplish a specific task.

The company in question changed its approach after analysts started to downgrade the stock despite a healthy prospect for the company's future. The CEO discovered that the analysts simply felt that the investor relations person at the company was not interested in giving them sufficient information to rate the company's stock. This led them to believe that something was wrong at the company. The investor relations person, on the other hand, was actually trying to do two or three jobs at the same time and simply could not keep up with the demands of the job. After this incident, the company hired two more professionals to handle the job properly, and its stock price shot back to where it should have been all along.

Time, like human resources and money, is also a critical factor in determining an organization's corporate communication strategy. Let's look at two approaches for dealing with the same problem involving the allocation of time.

In the case of the Japanese confectioner mentioned earlier, the company decided to produce a brochure (with the help of a communications consulting firm) describing its product more than two years before the piece was actually necessary. Over the course of two years, however, so much time was involved in getting everyone in the company to buy into the copy that was developed for the brochure, as well as the design, that it took over a year to produce an eight-page pamphlet. Much of the reason for the tremendous amount of time needed to develop this piece had to do with cultural differences between Japanese and American business styles.

For an American firm, the luxury of devoting such an enormous amount of time to such a simple project is usually unheard of. I have worked on similar projects for American firms that are produced from start to finish in a matter of weeks. But is this really a better approach?

The allocation of time, like the allocation of all resources, should be determined by what it will really take to achieve the company's objective rather than short-term solutions. In some cases, that might mean allocating more resources than the organization would like to achieve the desired result. But almost always, the organization is much better off allocating the resources up front rather than botching things up. Correcting mistakes in corporate communication can be a very costly proposition. As we saw in the Hooker Chemical case, the company's decision to put limited amounts of resources up front for dealing with the Love Canal crisis cost it far more in the long term.

Determining the Organization's Image Credibility.   Once the organization has set objectives for a communication and decided what resources are available to accomplish that objective, it must determine what kind of credibility it has with the constituency in question. An organization's image credibility is based on several factors. We will get into this in much greater detail in Chapter 4 when we talk about image and identity, but it is also a critical factor in the development of all communication strategies, whether related to image specifically or not. Primarily, credibility is based on the constituency's perception of the organization rather than the reality of the organization itself.

As an example, think about a university that is trying to generate positive publicity in the national press. If the university is not well known outside of its region, this might prove very difficult. Its image credibility in this situation would be very limited because national press representatives would have limited experience with the institution compared to an institution that already has a national reputation. Thus, no matter what kind of resources the university puts behind this effort, it will be an up-hill battle.

On the other hand, some institutions are uninterested in national publicity except when it is in their own interest. Salomon Brothers, for example, the prominent New York investment bank was well-known (as were all of the investment banks in the 1980s) for trying to avoid publicity at any cost. When it found itself involved in scandals in the early 1990s, the firm suddenly decided to become proactive rather than reactive in terms of its communication efforts. Given the limited image credibility it had with reporters, however (not to mention its lack of goodwill), this was very difficult to achieve. The constituency in question was not inclined to help Salomon meets its objectives because Salomon lacked credibility. Although the company was ready to put unlimited resources behind the effort, it nevertheless failed initially for reasons different from the example of the university mentioned above.

Thus, we can see that the amount of image credibility the organization has is an important factor in setting a coherent communication strategy. For simple tasks, this is not a critical problem. But in other cases, the amount of credibility the organization has built up can make a huge difference in determining the success or failure an organization has in achieving its objectives.

The three steps necessary for setting an effective organization strategy—determining objectives, deciding on the proper allocation of resources, and determining the organization's image credibility—are the building blocks upon which all other steps in the process depend. Once these are set in place, the organization can turn to an assessment of the constituents involved.

Analyzing Constituencies

Analyzing constituencies is similar to analyzing your audience when you want to plan a speech or write a memo. It involves determining who the constituency really is, what their attitude is toward the organization, and what they already know about the communication in question. We will look at each of these aspects of constituency analysis in turn.

Who Are Your Organization's Constituents?   Sometimes the answer to this question is obvious, but most of the time, it will take careful consideration to analyze who the relevant constituents are for a particular corporate message. Do not be fooled into thinking that it is *always* obvious who the main constituent is.

Once in an executive program, a vice president in charge of marketing told me a story from his personal experience that brought this story home at least as it relates to an individual communicating with someone else. The executive vice president that he reported to had decided on cutting the secretarial staff due to changes in communication patterns in the company. Most managers in the marketing department had voice mail and didn't need a secretary to answer the phone, used a computer with an electronic mail system, and needed a secretary for only the most routine tasks.

This vice president said that he had to write his plan for cutting the secretarial staff by almost two thirds in a memo to the vice president in charge of personnel. It involved laying off about five secretaries in the department over a period of six months. Many of them had been with the firm for several years.

As usual, the marketing v.p. typed up his thoughts in rough form on his personal computer and asked his secretary to print the final draft onto his letterhead. Although his secretary was not one of the five affected by the layoffs, she couldn't help but empathize with her colleagues of many years, and within an hour, the marketing v.p. had a revolt on his hands.

Now obviously, this gentleman didn't intend for his secretary to be a part of his constituency, nor did he stop to think about her reaction to the change when he asked her to print the letter to the personnel v.p. Nonetheless, she became a conduit to a more important constituency—the employees who would actually be affected by the plan.

This simple example on the personal level is very instructive to organizations seeking to communicate at a more macro level as well. Just as we cannot always control the flow of information to one constituency alone on an individual level, on the corporate level we run into the same set of problems.

We need then to think about the flow of information between the organization and a constituency, or set of constituencies, as a process with several layers. The first layer is the *main constituency* with whom we are actually trying to communicate; the second layer is often less obvious, and I will refer to it as the *shadow constituency;* and finally, another constituency needs to be addressed, which I will refer to as the *roadblock constituency*. Let's use an example to find out what I mean.

When the chairman of a major corporation decided to change the image of his company by creating a new logo in the early 1990s, the main constituency he wanted to appeal to were the customers the company hoped to attract. This constituency included about 50 percent of the U.S. population at the time. Over a period of five years all of the company's products would reflect the new image.

When the new logo was ready to go, however, the problems that developed are indicative of the difficulties organizations face in communicating with a single constituency. The company obviously wanted to tell everyone in America about the new logo and what it meant as a symbol for change in both the management of the company and in what was going on with its products.

Not everyone, however, agreed with the change. Some people liked the way it had always been. The old logo may even have held some nostalgic appeal for some audiences. In addition, the entrenched management at the company who had been around when the old logo was developed in the 1960s were also resistant to change. These naysayers were the roadblock constituency for this company in its attempt to change its image. Fortunately, the group was not large, and people came to accept the new logo; they liked it much more than the old one.

But, as I mentioned earlier, not all of the changes could be completed at once, so a shadow constituency also had to be considered. That group included the millions of Americans who would hear about the new logo and what it implied in the company's media blitz, but would run into the same old logo for the next several years. Again, by analyzing the constituencies beforehand, the company was able to think of ways to deal with this problem through some creative solutions involving communications. Although the company couldn't change the problem and everything else at once, it could acknowledge that this was a problem to the group who wouldn't see change for years.

What Is the Constituency's Attitude toward the Organization?

In addition to analyzing who the constituencies for a particular communication really are, the organization must try to assess what the constituents think about them.

We know from experience that it is easier to communicate with people who know and like us than it is to those who do not. The same is true for organizations. If the company has built up goodwill with the constituency in question, it will be much easier to reach the objective. The classic example, which has been used for several years as an example of good corporate communication, is Johnson & Johnson's ability to save the Tylenol brand in 1982, when poisoned capsules killed seven people in Chicago.

That the company was able to succeed against all odds (ad whiz Jerry Della Famina declared Tylenol impossible to save at the time, as did several other experts in communication) was a tribute to the hard work it had done before the tragedy (for which the company was not really responsible) actually happened. The company was known in the industry, among doctors, among consumers, and by the press as rock solid, willing to stand by its products, and do the right thing no matter what the cost. In this case, the cost ran into the hundreds of millions of dollars as the company recalled over 31 million bottles of Tylenol capsules.

Convincing people to buy a product that could be laced with cyanide is not an easy proposition. But because the company had the trust of many different constituencies, it was able to achieve its objective, which was to bring the brand back from the dead. If people hadn't trusted the company, or if they had questioned its behavior in any way, this would never have been possible.

What Does the Constituency Know about the Topic?

In addition to attitudes toward the company, we must also consider the constituency's attitude toward the communication itself. If they are predisposed to do what you want, then they are more likely to help the organization reach its objective. If they are not, however, the organization will have great difficulty in trying to achieve its goals.

Probably the most pervasive problem companies face is that people generally feel less positive about things they know nothing about. I remember going to a movie theater in New York City a few years ago where several different films were playing. I started talking to a young man and he asked me what I was going to see. When I told him, he said that the film was not worth seeing. I asked him how he could know this since the film in question had just opened that day. His reply was that he hadn't seen it, but he knew that he didn't like it! Maybe this is just an example of a crazy New Yorker (one wonders how he ever went to see anything), but I think that it represents the general nature of people to distrust things they know little about.

The Japanese confectioner that I mentioned earlier was a victim of the same bias as it tried to convince Americans to buy a product that was well known and liked in Japan but completely foreign to Americans. The company, Toraya, is one of the oldest companies on earth. It can trace its roots back to the 9th century, and the same family has been in control of the firm for 17 generations. In Japan, the firm is seen as the highest quality manufacturer of *wagashi,* or sweets as we would call them. Toraya has been serving the imperial family since its inception.

Given its long history and aristocratic roots, the president of the company assumed that the product would speak for itself in the U.S. market. Since no one else was around to compete with the firm, middle managers in charge of the U.S. operation assumed that its introduction of *wagashi* would be a huge success.

Unfortunately, they didn't think about how American palates would react to the taste of a sweet made out of red beans and seaweed. Most of the people who heard about the product couldn't even pronounce its name, and when they tasted the gelatinous form of the product, known as *yokan,* they were very negative about the experience.

To get consumers in the United States interested in the product, the company had to educate people about the role of *wagashi* in Japanese history, and its exclusivity as demonstrated by its aristocratic roots. A colleague who tasted the product early in the process of its introduction to the United States likened the experience to the first people who tasted caviar or espresso. It tastes horrible until you realize the importance of the product in terms of its socioeconomic significance.

Companies that try to sell an idea to the public are always in danger of failing as a result of the negative information people may have from previous experiences as well. For example, when the company that sold Yugos, the Yugoslavian car, first came onto the market in the early 1980s, people felt that Yugos were a cheap novelty item, and there was even talk about them being a kind of Volkswagen Beetle for the 80s. Then the product started to fall apart, and the company went bankrupt. Despite repeated attempts to save the product, people were not likely to trust the firm again, and opted to stop buying Yugos. The company folded when the Yugoslav war erupted.

Thus, after a firm has set objectives for its corporate communication, it must thoroughly analyze the constituencies involved. This means understanding who the constituency really is, finding out what their attitude is toward the organization, and determining what they already know and feel about the communication in question. Once this is accomplished, the organization is ready to move to the final phase in setting a communication strategy: determining how to deliver the message most appropriately for the constituency.

Delivering Messages Appropriately

Delivering messages appropriately involves a two-step analysis for companies. They must decide *how* they want to deliver the message and *what* approach to take in structuring the message itself.

Determining the proper communication channel is more difficult for organizations than it is for people. For an individual deciding on a channel, the choices are usually limited to writing and speaking, with some variation in terms of group or individual interaction. For organizations, however, the channels available for delivering the message are several. For example, the company looking to reveal a change in top management may decide to announce it through a press release, which gets the message out to a broad set of constituents. It may also decide to announce the change in a memo to employees.

This simple example alone, however, has multiple variations. Should the press release go to local media or national media? If the company is multinational, should it get the message out on an international newswire, such as Reuters? Should the message go to employees through visual communications since many companies today have satellite hookups for far-flung operations? Then there is the whole question of timing. Should the employees hear about it first? Should the story be given to one reporter before all others on an exclusive basis?

Each time a corporate communication strategy is developed, the question of which channels to use should be explored carefully before proceeding. But the company should also think about the best way to structure the message and what to include in the message itself.

According to most experts in communication, the choices about how to structure the message fall into two categories: direct and indirect structure. By direct structure, I mean saying exactly what you mean rather than trying to hide the message or building up to the message through a series of communications. Indirect is the reverse; you do not say exactly what you mean in the communication.

When should a company choose to be direct and when should it decide to be indirect? Normally, my advice to any organization is to be as direct as you possibly can with as many constituencies as possible. Indirect communication is confusing and harder to understand than the direct approach. Take the example of Nissan when it first introduced the Infiniti series in the United States. Instead of just coming out with photographs of the new cars (as it does now) the company took a more indirect (and typically Japanese) approach by showing impressions of landscapes and creating a mood without once showing the public a product. As compared to the approach its direct competitor, Toyota's Lexus, took by showing the traditional pictures of cars, this was a creative success. Unfortunately, it didn't help sell many cars. What the company was trying to do was to create an image (see Chapter 4 for more on this as it relates to Nissan) through this type of advertising, but this mixture of product and image advertising was completely lost on the American public.

The same problem arises when a company finds itself in some sort of trouble. Traditionally, the response to questions when problems came up was "no comment." Today, this indirect approach simply doesn't work with a public hungry for the next sound byte and scores of media hounds looking for a good angle on the story. Usually, saying that the company cannot talk about the situation until all of the facts are in is better than just saying "no comment" or nothing at all. But managers are often influenced by lawyers who are only thinking about the legal ramifications of saying anything in litigation-oriented American society. Deciding to be direct often means taking the court of public opinion, which is often far more important, into consideration as well.

Creating a coherent corporate communication strategy, then, involves the three-step process we have discussed in detail above: defining what the organization's overall strategy is for the communication, analyzing the relevant constituencies, and delivering messages appropriately.

The Corporate Communication Connection to Mission

By creating a coherent strategy based on the time-tested theories we have presented in this chapter, the organization is well on its way to reinventing its handling of communications. Just as important for the firm, however, is its ability to link the overall strategy of the firm to its communication efforts. Michael Porter set the agenda for discussion of strategy in 1979 with his *Harvard Business Review* article "How Competitive Forces Shape Strategy."[1] Managers looking toward the development of strategies in the 1990s need to think about how external forces shape its strategy as well.

One of the most compelling examples of this phenomenon is the effect that environmental matters have had on industry. Although companies are not always legally bound to clean up their act with regard to the environment, they are often morally bound to do so by groups willing to pressure them into doing the right thing. While this may not be their

---

[1] Michael Porter "How Competitive Forces Shape Strategy," *Harvard Business Review,* March-April 1979, pp. 137-145.

primary interest in terms of overall strategy, it becomes a priority in the end.

How the organization's overall strategy will be affected by external forces is determined by what industry the firm is in, where it does business, and how public its operations are. But in addition to thinking about coping with competition, the question of how the firm will be perceived externally must be considered. Just as the company's awareness about competitive forces makes it less vulnerable to attack from competitors, its awareness of external forces also makes it less vulnerable to attacks that can easily affect its position in its industry.

My recommendation is for a firm to consider its corporate communications effort while it is developing its overall strategy as manifested in the company mission statement. By doing so at the inception of its overall strategy, the firm avoids repercussions later. Since all organizations operate at the behest of the public will, this egalitarian approach to communications will be much appreciated by a society that has come to depend on its organizations more than ever before.

CASE
BROWN & SHARPE

John Gordon, director of industrial relations for Brown & Sharpe Manufacturing Company, drove up to the barbed-wire fence of his company's Precision Park facility one morning in early June 1982. The entrance surrounding the Rhode Island manufacturing concern's major plant looked more like a prison than a machine tool operation. A strike by the International Association of Machinists (IAM) was then in its seventh month. A particularly violent winter and spring had passed as a result of the company's decision to hire replacements in February 1982, four months after the strike began (see Exhibit 2–1).

As Gordon drove past the vast array of state, local, and company-hired security guards, he thought back to a phone call he had received the night before from Dick Jocelyn, Brown & Sharpe's manager of labor relations. Apparently, the IAM had just hired a sophisticated labor organizer from New York named Ray Rogers. Rogers was head of a consulting firm called Corporate Campaign, Inc.

Jocelyn was concerned because Rogers's Corporate Campaign tactics had been instrumental in forcing the J.P. Stevens & Co. management to recognize the textile workers union after a 17-year struggle. These tactics included the rallying of community, religious, and political support. In addition, Rogers's campaigns were covered extensively by local and national media. For example, the J.P. Stevens organizing fight appeared in the pages of local papers in South Carolina and in the national business press—*The Wall Street Journal* and *Business Week*. In Jocelyn's view, the man was dangerous.

When John Gordon and Dick Jocelyn met for their daily session that morning, they re-solved to work out a strategy that would minimize the effect of Rogers's unorthodox tactics. Among their many concerns was how to respond to the inevitable media coverage that was about to descend on the company.

Brown & Sharpe History

The multinational machine tool company began as a watch and clock-making venture. In 1833, father, David, and son, Joseph R. Brown, opened their business in Providence, Rhode Island. Apprentice Lucian Sharpe joined the firm in 1848 and formed a partnership with the younger Brown in 1851.

The B&S partnership became a renowned technological pacesetter. The partners produced the first Vernier caliper, sewing machines and needle bars, the first universal milling machine, the universal grinding machine, the formed-tooth gear cutter, and other products including horse hair clippers. Brown, a brilliant inventor, developed many products that remained virtually unchanged over the next century, while Sharpe ran the business operations.

B&S incorporated in 1868 and soon shifted its priorities to meeting demand. For the next 50 years, plants were expanded or built, and employment swelled. By 1920, over 7,500 Rhode Islanders worked for the company. The business, however, was cyclical and followed national economic trends (see Exhibit 2–2). The all-time employment peak of 11,119 occurred during World War II; the all-time trough of 1,295 occurred during the Great Depression.

Current Chairman Henry D. Sharpe, Jr. (Lucian's grandson) first became corporate president in the 1950s. When he took control,

EXHIBIT 2-1

BATTLE ZONE: Using a "pepper fogger," police spray tear gas over strikers blocking the main entrance to the Brown & Sharpe plant in North Kingstown this morning.

SOURCE: *The Evening Bulletin*, "Violence at Brown & Sharpe" (Providence, R.I.: Providence Journal Co., March 22, 1982). Photo by Jim Daniels.

he was 26 years old and a budding journalist. By the 1960s, the company moved corporate headquarters from Providence to Precision Park in North Kingstown, joined the New York Stock Exchange, and acquired a foreign subsidiary.

Both Chairman Sharpe and President and CEO Donald Roach were active leaders in the Rhode Island community. Sharpe served as a Brown University trustee and as a *Providence Journal-Bulletin* director. Roach, a Harvard Business School graduate, served as director of the second largest state bank—Rhode Island Hospital Trust National Bank.

During the 1970s, Roach introduced computer technology into B&S products. In 1978, the B&S DigitCal replaced the 19th century caliper as a precise measuring device. The Dig-

itCal was the first such microchip tool placed on the market anywhere. By the 1980s, lines of business included pumps, machine tools, and measuring devices. Manufacturing operations were located stateside in Rhode Island, Michigan, and North Carolina, and abroad in Switzerland, the United Kingdom, and West Germany.

President Roach attempted to reduce general business cycle effects on the company. As early as 1972, he advocated bridge building, which minimized work force reductions and built inventories during economic downturns. Over 500 employees' jobs were saved within the next two years. Roach's interest in employee effectiveness led to a company study in 1979–80. The industrial relations staff studied B&S's Rhode Island operations and found that

EXHIBIT 2-2

	1982	1981	1980	1979	1978
Cyclical Trends as Reflected in Recent Financial Data					

Five Year Financial Data (Historical, in thousands except share and employee data)

	1982	1981	1980	1979	1978
Net Sales	$149,827	$205,356	$227,472	$193,250	$148,540
Net Income	(13,547)	6,040	13,649	10,494	5,271
Share Price (yr. end)	10.630	18.000	28.000	27.125	13.640
Cash dividends declared per share	.6800	1.3200	1.200	.9000	.5833
Number of employees (yr. end)	3,032	4,089	4,172	4,147	3,532

Five Year Financial Data (Historical, reclassified to reflect the effects of discontinued operations)

	1982	1981	1980	1979	1978
Net Sales	$143,770	$195,018	$216,312	$182,420	$139,271
Net Income	(12,039)	5,909	13,025	10,133	5,165

Five Year Financial Data (Average 1982 dollars, current costs, reclassified to reflect the effects of discontinued operations and to conform to SFAS70: Financial Reporting and Changing Prices: Foreign Currency Translation)

	1982	1981	1980	1979	1978
Net Sales	$143,770	$206,972	$253,386	$242,582	$206,056
Net Income	(15,184)	347	7,870	6,081	NA
Share Price (yr. end)	10.63	18.49	31.33	34.11	19.43
Cash dividends declared per share	.68	1.40	1.41	1.20	.86

employee motivation and productivity could be improved.

Human Resource Development at B&S

Industrial relations director John Gordon viewed employee effectiveness as a management problem. Gordon, a Columbia MBA and former Ciba-Geigy Pharmaceutical human resources manager, defined motivation as "the desire by an employee to want to do what you want him to do." He divided motivation into a commodity element and a discretionary element. The employees' commodity element was their ability to "perform to the minimum acceptable standard to avoid being discharged." The employees' discretionary element, however, was their willing cooperation to "do things beyond minimum expectations." Gordon sought to capture the discretionary element (see Exhibit 2–3).

After completing the management study, B&S started to implement its human resource plan. The company founded a newspaper to communicate corporate concerns. The newspaper included messages from president Roach and divisional managers; employee recognition for cost-saving suggestions, good work, and athletic league participation; and articles about the effects of local, national, and international events on the company. In the newspaper, Roach expressed his concern with Rhode Island's extraordinarily high workers' and unemployment compensation costs, as well as increasing energy costs. The B&S president also emphasized the company's need to compete with the Japanese machine tool industry that was rapidly gaining its share of the American market. To respond to these problems, the president sought improved employee motivation and productivity. He declared:

EXHIBIT 2–3

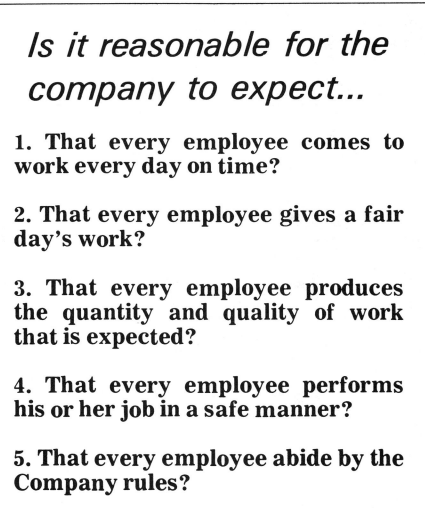

Is it reasonable for the company to expect...

1. That every employee comes to work every day on time?

2. That every employee gives a fair day's work?

3. That every employee produces the quantity and quality of work that is expected?

4. That every employee performs his or her job in a safe manner?

5. That every employee abide by the Company rules?

SOURCE: From B&S news, 9/80.

(continued)

EXHIBIT 2–3 (*concluded*)

Would Brown & Sharpe be a better place to work...

1. If all employees knew exactly what's expected of them?

2. If every employee who failed to meet the performance standards was helped to meet them?

3. If every employee did not have value judgments made about him or her as a person, however poor the performance might be?

4. If every employee was given the fairest possible break and was given the benefit of the doubt when a doubt exists?

5. If every employee "belonged" as a member of a section and a department, knew what the goals were, and knew how each was doing?

6. If every employee was treated as an individual and approached in terms of his or her individual needs?

7. If every employee knew where he or she fits in the organization?

8. If every employee was told how he or she was doing?

9. If the Company listened to what employees say without recrimination, even when what employees say is negative?

10. If every employee was recognized for his or her contribution?

11. If every employee was asked and given the reason why, rather than being told?

12. If every employee was developed until he or she was making the optimum use of his or her capabilities?

SOURCE: Brown & Sharpe *News*, September 1980.

First, we intend to keep everyone much better informed about the business. . . . This newspaper is an important first step in that direction. We have also started a newsletter for supervisors. . . .

Second, we will also try to do a much better job of listening. The vice presidents and I will start holding small group meetings. . . .

Third, all managers will be invited to attend a series of sessions . . . [about] working together more effectively.

According to Gordon, employees recognized these managerial efforts. He said that they sensed management was trying to change.

Union leaders said they saw the program as representing another managerial effort—to destroy the union. They viewed the company's new emphasis on individuals as an antiunion ploy. In particular, they claimed Roach complicated employee grievance procedures—leading to increasing arbitrations and a deteriorating labor-management relationship.

According to Bob Thayer, business representative for the local district of the International Association of Machinists and a former B&S employee:

Something started to change in 1975. The latitude of industrial relations to adjust difficulties was getting condensed. The grievance procedure was being bastardized, and the case load to personnel was on the increase.

In short, the labor leader saw a deterioration in the previously cordial relations with management.

Thayer pointed to public evidence of management's changing sentiments. In the August 1981 company newspaper, management described two companies and asked, "Which is the better company?" (see Exhibit 2–4). Labor interpreted Company A as a nonunion prototype and Company B as the existing union shop. The comparison inflamed labor leaders. Representative Thayer sent a letter to Gordon in response, but never received a reply (see Exhibit 2–5). Thayer claimed the "ivory tower" management had revealed its antiunion attitude.

Labor Relations at Brown & Sharpe

Prior to the 1970s, labor relations at B&S were notably free of the strife that was to make the 1981 strike the largest and longest running strike in the United States. Labor characterized relations with management prior to 1975 as firm but fair. Aside from some minor skirmishes during World War I and again during Henry Sharpe, Jr.'s first year as president (in 1951), the company had never faced a prolonged strike.

Contracts were renewed every two years until the 1970s. In 1975, the company endured an eight-week strike. Since the company settled with the union just before unemployment benefits were to be distributed, labor felt that management wanted the 1975 strike. Labor leaders felt that a strike was B&S's easy and cheap way to deal with a downswing in the industry at that time.

Although the 1977 negotiations were settled without a strike, the 1979 negotiations led to a three-day walkout. With the national economy in an upswing, management felt that the union was able to win a generous settlement. Labor felt that the 1979 strike would never have happened if "those charged with responsibility in 1979 had full latitude to negotiate a contract," said Thayer, who was then president of the B&S local. "The direction was coming from top management, not labor and industrial relations directors."

Negotiations: 1981. As management approached negotiations in 1981, they felt confident about conducting successful collective bargaining sessions with labor. According to President Roach, everything was done correctly. First, B&S offered a generous wage

Exhibit 2–4

Which Is the Better Company?

As a Customer: **Which Company Would You Buy From?**
As an Investor: **Which Company Would You Invest In?**
As an Employee: **In Which Company Would Your**
                     Future Be More Secure?

	Company A	*Company B*
Management System	Efficient systems provide concise, accurate and timely information which supports sound decision making.	Outdated systems produce untimely and frequently inaccurate information that cannot be consistently relied upon in the decision-making process.
Management Style	High standards of performance expected, but style is supportive.	Standards of performance variable. Style is punitive.
Capital Investment	Long-term commitment to continued reinvestment in the most productive equipment.	Very little investment in new equipment. Result: low productivity and poor quality.
Research and Development	Continued investment in improved and new products to maintain and enhance competitive position.	Limited investment in new products resulting in reduced sales because of outdated product lines.
Communications	All employees know what the goals are and how they're doing. Management listens to employee concerns.	Management doesn't communicate anything and never listens to employee concerns.
Employment Stability	Employment is kept as stable as possible to the extent that the company can afford it. Reductions in the workforce, when necessary, are by performance.	Workforce expands and contracts based on business cycles. Extensive and frequent layoffs take place by seniority. Result: Many of the best performers are not retained.

package, with 11, 10, and 9 percent raises in three successive years. This offer far surpassed industry and general business standards. Second, the company emphasized its commitment to Rhode Island. Management claimed that workers were scared about B&S's possible departure, especially with the unhealthy business environment in the state. Yet B&S wanted a Rhode Island workforce that would be flexible and responsive to increasing foreign competition.

During the negotiations, management and labor were not concerned with the wage package; they primarily focused on two new "flexibility" articles. Article 15.2 declared company supervisors' rights to assign employees to specific tasks, as long as the work fell in the same labor grades, occupational codes, shifts, and

Exhibit 2–4 (*concluded*)

	Company A	Company B
Promotions	Earned on the basis of performance.	By seniority.
Wage Increases	Earned on basis of performance and contribution.	Not related to performance.
Flexibility	Employees extremely responsive in work assignments, transfers, and scheduling to meet both immediate and longer term business requirements.	Rigid work practices restrict the company's ability to respond quickly to changed conditions, raising costs and allowing competitors to capitalize on opportunities.
Labor Disruptions	Work stoppages virtually non-existent, allowing company to plan effectively and customers to rely on the company as a continuing source of supply.	Frequent work stoppages erode customer confidence in the company's ability to deliver on schedule, polarize the workforce, lower efficiency, and limit the company's ability to plan.
Quality	Increased sales result from company's high quality reputation. Strong understanding in all functions that quality of work is a key to success in the marketplace.	Prevalent "what-you-can-get-away-with" attitude results in customer skepticism about the company's concern for quality, reflected in a loss of repeat business and higher warranty costs.
Productivity	Continuing improvements in productivity have controlled product cost, allowing the company to price products competitively.	Limited improvements in productivity make the company a high-cost manufacturer, resulting in non-competitive prices for their products.

Source: Brown & Sharpe *News*, August 1981.

seniority groups. Management designed the article to stop what they viewed as inefficient job preference or machine seniority practices, where workers could decide what specific parts of their jobs to perform. Article 9.4(i) allowed for mandatory employee transfers. If no employees responded to B&S's request for temporary job volunteers, then the company would assign these jobs. The assignments would be limited to 30 days (maximum), and workers' seniority, based on their permanent jobs, would remain unchanged. Workers' pay also would remain unchanged, unless they filled jobs normally held by higher labor grade workers. In the latter cases, replacements' pay would increase during the assignments.

Labor did not understand why these flexibility articles were needed, how the revised

EXHIBIT 2–5

International Association of Machinists and Aerospace Workers
AFL-CIO

DISTRICT LODGE NO. SIXTY-FOUR

78 KENWOOD STREET, CRANSTON, RHODE ISLAND 02907
Tel. No. (401) 944-4580—4581

August 31, 1981

Mr. John Gordon, Director Industrial Relations
Brown & Sharpe Mfg. Co.
Precision Park
North Kingstown, R.I. 02852

Dear Mr. Gordon:

On behalf of all IAM&AW members employed at Brown & Sharpe Mfg. Co., I feel compelled to respond to the article - "WHICH IS A BETTER COMPANY?" - published in the B&S News of August, 1981.

It becomes obvious after reading the Article that the connotations and perceptions drawn are a direct attack on the collective bargaining system, recognized not only in this country, but universally, as a system that given its due, works in the best interest of all parties concerned.

Reference between Company "A" and Company "B" is a typical example of a Company without a collective bargaining agreement and one with an agreement.

The twelve items addressed in the article, even if they were given a positive view, certainly do not represent what collective bargaining has meant to Brown & Sharpe Mfg. Co. and its unionized employees.

The history of collective bargaining between the Company and the Machinists Union, given a careful review, reflect a posture between the parties best portrayed as when various challenges affecting the parties need addressing. Sound labor relations have been implemented,

---

articles would increase worker flexibility, or how they would help B&S respond to foreign competition. In fact, labor interpreted these articles as union-busting measures. Consequently, they saw a rapidly approaching dead end with management. They had cooperated, conditionally approving 85 percent of the company's demands. The union would not, however, approve the remaining measures, which they called a "death blow."

Management also perceived a dead-end attitude embodied in union Business Representative Thayer. Industrial relations director Gordon commented that although Thayer had worked at B&S previously, Thayer was unaware of recent changes and a refocusing of the workforce toward flexibility. Dick Jocelyn, a University of Rhode Island graduate who served as negotiator and labor relations manager, said he failed to receive any response on these flexibility articles from Thayer. As the contract expiration date approached, Jocelyn expressed shock at Thayer's refusal to extend negotiations.

Thayer saw management as arrogant and inflexible. Thayer stated that Jocelyn talked of

EXHIBIT 2–5 *(concluded)*

and examples of this are evident when one considers the move from the providence location to the new plant in North Kingstown. Also the adoption of the New Form Standards which were negotiated and adopted in 1953. More recently, a serious problem arose when McDonnell-Douglas removed Brown & Sharpe Mfg. Co. from its list of bidding manufacturers. As you know, when we mutually addressed these problems, both productive and worthwhile resolves benefiting all were attained.

For one to question a seniority system which is no more than a recognition of an employees service to the Company, is to suggest a system which does not recognize or value long service.

To question wage increases by contract vs. performance is totally an 18th Century viewpoint. Unions became a reality because those who determined earnings based on performance felt few, if any, were worthy of a wage increase.

I could continue on in rebuttal of this unjust article but I will choose what I think is a more productive approach. I would request that Brown & Sharpe Mfg. Co. review our total record of labor relations and hopefully they will recognize a work force that has always been responsive to placing Brown & Sharpe Mfg. Co. in a viable position in the marketplace.

In closing I would like to quote statements by former Presidents of the United States, Abraham Lincoln and Dwight D. Eisenhower:

Abraham Lincoln: "All that serves labor serves the national. All that harms is treason . . . If a man tells you he loves America, yet hates labor, he is a liar . . . There is no America without labor, and to fleece one is to rob the other."

Dwight D. Eisenhower: "Only a fool would try to deprive working men and women of their right to join the union of their choice."

Very truly yours,

Robert V. Thayer
Business Representative
district #64, IAMAW, AFL-CIO

RVT/v

"absolutes" and that he would not listen to negotiating strategies or compromises proposed by the union. Although Jocelyn did offer a one-week extension, Thayer felt that management's position on the issues as "absolutes" made an extension a futile effort. In addition, Jocelyn's last-ditch ploy—to send management's final offer directly to workers the day before contract expiration—signaled an unwillingness to modify agreements.

Union leaders also felt that Gordon, who sat in on negotiations, had a distaste for the union. "He showed his contempt and frustra-tion for us through his body language," said Thayer. From labor's perspective, Roach, Gordon, and the 1970s generation of management at B&S were out to get the union from the very beginning of negotiations in 1981.

The 1981 Strike. The International Association of Machinists' District 64 voted overwhelmingly to strike, effective October 18, 1981. The machinists began their daily picket outside B&S's Precision Park, and five were arrested within the first four hours. Local police stationed themselves nearby as did a private security force hired by the company. As the fall turned into a frigid winter, an increasing amount of violence occurred. Strikers were frustrated by the length of the walkout and by B&S's hiring of strike replacement workers. Nearly every day nails were thrown on the pavement in an attempt to stop management employees' cars. Everyone was fair game. Even the car driven by Gordon's secretary was attacked while she sat helplessly inside; strikers lifted and shook the car from side to side. According to newspaper reports, stones were often thrown at windows, and names were called, particularly at those workers whom strikers recognized.

Union leaders claim, however, that very little of the violence was caused by striking workers. They saw the company's inability to get an injunction, which would have placed the blame on strikers, as an indication that their ranks might have been infiltrated. One labor leader said, "I wouldn't put it past Gordon to hire someone to throw rocks at the appropriate time."

Strikers also suffered amidst the violence. Newspapers reported that a 62-year-old female striker died from a stroke after overexposure to the cold air. In February and March violent activity peaked, directly triggered by the arrival of replacement workers. When picketers continued to block the main entrance to workers on March 22, local police sprayed pepper gas at them. This event reminded local journalists of Rhode Island's labor struggles in the 1930s.

The B&S Environment: 1982. "When there's a strike, there's a level of group cohesion . . . that gives you a starting point," observed Gordon. Supervisors, nonstriking workers, and newly hired replacements all worked together to run operations as smoothly as possible and to protect the plant against the strikers.

Inside Precision Park, the focus was on business as usual. Supervisors concentrated on important contracts and also delegated more responsibilities. The supervisors came to understand their operations better than before the strike and discovered many possibilities for savings. Since everyone was needed to operate the equipment, management employees and strikebreakers assumed many responsibilities. In addition, Gordon explained that the replacements, hired through management referrals, rapidly developed company loyalty.

From the beginning of the strike, management employees also provided many strike-related services. They maintained daily surveillance of the property and photographed strikers' activities. Managers personally drove replacement workers through the picket line, according to Roach, because these workers bore the brunt of strikers' resentful attacks. Through good formal and informal communication, Gordon proclaimed, "Morale was never higher."

In his B&S newspaper column, president Roach stated that the B&S workforce could change its direction. He had living proof of employee flexibility, pointing in his column to those who readily changed their jobs according to production needs. Management, running the facility as part of strike contingency plans, had helped to create the business efficiencies Roach had sought.

Corporate Campaign, Inc. In June 1982, B&S managers learned that the IAM had hired labor organizer Ray Rogers to help the strikers. The managers were troubled by the potential power of Rogers's Corporate Campaign, Inc.

Rogers founded the Corporate Campaign in the late 1970s as an outgrowth of a concept that ultimately led the J.P. Stevens Company to accept unions at 10 of its southern plants in 1980. Working for the Amalgamated Clothing and Textile Workers Union (ACTWU) at the time, Rogers masterminded a successful strategy to disrupt J.P. Stevens's relationship with the corporate and financial community. Rogers's strategy was to apply pressure to financial concerns that did business with Stevens or that had Stevens's directors on their own boards. This pressure remained until those companies worked toward change in Stevens's labor policies.

Labeled as unorthodox by both advocates and critics alike, most of Rogers's tactics in part stemmed from methods developed and proclaimed by the late Saul Alinsky, a popular organizer in the 1930s and author of *Rules for Radicals*. Speaking at a major eastern business school in 1983, Rogers told a group of first-year MBA students:

> The overriding issue that should be raised to the highest levels of public and political debate—but never is—is who controls the flow of the huge concentrations of money and to what ends. The response determines whether we improve the quality of life for all living things or whether we face social, economic, and quite possibly nuclear, holocaust.

In an article Rogers wrote during the summer of 1981 for *Business and Society Review,* he stated:

> There are means other than long, costly strikes and boycotts to challenge powerful institutions that are irresponsible in their social and economic policies. I am referring to a "corporate campaign," an approach that should become as important a confrontation strategy in the future as strikes, boycotts, and other forms of protest have been in the past.
>
> A total corporate campaign considers all avenues of pressure and would include the possibility of a strike, a boycott, and other traditional tactics. However, these would be timed and coordinated as part of an overall conceptualized strategy to maximize their effectiveness. A corporate campaign attacks a corporate adversary from every conceivable angle. It takes on the power behind a company. It shows clearly how to cut off the lifeblood of an institution. Its propo-

nents recognize that powerful institutions are both economic and political animals and must be challenged in both the economic and political spheres. It moves workers' and poor people's struggles away from their own doorsteps to the doorsteps of the corporate power brokers.

The original corporate campaign aimed at helping workers represented by the Amalgamated Clothing and Textile Workers Union (ACTWU) gain union contracts at J.P. Stevens & Co. This campaign focused on the company's corporate headquarters and on those institutions heavily tied into Stevens interests through interlocking directorates, large stock holdings, and multimillion-dollar loans.

In the Stevens campaign we wanted to cause those institutions heavily tied in with Stevens interests to exert their considerable influence on the company to recognize the rights and dignity of the workers and to sit down and bargain in good faith. We realized, however, that the "targeted" institutions and individuals would exert their influence only when they realized it was in their own primary self-interest to do so. To make it in their primary self-interest we had to draw these institutions into the Stevens controversy—so that their own image, reputation, and credibility were seriously jeopardized with large segments of the population important to their overall growth and prosperity. The ultimate goal of the corporate campaign was, if necessary, to polarize the entire corporate and Wall Street community away from J.P. Stevens, thereby pulling that company's most crucial underpinnings out from underneath it.

A company like J.P. Stevens cannot survive in a vacuum; it must be able to continue to spread its influence within the corporate and financial community if it is to maintain a stable level of business, much less grow and prosper. Once corporate and financial America turns off against a company like J.P. Stevens, unless that company is bent upon its own self-destruction, there is no place for it to go but the bargaining table. None of the big institutions that fight organized labor wants to face extinction. They only have to be convinced that unless they recognize the legitimate concerns of the labor movement, they will lose a great deal more than they have to gain.

We must recognize that banks and insurance companies have great influence over other corporations. First of all, banks and insurance companies control enormous amounts of stock in other corporations. They have voting power over this stock and can vote against management if they do not like the direction a corporation is taking. They can initiate stronger action by dumping large amounts of a corporation's stock on the market. When major financial institutions hurriedly sell a company's stock, it signals to the rest of the financial community that there is something wrong with the policies and direction of the company. The stock will probably decline in value, and no one else will be in a hurry to buy it. Banks and insurance companies also have a critical influence over other corporations when they decide to extend credit, or tighten credit terms, or deny credit entirely. Finally, big banks and insurance companies influence corporate America as well as each other by having their directors sit on the boards of other corporations. In this fashion they can have direct say over the policies and actions of these companies, or they can threaten to leave the board.

On the other hand, officials of a company serving on the board of a bank or insurance company can have tremendous pressure exerted on them to change their policies or face being pushed off a board.[1]

Corporate Campaign tactics were used against other companies as diverse as Farah Manufacturing Company and the Yale University Bookstore during the late 1970s and early 1980s. By May of 1982, the IAM felt that it was time for Rogers to try his hand at Brown & Sharpe. The regional offices put Rogers in touch with the local IAM strikers; Rogers arrived in Rhode Island with his associates the first week of June.

June 8, 1982.   After several days of deliberation, management at Brown & Sharpe knew that they needed a detailed strategy to counteract Rogers's Corporate Campaign. Rogers had already spoken the previous weekend to 1,100 of the 1,600 striking workers at a mass meeting.

One of the concerns John Gordon and Dick Jocelyn considered at any early morning meeting was how to respond to the local and national media. Don Roach and Henry Sharpe, Jr. had already spoken with a New York public relations firm; both were undecided about whether to go on the offensive (as advised) or remain silent. Gordon's secretary interrupted the meeting to tell him that Peter Gosselin, a staff writer for the *Providence Journal-Bulletin*, was on the phone asking for a statement about Rogers' arrival. John Gordon took a deep breath.

---

[1] Reprinted by permission from the Business and Society Review, Summer 1981, Number 38, Copyright © 1981, Warren, Gorham and Lamont Inc., 210 South Street, Boston, Mass. All Rights Reserved.

3 An Overview of the Corporate Communication Function

In Chapters 1 and 2, we looked at changes in the environment that have created the need for a new corporate communication function. We also looked at the importance of using a strategic approach to communication. In the remainder of this book, we will talk about the fundamentals themselves.

Fundamentals for the study of corporate communication must include the elements that will make up the new function in organizations over the next decade. The next several chapters, then, will focus on the subfunctions of corporate communication: the functions within the new function itself.

To begin our discussion, however, we need to step back and look at the whole picture first. This chapter will trace the development of the new function in recent years. Then, we turn our discussion toward finding the most appropriate structure within organizations as well as determining the best reporting relationships. We will also look at each of the subfunctions as a way of introducing the several chapters that follow. Finally, we will look at how the new function can be integrated within the existing organization.

Let's begin by tracing the roots of the evolving corporate communication function.

From "PR" to "CorpComm"

The predecessor to what I am calling the corporate communication function grew out of necessity. Although corporations had no specific strategy for communications, they often had to respond to external constituencies whether they wanted to or not. As laws began to change forcing companies to communicate in many situations they hadn't confronted before, and the environment for business changed (see Chapter 1), the responses became frequent enough that someone who was not responsible for another function, such as marketing or administration, had to take control of certain aspects of communication.

This function, which was tactical in most companies, was almost always called either "public relations" (also known as "PR") or "public affairs." Typically, it would include an aspect to it that would attempt to prevent the press from getting too close to management. Like a Patriot missile, the old PR person was supposed to prevent troubles from getting in or out of the company. Thus, the term "flak" came into existence as a way to describe what PR people were actually doing: shielding top managers from "bullets" thrown at them from the outside.

Since the press was used to this sort of activity, and the public was less interested in the goings-on of business than they are today, the flak era of public relations lasted for many years. As companies needed to add other communications activities to the list, public relations personnel were the obvious choice. For example, in the 1960s it was not unusual to find public relations officials handling speechwriting, annual reports, and the ubiquitous "house organ" (or company newspaper).

Given that the majority of work in this area involved dealing with the press (television wasn't really a factor until the early 1970s), former journalists were typically hired to handle this job, at a director level, in most companies. The former journalist was often seen by his former colleagues as a turncoat, going over to the other side for a quick buck.

What the former journalist, turned flak, brought to the organization, however, was the first inkling of expertise in the area of communication. Most of the top managers in large companies, until very recently, came from very traditional backgrounds such as engineering, accounting, finance, production, or at best (in terms of understanding communication) sales or marketing. Their understanding of how to communicate depended on abilities that they might have gained by chance or through excellent undergraduate or secondary school training rather than years of experience. Given their more quantitative rather than verbal orientation in general, these old-style managers were delighted to have an expert communicator on board who could take the heat for them and offer guidance based on something other than seat-of-the-pants reasoning.

Thus, the abilities of the pioneers in the development of the corporate communication function were often far overrated. And, PR people were often deemed capable of turning bad situations into good ones, creating excellent relations with their former colleagues in journalism (who in reality often loathed the turncoats), and helping the chief executive officer (CEO) become a superb communicator. In some cases, this was certainly true, but for the most part, the journalists who left behind less than promising careers were not the answer to all of the company's problems in terms of communications. Thus, when things turned bad, they were the obvious ones to blame and easy scapegoats for irresponsible managers.

In addition to the inside PR people, outside counselors often helped companies that either couldn't afford a full-time person or needed an extra pair of hands in a crisis. The legends of the public relations field like

Edward Bernays, David Finn, Harold Burson, and more recently Robert Dillenschneider, helped the profession develop from its journalism roots into a more refined and respected field.

For many years, PR firms dominated the communications field, billing companies huge fees for services they simply could not handle in-house. Very few large companies were willing to operate without such a firm for fear that they might be missing an opportunity to solve their communications problems fairly painlessly by using these outside flaks. Some of the top public relations firms today, such as Hill and Knowlton and Burson-Marsteller in the United States, Shandwick in the United Kingdom, which also has the largest firm in the United States, and Cosmo PR in Japan still provide some of the best advice available on a number of issues related to communications. But, for the most part, the firms cannot handle the day-to-day activities required for the smooth flow of communications from organization to constituents.

Thus, as problems in the 1970s developed outside of companies, requiring more than the simple internal PR function supplemented by the outside consultant, the roots of the new corporate communication function started to take hold. The rise in importance and increased power of special-interest groups, such as Ralph Nader's PIRG, and environmentally oriented organizations contributed greatly to the need for companies to increase communications activity.

An example of this is the problems that oil companies faced as a result of the Arab oil boycott and embargo in the 1970s. The entire industry was under fire as consumers had to wait hours for a tank of gasoline while companies reported what many consumer groups and agitators like Ralph Nader felt were obscene profits running into the hundreds of millions of dollars.

This led Mobil Oil to develop one of the most sophisticated public relations departments the world had ever seen. Herb Schmertz revolutionized the field by using strategies for solving communications problems that no one had thought of before. For example, his series of advertisements, called issue ads (see Chapter 5 for more on this subject) which began to run on op-ed pages in *The New York Times* and *The Wall Street Journal* once or twice a week directly attacked the allegations of obscene profits and hoarding of oil to jack up prices. Instead of merely reacting to the allegations thrown at them, the Mobil issue ads put the burden on government, told why the companies needed hefty profits for oil exploration, and changed the discussion to focus on other issues that the company's CEO felt were important to shareholders.

Schmertz was given wide latitude to set up a communications department with a budget in the tens of millions of dollars that would change the nature of Mobil's communications effort from old-style public relations to the first significant corporate communications department. Schmertz, as a senior vice president of the corporation, was also one of the very few communications executives with a seat on the board of directors, which gave further proof of the company's commitment to an enhanced communication effort.

Similarly, companies in other industries also ran into difficulties that led them to think more seriously about their communications effort. For example, Bechtel Corporation, a multibillion-dollar construction company with a relatively low profile until the mid-1970s, found itself in the midst of a firestorm of communications activity over cost overruns and delays in its work on the Alyeska oil pipeline in Alaska and the San Francisco subway system.

Illinois Power company, a subject of a *60 Minutes* segment because of delays and cost overruns on a nuclear power facility, fought back the media by taping a response to the segment that included lengthy, albeit boring, explanations about what was really going on. The program used actual *60 Minutes* footage coupled with these explanations, which helped Illinois Power tell its side of the story to employees and shareholders.

As individual corporations and entire industries came under increasing public scrutiny and had to answer to a much more sophisticated set of journalists that now included hard-hitting television reporters like CBS's Mike Wallace, the old-style public relations function was no longer capable of handling the flak.

As a result, what at first seemed to be a ridiculous waste of resources at Mobil in the early 1970s increasingly became the norm in corporate America as companies poured millions of dollars into developing effective corporate communications departments. The question at many companies now focused on how to structure these new departments most effectively and how to fit the function into an existing system rather than deciding whether it should exist at all.

To Centralize or Decentralize Communications? That Is the Question

One of the first problems that most companies faced was whether to keep all communications focused by centralizing the activity under one senior officer at a corporation's headquarters or to decentralize activities and allow individual business units to decide on how to handle communications. The more centralized function provided a much easier way for companies to gain consistency and control for all communication activities at the top of the organization. The decentralized function, however, gave individual business units an opportunity to adapt the function to their own needs rather than the needs of the organization as a whole.

For companies as diverse and large as a General Electric, for example, the question was moot. There was no way such a huge, diverse organization involved in activities as different as aerospace and light bulbs could possibly remain completely centralized in all of its communication activities. The same was true for other organizations in different industries like RJR-Nabisco, which had to integrate units selling cigarettes with others selling cookies.

Perhaps, then, the best structure of all for large companies is some combination of a strong, centralized, functional area (with all of the subsets mentioned later in this chapter) plus a network of decentralized operatives helping to keep communications consistent throughout the organization while adapting the function to the special needs of the independent business unit.

This obviously presents problems for organizations in terms of reporting relationships, however. If the communications operatives report to their local managers, as they inevitably would, they will run into problems when the manager from headquarters disagrees with an action taken at the local level. On the other hand, if they report to headquarters, the operatives may not fit in with the rest of the organization at the local level.

These problems can often be handled creatively using some combination of both a strong decentralized control for all affairs related to communications throughout the company and the participation of local operatives who, as in the case of General Electric, act as reporters back to the headquarters. The problem of centralization versus decentralization across business units will be more or less important depending on company size, geographic dispersion, and the diversity of a company's products and services.

One final aspect of centralization versus decentralization needs to be addressed as well, however. In addition to the problems for companies with multiple business units spread throughout the world, companies looking to build their corporate communication function need to worry about how decentralized communications activities are at the corporate level as well. As we begin to look at each of the different aspects of the function, we will find that some of these activities are already handled through another functional area.

For example, the investor relations function could be in the treasury department, the employee relations function within the personnel department, and the customer relations function within the marketing department. All of these activities require communication strategies connected to the central mission of the firm. And, as we shall see later in this chapter, each of the activities can be classified as a subfunction of the corporate communication function itself.

So, how should the problem of centralization versus decentralization be handled? Obviously, the answer depends on historical reporting relationships, relative strengths of different departments, and how much the company wants to create a cohesive communication function. But most important of all may be where the function reports within the organization.

Where Should the Function Report?

Many polls taken over the last five years have consistently shown that a huge percentage of a chief executive officer's time is spent communicating with one or another of the company's constituencies. We estimate from our research that the percentage of time spent by CEOs is a whopping 85 percent, on average, across all CEOs at the Fortune 500 companies. This implies that the person who is most involved with both developing the overall strategy for communications as well as actually having to deliver the messages to constituencies is the CEO in most cases. It should come as no surprise then, that for most companies, I would recommend that the CEO should have a direct line to the corporate communications function. Without this connection, the communications function will be much less effective and far less powerful.

In many cases, however, we find the function, such as it is, reporting to the catch-all executive vice president in charge of administration. This person might also have responsibility for personnel, security, and buildings and grounds, for example. This presents tremendous problems for the communications function—especially if the EVP has little knowledge about or lack of interest in communications.

In other companies, we find the function reporting to a strategic planning function. Given what I said in Chapter 2 about the importance of tying communications to the overall strategy of the firm, we can see that this might benefit the growing corporate communication function.

Union Carbide Corporation, which is still dealing with the fallout from the Bhopal accident in India several years ago, recently transferred its communications responsibilities to the vice president of strategic planning. In a letter to executives, the chairman and CEO of the company, Robert Kennedy, said:

> The Corporation's strategic direction is a key element of our communication to shareholders, employees and the public at large. . . . It is therefore more important than ever to be open and consistent in our communications to all of these groups, to keep them informed of our progress as we implement strategy, and to make sure that we address the special concerns and interests of all the groups and constituencies with a stake in Union Carbide's future. . . . To ensure the closest possible alignment of our communications with management directed at strategic planning developments, the management of those functions is being consolidated under . . . [the] Vice President of Strategic Planning and Public Affairs.

Whether this arrangement will work or not for Union Carbide remains to be seen, but the idea of linking these two functions together is an interesting one for companies to consider. It certainly gives the organization an opportunity to link strategy with communications and preserves the direct connection with the CEO to whom the vice president reports.

Other links, or strategic alliances, with existing functions like strategic planning may be an answer for the CEO looking to keep the number of direct reports down to a handful of senior executives. This problem is often the biggest stumbling block to getting the corporate communication function plugged in at the top.

So, a strong, centralized function with direct connections to the chief executive officer is the best way for a company to ensure the success of its corporate communication function. In the next section of this chapter, we will focus on what the function should include.

The Functions within the Function

The best way to discuss the different parts of a modern corporate communication function is by going from the most global and strategic issues to the narrower aspects of the function. Thus, we will begin with a discussion of image and identity; then, we will look at corporate advertising, media relations, product publicity and customer relations, financial communications, employee relations, community relations and corporate philanthropy, and government relations. We will also determine how this function is equipped to deal with a crisis at the end of this section.

Several people have asked why I have chosen this particular grouping of subfunctions to include in the corporate communication function. First, these are subfunctions that I believe have a direct bearing on how the corporation will be perceived by its most important constituencies. Second, these subfunctions all have a primary focus on communication above all else. So, while customer relations helps support the marketing function without any doubt, it's primary goal is to create strong ties through communications with a critical constituency—the organization's customers. Not every company will be able to include all of the subfunctions that I suggest, but a majority of these functions must be included for the function to operate best.

Image and Identity

Hard to classify as a separate subfunction, an organization's image and identity strategy is the most critical aspect of any corporate communication function. What is the difference between image and identity, and how do they shape the operations of a corporate communication department?

Image is a reflection of the organization's reality. It is the corporation as seen by the eyes of constituencies. Thus, an organization can have different images with different constituencies. For example, cigarette companies might be reprehensible to many American consumers looking for a healthier lifestyle, but a delight to Phillip Morris shareholders reaping the profits from the sale of the same product. On the other hand, customers might have been perfectly happy with what Macy's had to offer in its many stores throughout the United States, but securities analysts were loath to recommend the parent company's stock knowing that inevitably it would enter bankruptcy.

Determining what the organization's image is with different constituencies is often less obvious than in the examples given above. The corporate communication department can conduct the marketing research a company needs to understand each constituency's needs and attitudes. Obviously the organization cannot always please everyone, but at least, by monitoring what constituencies are thinking about, they can consciously try not to create hostility with a particular group.

Unlike its image, however, the organization's *identity* should not change from one constituency to another. Identity is the visual manifestation of the company's reality as seen in the company logo, its buildings, its stationery, and even in employee's uniforms. The identity an organization chooses, consciously or not, creates an image in itself. It must be updated periodically, lest it gets stale and outdated, and its identity also constantly needs to be monitored for consistency.

An organization has some kind of identity whether it wants one or not based on these visual stimuli. People all over the world know what McDonald's golden arches represent on a store, what Coca-Cola's red can and white script lettering signify, and what the big yellow shell means in front of a gas station whether it's in Lagos, Nigeria or Providence, Rhode Island.

Since this subfunction requires a variety of skills, including the ability to conduct marketing research, to design attractive brochures, and to serve as a policeman in terms of identity standards, it might be spread around a couple of different functions in the absence of a strong corporate communication function. For example, the marketing research needed to determine a firm's image with various constituencies might be a minor by-product of the overall marketing research effort currently underway to determine customer attitudes toward particular products and services rather than the firm as a whole.

Determining how a firm wants to be perceived with different constituencies and how it chooses to identify itself is the first function of corporate communications. If the firm is making serious changes in its image or identity, this subfunction might very well be a full-time job for someone for a period of time.

At nearly all companies, outside counselors, such as Anspach, Grossman, Portugal or Siegal and Gale in New York City, would definitely be involved as well if the company is altering its identity. These changes might be merely cosmetic to keep the "look" of the company up-to-date, or they can be significant ones, such as a name change.

Corporate Advertising and Advocacy Programs

Image can also be reflected in a company's *corporate advertising*. This subfunction of corporate communication is very different from its product advertising or marketing communication function in two ways.

First, corporate advertising, unlike product advertising, does not try to sell a company's particular product or service. Instead, it tries to sell the company itself—often to a completely different constituency from customers.

For example, Beatrice ran an extensive corporate advertising campaign in the 1980s with the tag line: "We're Beatrice, you've known us all along." In these corporate ads, the company showed its many different product lines, which ranged from bras to spaghetti sauce, but its goal was not to sell more of these products with the ad campaign (even though that might have been a fortunate by-product) but rather to influence opinion leaders and potential shareholders about the company's viability and overall strategy.

Similarly, the aerospace and defense firms that advertise extensively in publications such as *The New Republic* are not trying to sell F-15s to liberals but to influence public opinion. In this way, the ads might make it easier for lawmakers to get approval for increases or allocations in the defense budget.

An important subset of corporate advertising is *issue advertising*. We discussed this earlier when we looked at Mobil Oil Corporation's corporate communication function. This type of advertising attempts to do even more than influence constituent's opinions about the company; it also tries to influence their attitudes about specific issues that affect the company. For example, in the 1980s insurance companies ran issue ads that tried to get government off of their backs. Mobil, in its extensive campaign, tried to influence how people reacted to giving one dollar toward presidential races by checking off the appropriate box on tax forms. Drexel, Burnham, Lambert tried to convince people that the firm was free from any wrongdoing in relation to insider trading allegations. And Johnson & Johnson used issue advertising to convince Tylenol customers that it was not responsible for poisoning people with its products.

This kind of corporate advertising is very risky. By taking a stand on a particular issue, the company is automatically creating a negative image with some constituency. But many companies feel that the risk is worth it to get its opinions into the marketplace of ideas. These campaigns almost always reflect the attitudes of the chairman and CEO as well as a majority of senior managers.

Even though product advertising is obviously the purview of most marketing functions in large companies, corporate advertising is run from the CEO's office or through strong corporate communication departments instead of through marketing. During the 1980s, this was the fastest growing segment of the advertising industry as senior officers tried to present a coherent company image for the financial community and opinion leaders. As budgets get squeezed in the cost-conscious 1990s, however, this kind of advertising is growing at a much slower rate.

Media Relations

The old public relations function, which focused almost exclusively on dealing with media relations, may be a thing of the past, but the subfunction we now refer to as media relations is still central to the corporate communications function. Most of the personnel for corporate communications will typically be found within this subfunction, and the person in charge of the communications department as a whole must be capable of dealing with the media as a spokesperson for the firm. Although the media relations subfunction started off as a flakking service for managers in response to requests from news organizations, it is much more active in setting the agenda for discussion of the firm in the media today in the best corporate communication departments.

New technology has helped companies communicate through the hundreds of media services available virtually anywhere in the world. Satellite up-links are available at most corporate headquarters, and companies can put their press releases out to wire services electronically without even making a single phone call today. Despite this, the relationship between business and media remains largely adversarial (as it should be), although positive relationships are much more common today between sources and reporters. Since both the media and business need each other, most companies try to make the best of these relationships.

Unlike other subfunctions we have discussed in this chapter, media relations has no other departments with a legitimate claim of any kind on its territory. Everyone would agree that media relations should definitely be handled by the corporate communication function.

Product Publicity and Customer Relations

Publicity related to products was also often a function of the predecessor public relations function. But, more typically, both product publicity and customer relations have traditionally been the purview of marketing departments. This subfunction coordinates and manages publicity relating to new or existing products and also deals with activities relating to customers.

Today, *product publicity* almost always includes sponsorship of events for major corporations, such as golf tournaments, car races, and even marathons. In addition, celebrities are often involved in these activities, which requires coordination within the company. Given how important such events and sponsorship agreements can be in shaping a company's image, corporate communications experts are often involved in setting the agenda.

Customer relations activities have increasingly become a part of corporate communications as a result of pressure groups among consumers that try to exert their influence on an organization. Rather than simply making sure the customer is happy with the product or service, as in the past, companies today must get involved in quasi-political activities with constituencies claiming to represent a firm's customers.

For example, the conservative Reverend Donald Wildmon has pursued a family-oriented agenda against a number of companies that sell products he deems unfit for families. Waldenbooks, which is the only American-owned major book chain in the United States was vilified for selling sexually explicit literature in its stores. By organizing conservative church groups, Wildmon was able to apply pressure on Waldenbooks to stop selling literature ranging from what most people would consider simply erotic to literature with bad language in it.

Companies must also monitor phone calls, answer mail, deal with product recalls, and provide traditional customer-oriented services at the same time.

Financial Communications

Also called *investor* or *shareholder relations,* this subfunction has emerged as the fastest growing subset of the corporate communication function and an area of intense interest at all companies. Traditionally, financial relations have been handled by the finance or treasury department, but the focus today has moved away from just the numbers to the way the numbers are actually communicated to various constituencies.

This subfunction deals with securities analysts on both the buy and sell side who are often also a direct source for the financial press, which this subfunction cultivates in conjunction with experts from the media relations area. Financial communications also involves direct contact with investors both large and small. And, every public firm must produce financial statements and annual reports, which are produced by financial communications professionals.

Given the highly quantitative message involved in all of these activities, as well as the need for individuals to choose their words very carefully to avoid any semblance of transferring inside information, this subfunction must be a coordinated effort between communications professionals and the chief financial officer, comptroller, or vice president for finance. Graduates from business schools with previous experience in finance and an aptitude for and interest in communication are finding this a growth area for jobs after graduation, as companies try to find the right mix of quantitative and verbal abilities necessary for the smooth operation of this subfunction.

Employee Relations

As companies become more focused on retaining a happy work force with changing values and different demographics, they have necessarily had to think more than in the past about how they communicate with employees through what is also often called *internal communications*. Today, companies must explain complicated health and benefit packages, changes in laws that affect employees, and changes in the marketplace that might affect the company in the future. In addition, training programs need to be explained, new employees need to receive orientation, and employees no longer needed at the company must be helped along in their job search—a responsibility many companies now consider an obligation to the community.

While many of the activities can be handled in the personnel (also called human resources) department, the communication itself and the strategy for communicating these ideas must come from communications experts in the corporate communications function. In the best of all cases, the personnel department would willingly seek out the advice of communications professionals within the firm to deal with these issues.

Community Relations and Corporate Philanthropy

Many companies have a separate subfunction in the personnel area to deal with *community relations* and a foundation close to the chairman that deals with philanthropy. I see the two tied very closely together as companies take on more responsibilities in communities where they operate. I also see the need for including this subfunction within the corporate communication function, given the importance of the constituency involved and the importance this has in shaping the image of the firm. Given that the personnel department has no legitimate claim on the area if a corporate communication function exists, this subfunction is almost always easily brought into the fold.

Corporate philanthropy has become increasingly important as companies try to do more than just give back to the community. In addition, firms feel an obligation to donate funds to organizations that could benefit the firm's employees, customers, or shareholders in some way. Examples of this include donations to universities that might be conducting research in the industry and organizations representing minority interests.

Government Relations

This subfunction, also called *public affairs,* is more important in some industries than others, but virtually every company can benefit by having ties to legislators on both a local and national level. Many companies have established offices in Washington to find out what is going on in government that might affect the company and influence the discussion. Because of its importance in some industries such as public utilities and other heavily regulated areas, government relations can be either a separate function altogether in some companies or tied to philanthropy in others. Sometimes, firms as an industry will establish separate organizations to deal with government relations. Electric companies have such a lobbying group, for example.

Again, the importance of this subfunction in terms of communication cannot be overestimated, which means that it should be a part of a strong corporate communications department.

Crisis Management

While not really a separate function, planned responses to potential crises need to be planned for and coordinated by the corporate communications function. Ideally, a wider group of managers from throughout the organization will be included in all planning for such eventualities.

How to Integrate a New or Expanded Communication Function

In my experience, the two best ways to integrate a new or seriously expanded corporate communication function within an existing organization are by including the change in a reorganization of the firm as a whole, and/or by getting the full support of the chairman, CEO, president, and board of directors. Any attempts to increase the scope of an organization's communication activities without such high-level support are destined to fail.

Despite such support, however, change, in general, produces problems in large organizations that managers must be aware of. A substantial body of literature exists concerning the design of organizations that might shed some light on how this particular kind of change can be achieved more smoothly. What experts in the organization design field tend to agree on is that an organization's design should:

- Create coordination among departments.
- Clarify responsibilities in an individual's job.
- Ease information flow and decision making.

Thus, in the discussion above, I have tried to discuss ways to create coordination between the corporate communication department and other areas of the firm. We have also talked at length about the importance of information flow in our discussion of communication strategy in Chapter 2.

Perhaps most difficult of all, however, is trying to clarify responsibilities in this emerging function. Unfortunately, corporate communications professionals must be willing to do a wide variety of activities within the function. As we look at each of these subfunctions in more detail, I will try to delineate the particular responsibilities professionals must be willing to accept.

Finally, we have not discussed how a particular organization's culture can affect the integration of this new function into an existing framework. This, of course, will have a tremendous influence on how the acceptance of the new function will proceed in the organization and how the process will be conducted. Although such factors are critical in thinking about an enhanced corporate communication function, I believe they are quite manageable and worth the effort to achieve success in this endeavor.

Case
Deltoid Corporation

Deltoid Corporation was a large, service-oriented conglomerate operating out of a sprawling campus-like setting in Columbus, Ohio. The corporation had five separate business units that included operations ranging from hotels and restaurants to software development for the airline and travel industries.

The CEO of Deltoid was the company's founder, Mr. Roger Baraniak. Baraniak developed the business from the one hotel he inherited from his father into the $5 billion business it had become by 1993. Over the years, Baraniak brought in professional managers at the vice presidential level to deal with sales and marketing, finance, operations, administration, and human resources. Each of the five business units also had a professional business manager (called senior vice presidents).

In the past, the company had managed its relations with the media through a director of public relations reporting to the vice president for administration. Linda Yoza, who held the public relations job for the last five years, came to Deltoid from a trade publication that covered the hotel industry.

In December of 1992, one of Deltoid's flagship hotels in Minneapolis burned to the ground killing 50 people and injuring over 75 others. Yoza rushed to the scene to manage the company's crisis communication plan. Over the next several days, the media heard only from Yoza. The company's message was that the engineering firm involved in constructing the hotel was at fault.

Back at company headquarters, Mr. Baraniak's independent public relations consultant tried to convince the CEO that Deltoid's position had to be more proactive. As public sentiment became more vocal, Baraniak realized that his consultant was right. Mr. Baraniak asked the consultant to develop a longer-term strategy for the corporation's communications efforts. The questions he wanted the consultant to answer included:

> Should we expand our communications department? What would a new department include? What reporting relationships would be best for the organization? Would it be wiser to spend more on consulting instead?

Linda found that her own position at the firm was becoming much more than just a public relations professional, and she put in a call to Mr. Baraniak to convince him to fly to Minneapolis and get personally involved with the crisis at Deltoid Hotel. She had no knowledge of the consultant's charge to revamp communications at Deltoid.

Case Questions

1. You are Linda Yoza. What would you say to Mr. Baraniak in view of what you have just read in the preceding chapter?
2. You are the consultant to Mr. Baraniak. How would you answer the questions he puts forth in the case, based on what you have read in Chapter 3?
3. You are Mr. Baraniak. What would you do to bring Deltoid's corporate communication function into existence?

4 IMAGE AND IDENTITY

In the previous chapter, we discussed the various components that make up the corporate communication function. In this chapter, we will look at the first and most critical part of the function: the corporation's image and identity.

Let's start by looking at an example of image at the personal level. We all choose certain kinds of clothing, drive particular cars, and wear special jewelry to express our individuality. The cities and towns in which we live, the music we prefer, the restaurants we frequent all add up to an impression, or identity, that others can easily distinguish.

Compare these two examples to see what I mean. A gray-haired gentleman sits in a Mercedes 500SL, dressed in a blue Brooks Brothers suit, wearing a gold Rolex President watch. Across the street sits a middle-aged man in a Toyota Camry, wearing blue jeans and a black turtleneck, who tells time with a Seiko digital watch. Even for people with very little understanding of American culture, these quick glimpses of the two men speak volumes about what they are like. And if we knew about where they live, their religion, and their occupations, we could form a much clearer identity.

The same is true for corporations. Walk into a firm's office and it takes just a few moments to capture those all-important first impressions and learn a good deal about the company. If the effort is a challenge to understand at the personal level, it is significantly more difficult within organizations. One reason for this complexity is that many potential identity options exist. A couple of years ago while teaching in Asia, my wife and I treated ourselves to one of life's great pleasures: a weekend in a suite at the Oriental Hotel in Bangkok. My Asian *Wall Street Journal* and *Herald Tribune* were ironed to eliminate creases; the hotel staff was omnipresent to the point of running down the hallway to open the door lest patrons should actually have to use their room keys; laundry arrived beautifully gift-wrapped with an orchid attached to each package; every night, our pillows were adorned with an English poem on the theme of sleep; and, outside the lobby, Mercedes limos were lined up ready to take us anywhere at any time of the day or night.

A few weeks later, I returned to the United States and was giving a lecture to a group of executives at a midwestern resort. A *USA Today* appeared on the outside doorknob squeezed into a plastic bag; the staff was invisible and unavailable to bring room service in under 45 minutes; my pillow was "adorned" with a room-service menu for the following morning and a piece of hard candy; the vehicle waiting to whisk guests to various destinations was a Dodge van; and for flowers, the resort provided plastic varietals in a glass-enclosed case that played the popular song "Feelings" when I lifted the top.

Both hotels have strong identities, both appeal to particular constituencies, and both provide roughly the same level of service using distinctive approaches. The choices each has made about their businesses are at the heart of what identity and image is all about. They contribute to and shape the image of these hotels and, more generally, convey the image and identity of any institution.

Just what goes into creating these impressions? How do organizations distinguish themselves in the minds of customers, shareholders, employees, and other relevant constituencies? And, above all, how does an organization manage something so seemingly ephemeral as an identity?

What Are Image and Identity?

As we discussed in Chapter 3, the *image* is a reflection of an organization's reality. Put another way, it is the corporation as seen from the viewpoint of constituencies. Thus, many different images can exist for an organization depending on which constituency is involved. Thus, to understand image means to know what the organization is really about and where it is headed. This is often hard for anyone but the CEO or president to grasp. What, for example, is the reality of an organization as large as Exxon, as diversified as Mitsubishi, or as monolithic as General Electric?

Certainly the products and services, the people, buildings, symbols, and other objects contribute to this reality. While there are inevitably differences in how the elements are perceived by different constituencies, it is this cluster of facts, this collection of tangible things, that provides the organization with a starting point for creating an identity.

The *identity* is the visual manifestation of the image as conveyed through the organization's logo, products, services, buildings, stationery, uniforms, and all other tangible bits of evidence created by the organization to communicate with a variety of constituencies. Constituencies then form perceptions based on the messages that companies send out in tangible form. If these notions accurately reflect an organization's reality, the identity program is a success. If the perceptions differ dramatically from the reality (and this often happens when companies do not take the time to analyze whether a match actually exists), then either the strategy is ineffective or the corporation's self-understanding needs modification.

Organizations can get a much better sense of their image (as conveyed through visual identity) by conducting research with constituents. This research should be both qualitative and quantitative in nature and should try to determine how consistent an identity is across constituencies. As an example, Arthur D. Little (ADL) found through research that its image was not clear to a variety of constituencies. Was the organization a consulting firm? A think-tank? Involved in engineering? Defense? By asking people what they thought about the organization, ADL was able to find out how its image was perceived and discovered that it was unclear.

While image can vary among constituencies, identity needs to be consistent. One constituency, for example, might see ADL as a consulting firm that is too involved in the defense sector and therefore might have a negative image of the company; another more conservative constituency might be delighted with the extensive work the consulting firm has done to help the defense industry become stronger over the last decade and might very well have a positive image of the firm. But, at least they both have the firm's identity right. It is involved in defense work and is a consulting firm. That could be either positive or negative, depending on whom you ask, but at least it's accurate.

The logo that the Tuck School adopted several years ago was carefully crafted to reflect what faculty and officers felt was the reality of the school: It is the oldest graduate school of business, it is prestigious—a member of the Ivy League group of schools, it is a part of a great university—Dartmouth, and it is elite. The symbol conveys all of these meanings, but they can add up to very different images, depending on whom you ask.

For example, some potential students might think that old and Ivy League mean stodgy or conservative; others might think that prestige is great and this is the best place to go for graduate business training. Whatever their decision about the school, the logo should reflect accurately what the place is all about. Then constituents can decide whether that is an image they like or not.

So, what does this discussion about image and identity imply for the organization looking to create a successful corporate communication function? First, given how aggressive every industry has become, with competition coming from all over the world and companies trying to manage with limited resources, a company's image and identity might be the only difference that people can hold onto from one company to the next. Is there really any difference between buying a tank of Texaco and a tank of Mobil gasoline? Given that the same distributor often sells the same gasoline to dealers in the United States, the answer is definitely no. Yet, despite that, consumers make distinctions about such generic products all the time based on nothing more that what the company is all about rather than the product itself.

If we look specifically at the two examples above, we can see clearly what I mean. Texaco recently spruced up the image of its gas stations by redesigning its logo and the stations themselves; everything is new, from top to bottom. In addition, the company is a major supporter of opera in America through its support of the Saturday afternoon broadcasts from the Metropolitan Opera in New York.

Mobil, on the other hand, hasn't changed its image in several years. Its gas stations probably could use the facelift that Texaco's all have had over the last decade. The company has long been a major supporter of public television in the United States, especially known for its support of the popular "Masterpiece Theater" series, which has been running on PBS for many years.

Now, when a consumer decides to buy gasoline, aside from the location of the gas station, the factors above are really the only differences they are buying from the two companies (given similar prices). Both tanks of gas will keep the car going, both tanks of gas have approximately the same octane rating, and both service stations will offer varying quality of service, depending on who the dealer-owner is. But if you watch PBS and like the notion that Mobil supports certain programming, you might want to buy gasoline from them because of the image you hold in your mind about the company. If, however, you are an opera fan and listen to the Texaco broadcasts regularly, this might actually convince you to buy your gasoline at their stations.

Consumers are only now beginning to make the kinds of distinctions that we are talking about based on notions other than the product itself, but this reliance on nothing more than image and identity will become the norm as products become much the same all over the world.

Is Corporate Identity a Trend?

Corporate identity may appear to be a recent trend, emerging from the need for definition in a complicated world, but, in fact, identity programs have been around for a very long time. In ancient Egypt, the pharaohs used their signatures as a symbol of their administration. Anyone who has been to Luxor can attest to the fascination Ramses IV had with his "logo." It appears virtually everywhere and is especially noticeable because his cartouche is primitive and bold, dominating earlier symbols on columns and buildings.

More contemporary historical examples of corporate identity are evident in the 18th-century U.S. and French revolutions. As part of those upheavals, both countries changed their identities with the development of new flags, national anthems, uniforms, and, in the case of France, with a new execution device: the guillotine.

During the middle decades of the 20th century, Nazi Germany terrified the world with its identity program. Although we regard the swastika today as abhorrent and probably the most negative logo imaginable, the same symbol obviously had strong, positive connotations to earlier generations of German nationalists.

In terms of individual behavior, the Latin cross and the Star of David are critical symbols in Western civilization. Throughout the world, they are instantly recognized and elicit a spectrum of emotional responses.

Symbols—whether a Pharaoh's cartouche, a nation's flag, or a sign of a person's religious commitment—are just one dimension of the identity picture. These visual manifestations receive an inordinate amount of attention because of our increasingly visual focus and the exposure this type of shorthand receives on television and in magazines, annual reports, and the endless barrage of brochures we see at work and at home.

And as a parallel, organizations, from start-ups to industry giants as well as not-for-profits and universities, give at least some thought to these issues. Yet, despite this awareness, a much smaller group of executives and managers understands how to create a coherent image and identity and exploit perceptions as an essential organizational asset.

Differentiating an Organization through Image and Identity

Why is image so important today? A coherent image and identity that fits the reality of an organization attracts employees, customers, and investors—the three primary constituencies for virtually every organization. This attraction occurs for the same reason that people, on an individual basis, are attracted to personalities with a clear image and identity. Consider movie stars as an example. Their image usually comes through some sense of glamour. The late Marlene Dietrich once observed, "Glamour is assurance. It is a kind of knowing that you are all right in every way, mentally and physically and in appearance, and that, whatever the occasion or the situation, you are equal to it."

That same sense of assurance attracts the three key constituencies we discussed earlier to organizations. Think about how self-assured certain organizations seem compared to others. For decades IBM represented an organization that seemed to know what it was all about, that would persevere forever. Its logo seemed to represent that stability, as did its managers who all adopted the same "Big Blue" corporate attire of white shirts and dark suits.

That same sense of an organization that knows what it is all about helps companies get through crises. Because Johnson & Johnson had such a clear image and identity as an ethically sound company, it was able to weather the Tylenol crisis in a way that other organizations of lesser stature could not. Drexel Burnham Lambert was brought down as much for its former image as a "radical" institution as it was for financial reasons. The same is true for Leona Helmsley who went to jail as much for her former image as the "Queen" of the Helmsley Palace as for her sins committed in regard to tax evasion.

So, a solid image can be attractive, but it is the sense of goodwill credibility (see Chapter 2) we talked about in terms of Johnson & Johnson that is most important. Social-power theorists French, Raven, and Kotter discuss the importance of credibility on a personal level. We can expand these ideas to apply to corporations as well.

Initially, constituencies have certain perceptions about an organization before they even begin to interact. The perceptions are based on what they have read about the organization previously, what interactions others have had, and what visual symbols they recognize. Even if you have never eaten a hamburger at McDonald's, you have certain perceptions about the organization and its products through vicarious experience. If the constituents have a high regard for the organization based on this initial impression, they are more likely to give you the benefit of the doubt in difficult times.

After interacting with the organization, the constituents may have a different perception. One bad interaction with an AT&T operator can destroy a relationship for a lifetime with a customer. That's why organizations today are so concerned with the quality of each and every interaction. The goodwill credibility that a company acquires through the repeated application of consistently excellent behavior will determine its image in the minds of constituents in a much more profound way than a one-shot corporate advertising campaign.

In addition to goodwill, organizations can differentiate themselves based on image through names and logos. They can also lose whatever image they have built up very quickly through impetuous changes in the use of names and logos. Nissan in Japan and UAL in the United States are two good examples of this phenomenon.

To consolidate the company's brands worldwide, an edict from Nissan's company headquarters in the early 1980s eliminated the well-known Datsun brand name from the U.S. market in favor of the company name Nissan. This name change took over five years to complete because dealers refused to pay for new signs and resisted the change. In addition, customers became confused. Virtually everyone in the late 1960s and early 1970s knew about the Datsun 240Z, and the company's line of small cars helped Americans get through the first oil crisis. After the name change, however, customers thought that Nissan was a subsidiary of Toyota, its arch rival. And, even after almost a decade with the new name, Nissan is still less well-known in America than the old Datsun name. Executives at United Airlines' parent company, UAL, tried to change the name of that company in the mid-1980s to Allegis. The vision of the CEO at the time was that the company would become a complete service from air to ground with hotels and rental cars as part of the mix. Despite the heavily hyped name change, however, directors at the company, and customers as well, saw UAL as first and foremost an airline rather than a broad-based travel organization. The name was changed back to the original and the CEO was out of a job within a few months' time.

Other examples abound. USX (formerly U.S. Steel) is still basically considered a steel company despite diversification. Sears is still a discount department store in the eyes of most people, even though it tried to become much more with the addition of brokerage services and an insurance company. This does not mean that change is impossible. Transformations most certainly do occur.

Managing the Unmanageable

The dual nature of identity—embodied in things yet inextricably tied to perceptions—creates a special dilemma for decision makers. In a world where attention is generally focused on quantifiable results, the emphasis here is on qualitative issues. Devising a program that addresses these elusive but very significant concerns requires an approach that balances thoughtful analysis with action. Here is a method that has been successfully used by many organizations I have worked with to manage the identity process.

Step 1: Conduct an Identity Audit

To begin, an organization needs to assess the current picture. How does the general public currently view the organization? What do its various symbols represent to different constituents? Does its identity accurately reflect what is happening, or is it simply a leftover from days gone by?

To avoid superficial input and objectively respond to these questions, consultants from the hundreds of "identity firms" conduct in-depth interviews with top managers and those working in areas most affected by any planned changes. They review company literature, advertising, stationery, products and services, and facilities. They also research perceptions among the most important constituencies including employees, analysts, and customers. The idea is to be thorough, to uncover relationships and inconsistencies, and then to use the audit as a basis for potential identity changes.

In this process, executives should look for red flags. Typical problems include symbols that conjure up images of earlier days at the company or just generally incorrect impressions. Once decision makers have the facts, they can move to create a new identity or institute a communication program to share the correct and most up-to-date profile.

Kmart serves as an example of what I mean. This company's discount stores are part of the American landscape, so much so that it is one of the most recognized corporations in the United States. Comedians on national television make jokes about the stores' "blue-light specials," and several films (most prominently, the Oscar-winning *Rain Man*) make reference to the stores as a symbol of inexpensive, low-end shopping. With over 2,000 stores located throughout the United States (80 percent of the population in the United States lives within five miles of a Kmart), visits from 180 million shoppers a year, and over $30 billion in sales, Kmart in 1990 had very few problems with simple recognition.

What it did have, however, was a symbol that reflected the Kmart of the 1960s. Like a worn-out suit of clothes, the logo seemed comfortable, but after almost 30 years, changes in the stores and throughout the organization motivated designers, vendors, customers, and reporters to ask CEO and Chairman Joseph Antonini to update the corporation's image and identity.

In this case, consultants began by conducting an identity audit. After talking with customers, vendors, suppliers, and securities analysts and examining the way in which the old identity was used, they determined that the retail identifier needed to be changed.

Kmart was no longer the same company represented in the original mark. In addition, attitudes about design had shifted tremendously over three decades. The result was a new logo that is now on every store, on all signs, and in all advertising and promotion. But that is not all. Preliminary to putting up the new sign, the company first spent several billion dollars to refurbish the stores so that as a single message, the change in symbol would be complemented by significant interior enhancements—visible changes that would be obvious to customers.

While the identity audit may seem a fairly straightforward and simple process, it usually is not. Often the symbols that exist and the impressions that result are not how the organization sees itself at all. Companies that are trying to change their image are particularly difficult to audit because the vision of top executives of what the company will be is so different from what the reality currently is. And often executives disregard the best research telling them how constituents' perceptions about the organization differ from their own. Such cognitive dissonance is the first challenge in managing identity for executives. The reality of the organization must be far enough along in the change process (as in the case of Kmart) so that the new image the company is trying to adopt will actually make sense, some day at least, to those who will encounter this company in the years ahead.

Step 2: Set Identity Objectives

Having clear goals is essential to the identity process. These goals should be set by senior management and must explain how each constituency is supposed to react to specific identity proposals. For instance: "As a result of this name change, analysts will recognize our organization as more than just a one-product company"; or "By putting a new logo on the outside of our stores, customers will be more aware of dramatic transformations that are going on inside." What is important is that emphasis be placed on constituency response rather than company action.

That's where problems often start. Most managers are much more internally focused—particularly senior managers—and thus have great difficulty getting the kind of perspective necessary to see things from the viewpoint of constituents. Consultants can certainly help, but the organization as a whole must be motivated to change and willing to accept the truth about the organization, even if it hurts.

In addition, change for change sake (as in the case of UAL, perhaps) or to meet some kind of standardization worldwide (which was true in the case of Nissan) is not the kind of objective that is likely to meet with success. Usually, such arbitrary changes are the result of a CEO wanting to leave his or her mark on the organization rather than a necessary step in the evolution of the company's image.

A positive example of clear objectives leading to necessary change is Kentucky Fried Chicken's recent desire to change its image and menu as a result of changes in American dietary habits. The strong corporate identity of this company worldwide (it has one of its biggest restaurants on Tienanmen Square in Beijing and can be found in remote corners of Japan) conjures up images of Colonel Sanders's white beard, buckets of fried chicken, salty biscuits, and gravy. To an earlier generation, these were all positive images closely connected with home and hearth.

Today, health-conscious Americans are more likely to think of the intense cholesterol, the explosion of sodium, and gobs of fat in every bucket of the Colonel's chicken. Thus, the company (a unit of PepsiCo Inc.) has recently tried to reposition itself with health-minded Americans by offering broiled chicken and chicken salad sandwiches. The company's goal was to change the old image and adopt a more healthful positioning.

To do so, executives decided to change the name of the 5,000 restaurants gradually to just "KFC." The obvious point was to eliminate the word "fried." While most identity experts would agree that it is very difficult to create an identity for a restaurant out of initials alone, this one has the well-known Colonel to go along with the change. While this change is still going on and cannot be evaluated yet as either a success or failure, the objective for this particular change makes a great deal of sense, which puts KFC in a better position for the nutritious 90s.

Step 3: Develop Designs and Names

Once the identity audit is complete and clear objectives established, the next phase in the identity process is the actual design. If a name change is necessary, consultants must search for alternatives. This is a step that simply cannot happen without the help of consultants because so many names have already been used that companies must be sure to avoid any possibilities of trademark and name infringement. But options for change can still number in the hundreds. Usually, certain ones stand out as more appropriate. The criteria for selection depend on several variables.

For example, if the company is undergoing a global expansion, the addition of the word "international" might be the best alternative. If a firm has a lot of equity built into one product, changing the name of the corporation to that of the product might be the answer, as happened when Consolidated Foods changed its name to Sara Lee.

The process of designing a new look or logo is an artistic one, but so many times executives can't help getting involved in the process. Everyone has an opinion about designs, and the choice is usually a matter of taste coupled with the excellent work of a professional designer. Despite reliance on professionals to develop designs, I have seen CEOs rely on their own instincts rather than the work of someone who may have spent an entire career thinking about design solutions.

One CEO that I worked with designed what he thought would be the perfect logo for his company on a napkin. After several weeks of design exploration by a reputable design firm, he kept coming back to that same napkin design over and over again. Until the designer finally caught on and came up with an exploration that resembled the napkin design, each of the suggestions was rejected. When the CEO saw his own idea come back at him, he was happy. Everyone agreed that it was not the best design, but it was adopted and is in use today.

In another case, the CEO took what was everyone on the design team's favorite exploration out on the road for a couple of weeks to show it around. The designer warned him not to do this because it would only complicate matters with everyone thinking he or she is an expert in logo design. When the team met again, the favorite design was scrapped because of the candid comments of a first-grade teacher who felt that the lopsided positioning of the letters in the design would affect young children's perceptions of correct lettering. One person who had no knowledge of design and no sense of what the company's goals were made the difference.

Obviously, there has to be a balance between the professional opinion of a designer and a manager's own instincts. Both need to be a part of the final decision whether a name change or just a new logo is involved. In some cases, designers and identity consultants are perfectionists or idealistic, presenting ideas that are unrealistic or too avant-garde for typically conservative large corporations. In the end, strong leadership must be exerted to effect the change, no matter what it is, for it to succeed.

Step 4: Develop Prototypes

Once the final design is selected and approved by everyone involved, consultants develop models using the new symbols or name. This is usually the most exciting part of the process for most managers. For products, prototype packaging shows how the brand image may be used in advertising. If a retail operation is involved, a model of the store might be built.

In other situations, the identity is applied to everything including ties, T-shirts, business cards, and stationery to see how it works in practice.

During this process, it is common for managers to again get cold feet. As the reality of the change sinks in, criticism mounts (as in the case of the school teacher) from some quarters because they have not been involved in the process and from others because they do not have a good sense of the evolution and meaning of the design. At times, negative reactions from constituents can be so strong that proposals have to be abandoned and work started all over again.

To prevent this failure, a diversity of people and viewpoints should be involved in the identity process. The one caveat is to avoid accommodating different ideas by diluting concepts. A company should not accept an identity that is simply the lowest common denominator. Two ways to deal with the task are either to let a strong leader champion the new design or set up a strong committee to work on the program. In either approach, everyone has to be informed and involved in the project from the beginning. The more people involved in the process from its inception, the less work necessary to sell the idea after much hard work has already taken place.

Step 5: Launch and Communicate

Given the time involved and the number of people that need to be included in the process, news about future changes can easily be leaked to the public. At Kmart, hundreds knew about the effort, and managers worried that the new logo would appear in *Advertising Age* or another trade magazine before the launch. Fortunately, the story stayed under wraps until the day of the announcement and was exposed only when a savvy photographer spotted hundreds of carts with the new logo sitting in a parking lot. Of course, he took pictures and promptly sold them to *USA Today*.

Sometimes such publicity is a positive event, as it can create excitement and a sense of anticipation. Still, chance occurrences are no substitute for a formal introduction of the company's new identity. To build drama into the announcement, public relations staff should be creative in inviting reporters without giving away the purpose. One company sent six-foot pencils and a huge calendar with the date of the press conference marked off.

At the press conference itself, the design should be clearly displayed in a variety of contexts, and senior executives must carefully explain the strategy behind the program. As additional communication tools, corporations might want to avail themselves of video news releases and satellite links (see Chapter 6). Whatever the choice, remember that presenting an identity, particularly for the first time, is a complex problem. It is much too easy to interpret the change as merely cosmetic.

Step 6: Implement the Program

The final stage is implementation. This can take years in large companies and a minimum of several months for small firms. Resistance is inevitable, but what is frequently shocking is the extent of ownership constituents have in the old identity. (Just think about how long it took to get lights in Wrigley Field.)

Usually, the best approach to ensure consistency across all uses for a new identity program is to develop identity standards. A standards manual shows staff and managers how to use the new identity consistently and correctly. Beyond this, someone in the organization needs to monitor the program and make judgments about when flexibility is allowed and when it is not. Over time, changes will need to be made in some standards, for instance, when a modern typeface chosen by a designer is not available for use everywhere.

Implementing an identity program is a communication process involving lots of interpersonal savvy to work best. Managers must plan for such eventualities beforehand rather than allowing situations to develop naturally and having to react to each one separately.

Conclusion

Most managers who have not participated in developing an identity program tend to underestimate its value. I have found that those on the financial side of the operation, for example, often think that such a process is silly and trivial. Some of this hesitation emerges from a lack of understanding about what corporate image and identity are all about and what they do for an organization. But such skeptics should understand that an inappropriate or outdated identity can be as damaging to a firm as a weak financial performance. People seek consistency, and if perceptions about a corporation fail to mesh with reality, constituents take their business elsewhere.

Executives, then, need to be fully aware of the tremendous impact of image and identity and they must learn how to manage this critical resource. Success in this area is a catalyst for and a symbol of change, the dynamic process that keeps companies thriving. Success also matures into pride and commitment—among employees, consumers, and the general public—irreplaceable assets in our intensely competitive business environment.

CASE
GE IDENTITY PROGRAM (A)*

Richard Costello, manager of Corporate Marketing Communications at GE, sat in his darkened office, flashing image after image onto the wall. What he saw did not please him. He was reviewing images gathered from across GE's wide range of businesses—images of advertising, packaging, in-house publications, brochures, stationery, etc. It was 1985, and Costello had recently become responsible for the GE monogram, a responsibility he had pursued, believing that the trademark drove the company's image. Even though Costello knew it was time to review the use of GE's 100-year-old logo, he was surprised at the range and lack of consistency in the images being projected. He began to formulate the case he would make to his superiors, and ultimately to GE's chairman, Jack Welch, to fund a reexamination of the corporation's identity.

Managing the identity of the largest diversified multinational company in the world is no small task. Founded by Thomas Edison, GE became a public company in 1892, about 20 years after the development of the light bulb. By the early 1980s GE held the number one or number two position in each of 14 key businesses ranging from aircraft engines and kitchen appliances to light bulbs, medical systems, and financial services. The company had 300,000 employees and grossed over $50 billion a year. A 1991 article in *Fortune* magazine described GE this way:

> Few corporations are bigger; none is as complex. GE makes 65-cent light bulbs, 400,000-pound locomotives, and billion-dollar power plants. It manages more credit cards than American Express and owns more commercial aircraft than American Airlines. Of the 7 billion pounds of

hamburger Americans tote home each year, 36 percent keeps fresh in GE refrigerators, and after dinner, one out of five couch potatoes tunes in GE's network, NBC.[1]

In 1981, Jack Welch became Chairman and CEO of GE and began radically restructuring the company's portfolio, selling off some of the most traditional businesses that were electrical, like the housewares business, small kitchen appliances, and televisions, and buying such diversified businesses as CGR, a French medical systems company, and NBC. Welch's firm leadership transformed GE into a lean organization prepared to meet the challenges of the contemporary global marketplace. But although Welch had turned the company around internally, from a visual standpoint, it looked like nothing had changed. The company's visual and naming systems were not communicating the qualities that Welch was conveying through his actions.

Paul Van Orden, former Vice President of GE's Consumer Sector, describes the motivation for the company to reconsider its identity:

> We had done some research over time that indicated, first of all, that some aspects of the monogram and the identity program appeared less up to date than we would like. Two, there was a subjective feeling among some of us that the "General GE Electric" approach appeared kind of old-fashioned. And the third element was the wide variation of application of terminology and business cards, letterheads, all that sort of thing. It was clear that everybody did pretty much as they pleased, so we were a long way from

---

[1] "GE Keeps Those Ideas Coming," *Fortune*, August 12, 1991, p. 41.

presenting any kind of a consistent face to our customers or to the public.[2]

In addition, the company had become so diversified, that the name "General Electric" no longer appropriately expressed the range of the company's products. The corporation had also purchased businesses with their own strong identities but had no system for evaluating how to integrate them into the corporation. For example, during the process of selecting a corporate identity consultant, the company acquired RCA, NBC, and Kidder Peabody. These acquisitions forced the company to face decisions it had not confronted before about how to associate well-known brands with the larger corporation.

Between the lack of visual consistency and the need for a system to deal with acquisitions, Richard Costello and Merle Bonthuis, Manager of Corporate Identity, had little trouble convincing senior management to fund a review of the company's identity and to hire a corporate identity consultant. After reviewing eight prominent identity consultants, Landor Associates was selected based on the following criteria:

- Their expertise in corporate/subsidiary/ acquisition identity systems
- Their international base
- A design portfolio which was varied and free from any style or "look"
- The chemistry, size, and vitality of the project team
- A strong marketing orientation

The bulk of Landor's involvement took place over a two year period. During the first six months of 1986, the project team carried out an extensive analysis of GE's identity situation. They conducted 145 individual interviews with executives covering 23 cities in the U.S. and in every continent in which GE was involved, 21 operating units, selected ad agencies, and GE's public relations firm. They reviewed all written information about the company that was relevant to image and identity matters and conducted a more extensive audit of visual materials to supplement Costello's mini-audit. Finally, Landor conducted a very thorough multi-national research study to test awareness and perceptions of GE among both business and consumer audiences. The information gathered was analyzed to develop design and communications criteria, as well as to develop an innovative strategy for the company from an identity standpoint.

The support of top-level management was essential to the success of the GE identity program. In the words of Patrice Kavanaugh, Landor's Account Manager on the project, "It's critical when you're involved in a corporate identity program that you're working at the very highest levels within a corporation. All of our experience indicates that if the top executive is either not involved or not aware of what's going on and supportive in the appropriate way, the program never goes anywhere."

Paul Van Orden agrees:

Before you embark on the program, or sometime early in the program, you've got to get some sense that you're going to get executive support. Senior executives identify themselves with what is and, for the most part, are somewhat reluctant to change identity unless you can demonstrate to them a compelling need. In our case, the most compelling need was internal, to get our act together and present a single face.[3]

At GE, Jack Welch went beyond personally supporting and mandating the program. To de-

[2] Interview with Paul Van Order, December 6, 1991, conducted by Laurie Poklop.

[3] Ibid.

velop as much upper management buy-in as possible in such a huge organization, Welch established what was called the Identity Advisory Council, comprised of the marketing or communications managers from each of the 14 primary businesses. Involved from the very beginning of the program, this group of approximately 25 individuals helped Landor set up management interviews at their respective businesses and provided the visual materials for the audit.

At every critical stage of the program, presentations were made to the Advisory Council before going on to senior management. This was a new way of working for Landor, who in most cases, reported to a single client contact. But Welch and his top managers knew that eventually the program would have to be rolled-out throughout a huge organization spanning many countries. They believed that the way to do this successfully would be to establish a task force and to involve them from the very beginning. "And they were absolutely right," says Kavanaugh. "Since it proved so successful, we've actually been recommending to subsequent clients that they form a council at the very beginning and get them involved. It really does pay off in the long run to do that, if the company's big enough to warrant it.[4]

Landor's research focused, first of all, on awareness of GE among the business community and consumers. They asked such unaided questions as, "Name some major international corporations." They found, not surprisingly, that GE had a phenomenally high awareness level among both businesses and consumers—a very strong asset to play upon. In terms of image, response was fairly consistent both internally and externally; the strength of the company was that it was very "solid" and "reliable," but it was seen as being somewhat "old-fashioned" and was still known basically as an appliance and light bulb company. Comparing GE to other major U.S. corporations—AT&T, IBM, 3M—the research showed that perceptions of GE were high on the quality of reliability, but fell short in terms of dynamism and innovation. Even though the company was involved in a wide range of businesses, it was not being given credit for them. Improving perceptions of GE's diversity became a critical objective of the program.

The company name held unquestionably high awareness. But General Electric, as a full name, was seen to be an increasingly inaccurate way to describe the company, because it wasn't just in the electrical business anymore. In fact, only 25 percent of sales were derived from electrical businesses.[5] The monogram itself, the GE symbol, was definitely seen as a symbol of reliability, but old-fashioned—not surprising since it had essentially not changed since its introduction in 1896.

In one area, management perceptions differed from those of the marketplace: overall company image. Management knew that the company was very diverse, while externally, it was seen as being fairly narrow. Internally and externally there was agreement that the company did not have a terribly dynamic image, though this was in contradiction to the reality that Jack Welch was creating. The results of six months of management interviews, visual audits, and research were analyzed and program objectives established. Through both design and naming, the new identity system would:

- Broaden awareness of GE's diversity so that people have a more *accurate perception* of the Company
- Maintain GE's image of *reliability* and

---

[4] Interview with Patrice Kavanaugh conducted by Peter Lawrence, June 18, 1991.

[5] Bartels, Donald H., "The GE Identity Program: A Historical Review."

improve perception of its *innovation* and *dynamism*

- Unify the company's visual and verbal expressions through a *consistent* and *high quality* application of the *contemporary* program standards[6]

Landor spent the next six months developing an innovative identity strategy for the company, both visually and verbally, that would meet these objectives. This was the most extensive program ever undertaken by Landor; they built what they called a "GE War Room" in their San Francisco offices and explored a wide range of design options from evolutionary kinds of change to breakthrough design solutions. Since this was the first time in 100 years that the company had reviewed its identity, GE and the Landor project team agreed that management deserved to see a selection of alternatives spanning the full spectrum of ideas.

As the first year of the program was drawing to a close, Landor presented three alternative solutions, each fleshed out with comprehensive examples of typical media—package designs, letterhead designs, truck designs—so that the Advisory Council and Jack Welch could easily imagine the consequences of various degrees of change.[7]

The most revolutionary solution abstracted the letters "G" and "E" into an altogether new monogram.

GE Typography

---

[6] *GE Identity Program,* Volume 1: Basic Standards, p. i.

[7] Bartels, p. 47.

Alternative number two placed the monogram's script lettering into a square mark and used a more traditional typeface.

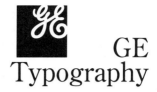

GE Typography

The third was an evolutionary change from the current GE identity (shown below). It left the monogram virtually intact, with very minor adjustments, and placed it in a new graphic environment with an italicized, sans serif typeface and a very fine "laser" line.

GE Typography

All three alternatives incorporated a single new naming scheme.

Problem

Imagine yourself in the position of Richard Costello. The three alternatives have been developed and presented by Landor Associates to upper management and the Identity Advisory Council, and you must recommend what you feel is the most appropriate solution. Your inclination is in the direction of revolutionary change. Management opinion is divided, and Welch has not indicated a preference. Landor would love to be known as the company that gave GE a totally new image, but isn't sure it's really the best thing for the company.

Issues to consider:

- How strong is the equity of the existing monogram, as a function of both awareness and imagery?

- How much change does GE need to communicate through its identity system in order to change perceptions of the company? Visibility is an issue here. A company which has high visibility can more readily communicate change than a company which does not.
- What other "tools" (besides identity) does GE have at its disposal to signal change?
- How would changing its identity help/hurt GE's marketing strategy? Short-term? Long-term?
- What impact would a dramatic change have on internal morale, given that a number of key managers had "grown up" with the monogram and felt it was a rallying point for all employees? Also, it was one of the few remaining links to the past which Jack Welch had not changed. How important is internal morale for a company like GE?
- How would the decision to change/not change impact GE's global competitiveness?

CASE
GE IDENTITY PROGRAM (B)*

For the final presentation to the Chairman, we developed three very finished systems: one that was evolutionary and the other two taking steps away from the traditional look to a very radical new approach which had nothing to do with the old identity. People could look at them and begin to get a sense of what each option might be like. In fact, that crystallized opinions very quickly. It was about 80-20; 20 percent of the management team, about 30 people in all, wanted to move to the radical end. They all tended to be in our high technology businesses. It didn't segment by age, by type of individual; it segmented by the business they were in . . . I was a believer in getting rid of the whole thing, blowing up the trademark. I was radical. I wanted to put a new trademark on the front door. A combination of Landor and the management kept us from doing that, and now, in retrospect, I really think it was the right thing to do.[1]

RICHARD COSTELLO

We were pretty excited, to be honest, about some of these breakthrough designs. Ultimately, however, it came back to the fact that the monogram had such tremendous equity and awareness levels and communications values. It was just impossible to walk away from it.[2]

PATRICE KAVANAUGH

To give Landor its due, they had done the alternatives in a really high quality fashion. They'd done packaging and signs and cards and letterhead and all that sort of thing. There was a vocal minority that thought we ought to take the more far out modification of the monogram, to the point that it was unrecognizable. Our concern was that we could lose all identity and that it would be enormously expensive to associate that new identity with all the equity that we'd built up through the monogram. That was the basis of the decision to make relatively small modifications in the actual appearance of the monogram. But there was whole-hearted support for the nomenclature and the cleaning up of our appearance and looking as one company.[3]

PAUL VAN ORDEN

Ultimately, the decision was made to retain the GE monogram—thus retaining that quality of solidity and reliability—and to communicate the qualities of dynamism and innovation through secondary devices enhancing the monogram. In other words, to "keep the baby, change the bath water."[4] Landor spent three-quarters of 1987 fleshing out the system to meet their original objectives.

Objective: Broaden Awareness of GE's Diversity so that People Have a More Accurate Perception of the Company

The new identity system gave GE a coherent branding and naming system; it established a logic which had previously been absent and facilitated decision making on branding and naming of components within a brand.

To address the reality of the corporation's

---

[1] Interview with Richard Costello conducted by Peter Lawrence, June 18, 1991.
[2] Interview with Patrice Kavanaugh conducted by Peter Lawrence, May 9, 1991.

[3] Interview with Paul Van Orden, December 3, 1991, conducted by Laurie Poklop.
[4] Interview with Richard Costello by Peter Lawrence, June 18, 1991.

diversity, Landor recommended that in its external and internal communications, the company no longer call itself General Electric, but simply GE. This change was supported by research in which two thirds of the people who named GE, when asked to name some big companies, called it GE, not General Electric. So the change would not cause confusion.

To make the company appear leaner and simpler, both visually and verbally, a plethora of formal organizational names being used in advertising, brochures, business cards, etc., were shortened to very concise descriptors of competencies. To the degree possible, the rule was to use the highest level of competence that made sense for a particular business, i.e., GE Aerospace, GE Plastics, GE Aircraft Engines, GE Financial Services, etc. While people would not remember that GE was in hundreds of businesses, by using these concise competency terms, it was hoped that they would build awareness of 15 or so areas of business, thus communicating the company's diversity.

Former Organizational Name	New Communicative Name
General Electric Aerospace Business Group	*GE Aerospace*
General Electric Aircraft Engine Business Group	*GE Aircraft Engines*
General Electric Major Appliance Business Group	*GE Appliances*
General Electric Financial Services, Inc.	*GE Financial Services*
General Electric Lighting Business Group	*GE Lighting*
General Electric Medical Systems Business Group	*GE Medical Systems*
General Electric Motor Business Group	*GE Motors*
General Electric Power Systems Business	*GE Power Systems*
General Electric Semiconductor Business	*GE Solid State*
General Electric Plastics Business Group	*GE Plastics*

A similar logic was used internally to simplify functional titles, which supported the direction of the company to become less bureaucratic. For example, the person in charge of the major appliance business had been called Vice President and General Manager of the Major Appliance Business Division. Under the new system, that person's title became Vice President, Major Appliances.

> We were striving internally to become less bureaucratic, to have fewer layers of management structure, increasing the span of control of the manager, so that instead of having 7 people reporting to a manager, we have 15 or 16. We were cleaning up the processes so that there were fewer approvals. Cleaning up the way we identified ourselves internally went with the grain of that thought. This was another step in being less of a bureaucratic, cumbersome company. We're cleaner, we're one, we're going to have more simple identification of our business.[5]
>
> PAUL VAN ORDEN

Next came the issue of how the company would deal with acquired brands. Patrice Kavanaugh gives the following description of how corporations deal with branding issues:

> There are basically two extremes, if you think in terms of a spectrum. On one extreme, you have a company like IBM, where the brand that's used at the corporate level is also the brand that's used at all their product levels. The opposite extreme is represented by Bristol Meyers or Proctor & Gamble, where the corporate brand is completely invisible to the public and, all of their visibility is exclusively through their brands. It allows them to create two brands in the same category, like Bufferin® and Excedrin®, which compete against each other and thereby increase the company's overall market share.
>
> Then you have companies that do a mixture

---

[5] Interview with Paul Van Orden, former GE Vice President, on December 6, 1991.

of the two. Disney, for example, has some of its products and brands share the corporate brand while others don't. For example, Touchstone, the more mature theme film brand, has no relationship back to Disney, because they're trying to create some separation.

It can be very difficult to support the Bristol Meyers strategy, because you have to have lots of promotional dollars to support all those brands. And an IBM-type strategy can be just as difficult unless you're in one business that allows you to expand as much as you want to remain viable. So, most companies end up somewhere in between.[6]

GE historically had been where IBM was, but it was moving. The question was, how far would it move and how? Landor developed five levels of identification which GE could use to identify every conceivable business it would ever enter or acquire: (Examples shown are for purposes of illustration only.)

1. GE linked to a competence term. Encompassed 80 percent of GE's businesses.

GE Investment Banking

2. The monogram + proper name. Used when it is beneficial to retain the affiliate's existing name and a lesser degree of association with GE is desirable.

GE Kidder Peabody

---

[6] Interview with Patrice Kavanaugh conducted by Peter Lawrence, May 9, 1991.

3. GE monogram endorsement. Used if the company acquired a business with powerful brand which would still benefit from being linked to GE.

Kidder Peabody

---

4. GE verbal endorsement. Used if an acquired company had strong equity in both its visual and its verbal expression, or if for other reasons the company didn't want GE so closely tied to it.

Kidder, Peabody&Co.

GE Financial Services

5. GE invisible. Used in cases where there is no benefit in linking GE with an affiliate. NBC is an example of this. Concerned that GE would be seen as controlling the news if it linked itself too closely to NBC, it was decided to retain NBC as a separate entity.

Kidder, Peabody&Co.

To help the company determine which level is appropriate for a business, Landor developed an elaborate decision tree addressing business, industry, image, and identity issues. In terms of business issues, questions are asked such as: Do you have control over this organization? Are you committed to this business? If GE doesn't control an acquired company, it is recommended that they not link themselves too closely to it, because they risk losing control of their image. In terms of commitment, GE had historically gotten in and out of several businesses. This system allowed GE not to link itself too closely to a business it was not committed to for the long term.

Through its extensive research, Landor rated the image value of particular industries. For example, aerospace, communications, and medical systems industries were rated with a high image value for the targeted qualities of dynamism and innovation, while appliances, construction equipment, and financial services provide a lower image value for these traits. Because the company is trying to communicate that it is dynamic and innovative, if they were acquiring a company in an industry that is not particularly dynamic, a lower level of association with GE would be appropriate. Similarly, through research, Landor developed ratings of performance expectations of GE in a range of industries. Whether or not GE is likely to be thought of as doing well in a particular industry would lead to higher or lower level of association.

Finally, in terms of identity issues, questions are asked such as: Is the equity of the affiliate's existing identity strong or weak? Is awareness of the name and logo high? Is the name associated with a leadership position in terms of product and service quality? What would be the impact on the company if GE were prominently associated with the affiliate? A negative association always leads to a higher level (#4).

Objective: Maintain GE's Image of Reliability and Improve Perception of Its Innovation and Dynamism

The GE Identity Program Manual succinctly describes how the new GE signature communicates the qualities of reliability, innovation, and dynamism:

Reliability is conveyed by:
- Continuing use of the monogram, a 100-year-old symbol that is familiar and trusted.

- Standardizing the color of the monogram to platinum grey, creating a classic and distinguished presentation
- Using a serif typeface, ITC New Baskerville, suggesting traditional qualities

Introducing a line of built-in appliances designed for people who dislike unnecessary irritation.

Dynamism and innovation are conveyed by:
- Using a signature that provides a contemporary environment for the monogram. The Graphic Signature features:
  (a) *The Laser Line,* suggesting high technology
  (b) *The italic typeface Univers,* suggesting forward movement
  (c) *An asymmetrical layout,* conveying movement with its visual tension

GE Plastics

_____

We bring good things to life.

_____

- Selectively using a portion of the monogram on a large scale—the dynamic monogram—suggesting the Company is "too dynamic to be contained."[7]

_____

[7] GE Identity Program, Volume 1: Basic Standards, p. ii.

Objective: Unify the Company's Visual and Verbal Expressions through a Consistent and High Quality Application of the Contemporary Program Standards

The Landor design team worked out applications for every conceivable visual and nomenclature situation—print advertising, brochures, stationery, checks and business forms, trucks, packaging, signs, and exhibits. At this point, the Advisory Council broke into small groups to help define the breadth of each media category and the practical limitations and requirements imposed by each kind of application.[8]

The most tangible deliverable Landor presented to GE was a two-volume manual documenting all the standards. The first volume, distributed by late autumn of 1987, was devoted to general standards and trademark applications. The second was devoted completely to applications and followed a few months after the first. Because GE had so many businesses spread throughout the world working with so many consultants, they felt it was important to show as many examples as possible, leaving as little as possible to people's

imaginations. The manual was designed as an out-sized loose-leaf notebook. The large format allowed space for the necessary displays and specifications and indicated the importance of the program. In addition, the loose-leaf format permitted economical printing of any adjustments and additions that might be made to the standards.

By early 1988 each business began implementing the standards of the new corporate identity system, supported by a communications manager who had participated firsthand in the development of the program through the Advisory Council. Each business was responsible for developing its own roll-out schedule. Schedules were influenced by such factors as current budgets, new product launches, a new advertising campaign, etc.

Media that are the most easily and economically implemented—such as stationery, print advertising, new brochures, etc.—were the first converted to the new identity system. Other media that are more expensive to implement—such as signs and vehicles—were converted once funds could be allocated or according to pre-existing maintenance schedules. For example, if a vehicle fleet was due to be repainted in 12 months, then it would be converted to the new look at that time. In this way, GE instituted a "rolling change" for the

[8] Bartels, Donald H., "The GE Identity Program: A Historical Review," p. 50.

new identity system. That is, its various media were implemented over a period of time, rather than all at once; thus, the implementation was carried out as cost efficiently as possible.

GE's businesses were introduced to the program standards via on-site Identity Introduction presentations. For each major business, in the United States and at several international locations, GE corporate identity management and Landor presented an overview of the program standards to selected marketing and communications managers and their staffs, as well as key outside vendors. A subsequent question and answer session addressed the program standards.

Shortly after these presentations, the manuals were distributed throughout the company to the appropriate individuals and implementation began according to each business' roll-out schedule. In addition to the manuals, posters were distributed summarizing the program for display in office/studios. A videotape was produced, detailing highlights of the development process and strategy; this was distributed widely inside the company.

One of the largest businesses, GE Appliances, established its own internal corporate identity council. Vic Alcott, Manager of Advertising and Design for GE appliances, had been a member of the Advisory Council. Implementation of major areas of the identity program came under his responsibility. To accomplish this, he brought together a team of about a dozen people representing design, purchasing, sales, promotion, consumer service, and patent council. The group stayed in place for approximately two years and worked to execute the program, keep a lid on costs, and develop a sense of ownership of the plan among employees with various departmental responsibilities.

One of the biggest challenges from the beginning was what I call the cost equation. You can't tell management you need X million dollars to imple-

ment some corporate identity program. You still have to meet bottom line goals. So how do you phase it in and begin to execute it as quickly as possible and make it very visible, but not generate a lot of incremental cost? I saw that as our number one challenge.[9]

VIC ALCOTT

Some changes were easier to implement fairly quickly, like adapting the type style and signature guidelines in advertising. Other changes took place according to regular schedules. For example, in exhibit design, new shows are continuously designed throughout the year, and elements such as dynamic monogram were integrated fairly quickly. Other changes, such as those effecting product or vehicle design, were more long-term. The program effected product design in terms of graphics and terminology which appeared on appliances. Similar to the principles of the simplified nomenclature system, the basic criteria governing words and graphics on products are that they will create an overall statement of quality and innovation and will communicate to the user how to use the product. They will have functional copy, not promotional copy. Particular graphic elements are evaluated as to their effectiveness on individual products. For example, a thin, laser red line on a microwave oven helps to create a streamlined appearance.

Once the team had communicated the guidelines internally, it took on the challenge of implementing the program with external suppliers. To do this, they distilled the two-volume identity manual into approximately 50 pages, covering the highlights of each of the basic media. Then they held a seminar with 40 to 50 of their major suppliers and got them to begin working with the system— "put it into real day execution."

---

[9] Interview with Vic Alcott, Manager of Advertising and Design, GE Appliances, December 2, 1991.

Getting it under control; simplifying it; making whatever modifications had to be made along the way; making sure that it doesn't get out of line from a financial perspective; and getting people to feel comfortable with it and therefore take ownership: these are the key ingredients of making a corporate identity program work well in the real marketplace quickly.[10]

Landor continued to work with GE on "identity system maintenance"—monitoring the implementation of the identity system through on-site workshops conducted at each of the 14 major businesses approximately every 18 months. Over a period of several months prior to the workshops, Landor evaluated visual materials produced by each business, then reported back the results to each group. Through a slide presentation, Landor presented, first, how the identity system was being implemented company-wide and, second, how the particular business was performing in terms of following the identity guidelines. Workshop participants were also encouraged to bring materials to the workshops for on-the-spot consultation. In the first such Identity Review, which took place in 1989, a few businesses showed excellent results, while as a whole the company's implementation was judged to be very good, particularly considering its decentralized organization structure.[11]

According to Patrice Kavanaugh:

The workshops are really effective in motivating people to continue following these guidelines. They are a reflection of the corporation's ongoing commitment to the identity program, and help keep the program on track. Identity is like any other corporate asset. You have to give it attention and maintain it over time. These workshops seem to be an effective way to do that.[12]

Has the GE Identity Program been a success? The following comments represent a variety of perspectives on the value of corporate identity:

Paul Van Orden, Executive Vice President, GE:

The GE identity, as former chairman Owen D. Young once said, "may be our least tangible yet most valuable asset." To sustain the number one or number two position of all our businesses in today's tough business environment, we must leverage every asset and competitive advantage we own. We can't afford to be misunderstood; we can't afford our leadership position to be overlooked.[13]

Richard Costello, Manager of Corporate Marketing Communications, GE:

I could argue quite vigorously that there has been significant day to day cost savings by implementing a clean, clear, orderly, narrowly defined program. We have had millions of dollars being spent on people reinventing the light bulb, or more specifically, reinventing how you do a sign outside. By limiting choices, we've improved not only the quality of the output, but we've improved productivity as well. When we audited business cards and stationery, even in corporate headquarters, there were 10 different designs. So even at that very pragmatic level of standardizing stationery, there is a cost savings.

At a strategic level, I would argue that the company had done a superb job over a century of creating whatever it was that people perceived and valued about GE. That was the reason that we decided to keep the monogram—because there's 100 years of investment behind that. However, over that time there had been some practices or just simply sufficient changes that it was not as appropriately positioned for today's world and today's company as it might have

[10] Ibid.
[11] Ibid., p. 52.
[12] Interview with Patrice Kavanaugh conducted by Peter Lawrence, May 9, 1991.
[13] Bartels, p. 46.

been. So I would argue that we then invested for a couple of years a significant sum of money, that in the scheme of a $50 billion corporation is peanuts, to position ourselves for the next 20 years.[14]

Vic Alcott, Manager of Advertising and Design, GE Appliances:

As we began to expand it internationally, through working with customers or acquiring new companies on a global basis, one of the first things they say is: Isn't it remarkable, all you people at GE have the same business card? It's such a simple thing, but what it says to people on the international scene is that here's a company that is concerned about its identity; no matter how big or small, it is communicated. Be it a business card or an expensive product display or a television commercial, there is a clear, single idea that you get about this company from all those media. It pays off as it begins to get bigger and broader.

If your objective is to establish an image for a brand as being a leader in a given industry, and as one that provides genuine relevant innovation in its product to that industry and maintain a very high quality standard of execution that has a rub off in sales and margins, and profitability over time. It's hard to single out that that was the result of a given signature or graphic system, but the fact remains that that forces the consistency which results in an executional quality and a perception of a customer when they look at all those products and they see that design consistency. It pays off, it builds, it has added value.

Roger Morey, Vice President, GE Motor Sales:

Ten years from now, we'll look back and realize the identity program is one of the best things the company ever did.[15]

Patrice Kavanaugh, Account Executive, Landor Associates:

The hardest job I think we have to do in "selling" companies on the value of design is proving its value to the bottom line. If you've got dozens of consulting firms, design firms, and in-house designers constantly creating new looks and coming up with new themes, all of that time and effort and energy costs the company money. If you come up with a set of guidelines that establish consistency, while still allowing sufficient flexibility, you're giving people a template. Our argument is that, giving them that template, one, you're insuring that the company is communicating what the corporate message is, but two, they're further up on the design line than they would be if they were always starting from ground zero.[16]

[15] Bartels, p. 52.

[16] Interview with Patrice Kavanaugh conducted by Peter Lawrence, May 9, 1991.

* © 1992 Corporate Design Foundation. This case was written by Laurie Poklop under the direction of Peter Lawrence, Chairman, Corporate Design Foundation. Reprinted by permission.

[14] Interview with Richard Costello conducted by Peter Lawrence, June 18, 1991.

5   THE CORPORATION IS THE MESSAGE

In the preceding chapter, we discussed the importance of creating a coherent image and identity. Of the many options available to organizations, paid corporate advertising is the easiest and fastest way to communicate about an organization's image. As a result, about half of the largest corporations in the United States today use some form of corporate advertising.

In this chapter we will study the role of corporate advertising in a corporate communications program and how it can shape an organization's image by first defining what corporate advertising is, then looking back at its history, determining who uses this form of advertising and why, and ending with the question of whether to use it or not. Given that the corporate world seems to be evenly split on the issue, some guidelines may help organizations to come to the right conclusion.

What Is Corporate Advertising?

Corporate advertising can best be defined as paid use of media that seeks to benefit the image of the corporation rather than just its products or services. Some would say that it is a form of paid public relations or corporate communications as opposed to unpaid public relations, which we will talk about in the next chapter as we study how organizations can use the media to enhance their image.

A major difference between corporate and product advertising also comes from looking at who pays for each of the two types of advertising. Typically, the marketing department would be responsible for all product-related advertising and would pay for such ads out of its budget. In the case of corporate advertising, however, the ideal place for such responsibility is the corporate communications department. More typically in the absence of a strong function in most companies, we find that corporate advertising is paid for by the chairman and/or CEO's office. This points out the importance of tying corporate advertising to top management. It also explains why we often see the CEO included in such ads as he or she tries to shape the organization's image.

First and foremost, corporate advertising should strive to present a clear image and identity for the organization. It should definitely not promise more than an organization can really deliver, and it must be based on a careful assessment of the overall communication strategy for the organization (see Chapter 2 for more on strategy).

Corporate advertising tends to fall into three broad categories: (1) image enhancement, (2) financial enhancement, and (3) issue enhancement. Let's take a closer look at each of the three categories to get a better understanding of what this kind of advertising is all about.

Advertising to Enhance an Organization's Image

We have already discussed in the previous chapter why organizations need to enhance their image with a variety of constituencies. Some of the most important criteria that companies use to decide about corporate advertising stem from what they learn when they analyze their image with constituencies. If the organization's image is, in reality, very different from how they are perceived, they will want to communicate about those differences through the use of a corporate advertising campaign.

Over the last 10 years, many companies have decided to use corporate advertising aimed at image enhancement primarily as a result of structural changes that have taken place at the organization. As companies have merged and become more disparate, for example, they have had to explain what they are all about to constituents who may have known them quite well in an earlier incarnation but are struggling to figure out what the new organization is all about. These typically larger organizations often need to simplify their image to unify a group of very disparate activities.

Organizations also use image advertising to change impressions about themselves. In the last chapter we looked at how Kmart tried to change its image by redesigning its stores and creating a new logo. In addition, the company has created an image-oriented advertising campaign for television featuring chairman and CEO Joseph Antonini walking through a refurbished store with the new look. The primary goal of this campaign is to change an erroneous impression that people have about this large discount retailer. Corporate advertising can be a very efficient means to change impressions about large organizations if changes have really taken place.

Each year, *Business Week* magazine gives awards to the best-remembered corporate advertising campaigns. In 1992, one of its awards went to Fujitsu Ltd., a Japanese computer, communications, and microelectronics firm. It's campaign was fairly typical of the sort of image enhancement that companies try to use if they are not well known with a particular constituency. The headline for this particular advertisement was: "How a $21 billion technological giant manages to remain virtually anonymous." The copy goes on to say:

> It's true we've spent the last half century pushing the envelope of technology harder than we've pushed our name. Our commitment to R&D (over $2 billion last year alone) has helped make us the world's second largest computer maker. And our advances in communications and microelectronics have always taken priority over publicity. Today, our capabilities range from hand-

held computers to high-speed fiber optics. We make disk and tape drives for many of America's leading computer manufacturers. Transistors that made direct broadcast satellite systems possible. And more of the application-specific ICs for modern computers and electronics than anyone in the world. You'll find our name in over 100 countries. Now we're making a name for ourselves in America.

Notice that Fujitsu does not mention anything about its Japanese roots (perhaps so evident in the name, that they need not bother), but instead tries to position itself as a global company with much to offer American business.

The benefit of such a campaign is very hard to measure, which is why corporate advertising tends to be rather controversial. Will the Fujitsu ad have a specific effect with a specific audience? Does anyone but the companies involved with this technological giant need to know about Fujitsu? While no one can really measure the effects of this campaign, we can assert that any company trying to position itself with a particular image in the minds of constituents will have an easier time building credibility than those who do not. Thus, Fujitsu's corporate ad cannot really hurt the company, and it might do quite a lot of good in building goodwill with constituents.

Advertising to Enhance Investment

Later in this book (Chapter 7) we will look at the importance of a strong investor relations function within the corporate communications department. One of the methods that companies use to enhance their image in the financial community is to use financial-relations corporate advertising campaigns. This kind of corporate advertising can stimulate interest among potential investors for a company's stock. Analysts are a particular target of this type of advertising. Given the hundreds of companies analysts must study, a good corporate advertising campaign can stimulate their interest and make a statement about the company's dynamism.

Some corporate advertisers also assert that a strong financially oriented corporate advertising campaign can actually increase the price of a company's stock. A W.R. Grace campaign that ran in the early 1980s is often cited as evidence of this potential. The television campaign, which ran as the company's "Look into Grace" series, highlighted the company's financial and business attributes and then asked "Shouldn't you look into Grace?" Attitude and awareness studies of the ad campaign in test markets showed that awareness and approval ratings were much higher after this campaign ran.

In addition, the company's stock price increased significantly during the test campaign, although it did not go any higher with later campaigns. Corporate advertising expert Thomas Garbett, writing in the *Harvard Business Review* stated that:

I interpret the relationship between corporate campaigns and stock pricing this way: advertising cannot drive up the price of a reasonably priced stock and, indeed, doing so might not be entirely legal; it can, however, work to ensure that a company's shares are not overlooked or undervalued.[1]

Professors at Northwestern University tried to study this trend using econometric analysis of the link between corporate advertising and stock price. They determined that, indeed, corporate advertising does have a statistically significant positive effect on stock prices. They further determined that the positive influence from such campaigns averaged 2 percent and was particularly strong when the market was in a bull phase.

The implications of this study, if true, are very exciting for companies that may consider their stock to be undervalued. Even a 1-point increase in the stock price can run into the tens or hundreds of millions of dollars for large companies with many shares of stock outstanding. In addition, an improvement in stock prices that improves the company's price-earnings ratio can present opportunities for stock options and dividends for employees. And the effect on bonds is equally impressive considering the impact even a slight improvement in a company's rating can have on a large bond offering.

Although financially oriented corporate advertising campaigns are really just a subset of image-oriented ads, they can usually be identified by the presence of a chief financial officer's name and address appearing with the ad or a mention at the end of the ad for interested parties to write for copies of the company's annual report.

Advertising to Enhance Impressions about an Issue

This kind of advertising is typically called issue or advocacy advertising and is used by companies to respond to external threats from either government or special-interest groups. Issue advertising is usually argumentative, deals with controversial subjects, and is directed at either specific or general targets and opponents. The company is always presented in a very positive way and the opponent in a very negative way. It is a form of corporate debate leveled primarily against those who seek to change the status quo.

Many companies started using issue advertising in the late 1970s and early 1980s to meet the challenges presented by what most corporate executives would agree is an antibusiness sentiment that pervades the media. By taking issues directly to the consumer, companies could com-

[1] Thomas F. Garbett, "When To Advertise Your Company," *Harvard Business Review*, March–April 1982, p. 104.

pete with primarily print journalists for a share of the reader's mind. As a result, these advertisements are often purposely placed on op-ed pages in prominent newspapers such as *The New York Times* and *The Wall Street Journal.* Perhaps the most famous example of this kind of advertising is Mobil Oil's series of issue advertisements, which have run for over 20 years. What began as a dialogue about the oil embargo in the early 1970s has expanded to become a sort of bully pulpit for this powerful organization as it tries to advocate positions on a wide variety of topics.

Many other organizations have also adopted this "op-ed" style for their advocacy ads including United Technologies (which ran several ads during an unsuccessful takeover attempt in the early 1980s), and Amway, which typifies the current trend toward a more positive approach among companies for dealing with environmental issues. Amway recently ran a series of ads that tried to position the company as bullish on the environment. One ad had a photograph of five Amway distributors and the headline: "Find the Environmental Activist." The copy goes on to explain that everyone in the ad is an environmental activist and that all Amway distributors are committed to the cause of environmental awareness. The tag line reads: "And you thought you knew us."

This advertisement also points out the problem, however, with much issue advertising. As David Kelley pointed out in an excellent essay on the subject of issue advertising in *Harvard Business Review* most companies ". . . pay too much attention to the form and too little to the content of the message." Does the tag line in the Amway ad, for example, imply that "You thought we were a bunch of polluters because we specialize in detergents that come in huge containers?" Or does it mean that "You thought we were just selling detergents when what we are really doing is protecting the environment?" In either case, the advertisement seems to be playing into the hands of critics rather than setting the agenda for the argument. Since the advertisement is so short, it never gets across the point that I think this company is trying to make. That is, they would like to argue directly with critics who charge Amway with environmental neglect.

Kelley points out in his HBR article that such a modest approach (unlike the more heavy-handed approach that Mobil has taken over the last 20 years) comes across as arbitrary and leaves the reader more suspicious than before. He goes on to say that:

> If we can judge by numerous corporate advocacy campaigns, speeches by top executives, and discussion in business publications, the defenders of business feel constrained to operate within a framework for discussion that is skewed against the free market system and corporate enterprise. Simply put, the critics of corporations have been allowed to set the terms of the debate in which everything concerning business is argued.
>
> Accepting this framework is a fundamental mistake. Philosophy has long

taught that assumptions granted at the outset of any argument help determine the success or failure of a particular point of view. These assumptions set the framework for argument and determine how the issue is stated, who has the burden of proof, what facts are relevant and how they are evaluated, which arguments seem convincing and which miss the point, what questions critics will ask and what they will accept as valid answers.

Unless business challenges the fundamental assumptions that define the framework in which we currently debate social and economic issues, it can expect nothing more than occasional local victories in the marketplace of ideas—bull rallies in a primarily bear market. . . .[2]

The problem is that most companies are much more conservative than their adversaries, which means that their arguments almost always fall short of the mark. It is extremely difficult for a large corporation that seeks to have positive relations with a variety of constituencies to take on a tough issue in the marketplace of ideas without offending someone. As is true for most politicians nowadays, most companies end up trying to please everyone and thus make it easier for opponents to present a more coherent argument.

Therefore, unless the company has been terribly wronged by an adversary who has received lots of media attention, it should proceed into the world of issue advertising with extreme caution mindful of the dangers that await despite its ability to put much greater resources into the argument than their adversary. If the company decides to do it, top management must have the courage to argue forcefully for its ideas and must not be afraid to alienate certain constituencies in the process. For example, when the major booksellers took on the conservative groups advocating a cleansing of their shelves of all "dirty" books, they won the argument with those advocating first amendment rights, but lost with family-oriented fundamentalist groups.

Now that we have had an opportunity to learn what corporate advertising is all about, lets take a look at its history over the last century.

The History of Corporate Advertising in America

Oddly enough, one of the earliest corporate advertisements was actually issue oriented. According to expert Thomas Garbett, the earliest corporate ad, paid for by the American Telephone and Telegraph Company, started its run in June of 1908. The ad had as its headline: "Telephone service,

---

[2] David Kelley, "Critical Issues for Issue Ads," *Harvard Business Review,* July–August 1982, p. 81.

a public trust,'' and went on to defend the company's point of view as follows:

> The widespread ownership of the Bell Telephone System places an obligation on its management to guard the savings of its hundreds of thousands of stockholders. Its responsibility for so large a part of the country's telephone service imposes an obligation that the service shall always be adequate, dependable and satisfactory to the user. . . . There is then in the Bell System no incentive to earn speculative or large profits. Earnings must be sufficient to assure the best possible service and the financial integrity of the business. Anything in excess of these requirements goes toward extending the service or keeping down rates. . . .

Obviously, even in the early part of the century, AT&T had to defend its (former) monopoly status and the assumption that it couldn't possibly be acting in the public's interest given the lack of competition. As a result of reading the advertisement, the company hoped that the public would have more faith in the company and its honest intentions.

A decade later many different companies were running corporate advertisements, according to textbooks from the period. In fact, Herbert F. deBower's 1917 textbook, *Modern Business*, defines this type of advertising in a way that still applies today:

> Copy that is intended to make people ''think something'' is termed ''molding public opinion'' copy. It is used for pure publicity—to direct public sentiment for political or legislative purposes, and frequently to advertise an industry. An advertisement which aims to induce a general impression favorable to some policy, act, or product, obviously employs copy designed to influence public opinion.[3]

By midcentury, ''institutional advertising'' as it was called was widely used throughout the United States. Garbett describes one of the most interesting reasons for the increased use of this form of advertising during World War II:

> [Corporate] advertising was broadly used during the [second world] war. Although few peacetime products were available for sale to the public, some advertisers realized that if they stopped advertising for several years, it would be difficult to regain their prestige after the war. A younger generation of consumers would come into the market unfamiliar with their products. The advertising of the period frequently took the form of telling what the company was manufacturing for the Armed Forces . . . In many cases the advertisers expressed regret that their products were not available to the public and promised improved products after the war. . . .[4]

---

[3] Herbert F. deBower, *Modern Business*, vol. 7, ''Advertising Principles'' (New York: Alexander Hamilton Institute, 1917).

[4] Thomas F. Garbett, *Corporate Advertising* (New York: McGraw-Hill, 1981), p. 9.

One advertisement that captured the essence of what companies were doing was a hybrid product and image ad. Lucky Strike cigarettes at the time had a green package that was made from some copper derivative. The cigarette company was forced to give its copper over to the government. In changing its packaging to white from green, the company adopted an innovative ad campaign with the headline: "Lucky Strike goes to war!" And Shell Oil stated in its advertisements that: "War production speeds ahead on Shell Industrial Lubricants."

After World War II, corporate advertising faded from view until its revival in the 1970s when oil companies found themselves battling the general public over the issue of "obscene" profits during the oil crisis. As special interest groups gained power throughout the 1970s and 1980s and media interest in corporations increased at the same time, companies again turned to corporate advertising. Today, it is one of the fastest growing segments of the advertising industry, generating over $1.5 billion in billings at the beginning of the 1990s.

Who Uses Corporate Advertising and Why?

According to recent studies, about half of the largest industrial and nonindustrial companies in the United States have corporate advertising programs of one sort or another. Usually, a direct correlation exists between size and the use of corporate advertising—the bigger the company is, the more likely it is to have a corporate advertising program. Since big companies tend to have more discretionary income, this makes sense. In addition, larger companies tend to be more diversified and thus have a greater need to establish a coherent image out of disparate activities.

In addition to size, we can see trends in the kinds of industries that are most likely to use corporate advertising. Typically, the more problematic the industry, the more likely we are to find corporate advertising widely used. This explains the heavy use of corporate advertising among cigarette companies, which have health-related issues to deal with; among oil companies, which have environmental issues and the issue of excessive profits to face; among insurance companies, which are seen as charging too much for too little and face regulation such as we have seen develop in California and other states over the last few years; among utilities, which face potential regulation as well, and are basically monopolies; and among all large industrial companies as a result of the byproducts that tend to come from the manufacturing process.

Overall, heavy industry spends more on corporate advertising than consumer-packaged goods firms, which lead all other industries in terms of product advertising. This may be related to the presence of a strong marketing focus, which tends to scoff at the importance of developing a strong corporate image rather than focusing on the four "Ps" of product, price, promotion, and place (distribution).

The lack of a clear image that can come with a good corporate advertising program, however, can hurt packaged goods companies as well. Procter & Gamble had for years downplayed the importance of creating a corporate image and instead focused on pushing its products as independent entities. When the company became embroiled in a controversy surrounding its logo, which rumors implied was connected to devil worship, the lack of a clear corporate image added fuel to the fire as the company sought to establish that it was in fact a good corporate citizen with no ties to the devil.

It is surprising that companies in certain industries shun corporate advertising given the potential threats that exist. For example, one can imagine that cable companies will find a very hostile environment if they ever become part of a controversy. Most people have a very negative impression of the industry and its poor service. More extensive use of corporate advertising could help the industry change that poor image and at the same time build a reservoir of goodwill for tough times ahead.

Finally, many companies use corporate advertising today to trumpet their philanthropic activities. These advertisements typically create bizarre associations between otherwise diametrically opposed sectors of society such as cigarette manufacturers and the arts (Philip Morris), opera and oil (Texaco), and supertanker manufacturers and blue whales (Samsung).

Philip Morris, for example, has spent hundreds of millions of dollars to support the arts and runs advertisements regularly to explain its involvement. A recent two-page spread in the Sunday *New York Times,* showed the company's support of an exhibition at New York's Jewish Museum entitled: "Bridges and Boundaries: African Americans and American Jews." The advertisement has a list of all the Philip Morris companies at the end and the tag line: "Supporting the spirit of innovation." While it is often hard to see the direct benefit of such an advertisement, it clearly strives to create goodwill among some constituencies.

Although we can see that many different kinds of companies use corporate advertising, many more do not. The debate about whether to invest the amount of time and money involved will continue, particularly during difficult economic times. But it remains one of the most efficient ways to get the corporation's message out in the best possible light without any distortion.

Should Your Company Use Corporate Advertising?

Given what the medium has to offer, most large companies should certainly answer yes to that question for a variety of reasons that I will go into in the remaining part of this chapter. But I can also think of many reasons why certain companies should stay clear of corporate advertising.

For example, I recently spoke with senior executives at a company that makes snuff. This tobacco product produces sales and profits that are the envy of executives everywhere. Yet, the use of tobacco to produce the product causes anxiety for the company's top management. Even though no connection has ever been established between the use of this product and cancer in the way that it has certainly been for cigarettes, the snuff manufacturers are the recipients of bad press generated by a few court cases that the companies easily won. As the attention has died down, these companies might consider trying to bolster their image with certain constituencies through the use of corporate advertising. But, in my view, that would be exactly the wrong thing to do given the overwhelmingly negative view that most Americans have about anything related to tobacco. Sometimes, it's best to leave well enough alone.

As we think about the more positive side, however, we should first determine what companies might conceivably get by investing in a corporate advertising campaign. In general, most companies should be able to increase sales of products and services, build goodwill among the general public, help retain and recruit employees, and enhance the financial situation at the company.

Increase Sales

The relationship between corporate advertising and sales is less clear than it is for product advertising and sales because the objectives for this kind of advertising are meant to do other things that may eventually boost sales but should not directly do so. This creates a problem for managers trying to introduce corporate advertising into companies that have a heavy financial orientation. The numbers-oriented manager will often use the lack of a direct connection between corporate advertising and sales as the best reason to keep away from it.

According to Garbett, the relationship between sales and corporate advertising also depends on the class of products in question:

> The relationship between corporate advertising and sales appears to vary by product class. For example, the effect on the sale of frequently purchased packaged goods is less than on high-priced industrial goods. Similarly, simple low-technology products probably will not benefit from corporate ad programs to the extent that high-technology items will. In high-tech, customers place a great deal of importance on the reputation and expertise of the manufacturer.

Given that the relationship between corporate advertising and sales increases is at best secondary and at worst nonexistent, this should probably not be used to justify the expenditure of a campaign.

Create Goodwill among Constituents

As a way to increase the account that holds goodwill for the corporation, however, corporate advertising is an excellent investment. As we discussed in the last chapter, companies cannot avoid having an image. Every organization has an image even if it does nothing to create one consciously. And the less people know about an organization the more they are likely to distrust it (the same is true for individuals). As a result, it is best to create the right image in your own words, using the media you want to use rather than relying on third parties to do the job for you.

The best corporate advertising creates goodwill by letting constituents in on what the organization is all about. Amoco Chemical Company's recent campaign, which won an award from *Business Week,* is a good example. The ad has a picture of an airplane landing at night with the headline: "Amoco Helps Make Coming Home a Little Safer." The ad goes on to explain that the lighting masts use durable resin compounds based on material from Amoco Chemical. While the advertisement is visually appealing, what makes it memorable, and therefore most likely to generate goodwill, is the idea that chemicals are used for things most people don't even think about that make our lives better. The tag line reads: "The chemistry is right at Amoco," which is also memorable. Knowing more about what Amoco does through advertising such as this prevents people from thinking of Amoco as a producer of terrifying waste that might leach into our backyards.

Help Retain and Recruit Employees

One of the most critical communication activities for any company is communicating with employees. But communicating with them through corporate advertising is an indirect way of building morale among employees as well. Since large companies today are so complex, corporate advertising can explain in very simple terms what the overall strategy of the firm is. In addition, the conversation with employees gets "overheard" by other constituents as well. So, while it makes employees feel good to hear about the career opportunities in their own firms, it also helps to build goodwill among the general public.

In addition, corporate advertising makes employees feel better about their companies because other people who know them will see the advertisements. Trying to quantify this is also very difficult, however. Garbett says that:

> Putting a dollar figure on the savings attained by reducing employee turnover is difficult. Some say you should add recruitment and training costs, next multiply by the turnover rate, and then estimate the percentage of employees who might be persuaded to stay if they felt more positively about the company. Whatever the real figure, if corporate advertising can effect even a modest

reduction in turnover, the saving to a large corporation is well worth the expense and effort of a campaign.[5]

Such advertising also helps companies attract the best and the brightest both at the entry level and for senior positions. The excitement that a good corporate advertising campaign can create among both potential and current employees should not be underestimated.

Enhance the Financial Effort

Finally, corporate advertising can enhance the financial situation of companies. As we discussed earlier, financially oriented corporate advertising may actually help companies increase the price of their stock if the company is undervalued, increase the price-earnings ratio, and increase bond ratings.

However, the most important function that corporate advertising can serve in terms of relations with the financial community is to create awareness among analysts. This is especially true for less-well-known companies that are not the subject of interest for the handful of investors that cover various industries. While this constituency may not be easily influenced and will certainly rely primarily on what the numbers say, they cannot help seeing a powerful corporate advertising campaign as a sign that something significant is going on in the company. Since most corporations today do not have unlimited resources, analysts rightly conclude that the advertising must exist to highlight changes or improvements at the company. And, as we shall see in Chapter 7, familiarity with the company also helps make the job of investor relations personnel easier.

Conclusion

While many companies may decide against a corporate advertising campaign simply because one cannot prove that it will work to the company's advantage, many others will leap into the fray simply to enhance the egos of senior managers. Both are wrong in their approach. As I have tried to show in this chapter, corporate advertising can help companies get their message out to a mass audience quickly and efficiently, but at a rather high price. The decision to run a campaign, then, should be based above all else on the overall communication strategy of the firm. If it needs to be a part of the corporate communication effort because the company's image is changing, or if it is used to change an erroneous assumption about the company, it can be a tremendous resource in positioning the organization for future success.

---

[5] Garbett, p. 120.

Exercise

Based on what you read in this chapter, evaluate the five advertisements (Exhibits 5–1 through 5–5) that follow by answering these questions:

1. What is the purpose of each advertisement?
2. Are they corporate advertisements or product advertisements?
3. If corporate ads, what kind are they?
4. What constituencies are the ads aimed at?
5. Pick one of the ads and write a memo to the vice president of corporate communications explaining how you would improve the ad based on what you have just read.
6. Develop a concept for a corporate advertisement that your organization/school could use to market its image.

EXHIBIT 5-1

To the birds, it matters very little that these boxes
of recycled paper reflect a child's creativity and involvement.
But to the environmental education program that
distributes these take-home nests, and Phillips Petroleum,
who sponsors them, it matters a great deal.

Because as life unfolds inside these cardboard walls,
so too does an enduring understanding and respect for the
wonder of it all. Helping students realize a greater awareness
and responsibility for the environment.
And confirming our belief that when you teach a
child about nature, he learns facts about nature.
But bond a child with nature, and he learns to care.

PHILLIPS PETROLEUM COMPANY 66

For more information about the Bird Box Program and what we are doing to protect our environment, write: Bird Box, Phillips Petroleum Company, 16C4 Phillips Building, Bartlesville, Oklahoma 74004.

Exhibit 5–2

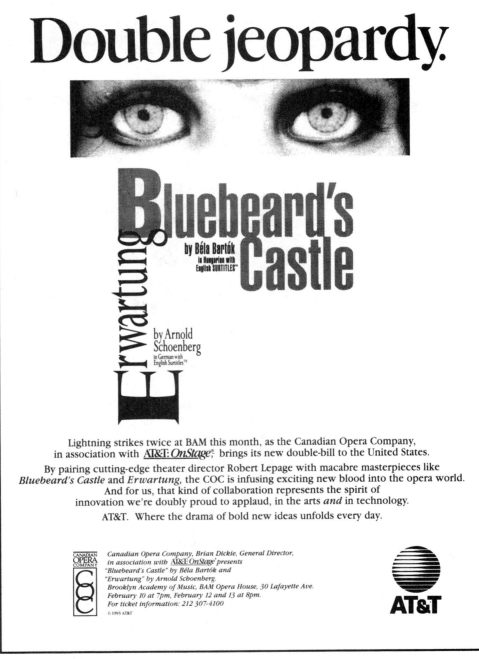

EXHIBIT 5–3

Some People Have A Different Idea Of How A Classroom Should Look.

The floors aren't hardwood but soft sand. And the only ceiling is the sky. This is Cape Henlopen State Park in Lewes, Delaware and this is Cindy Dean's fourth-grade classroom.

Through the efforts of students digging, seining and exploring tidal pools, Cindy's class boasts an aquarium containing blue crab, calico crab, fiddler crab, shrimp, baby lobster, conches, oysters, squid and snails. The students use their catch to study classification schema, molting, the food chain and the ecology of the Delaware Bay.

"Collecting live specimens is the highlight of the year because it helps the students realize that what they learn in school really applies to the world around them," says Cindy. "Suddenly science is more than a class. It's real life."

For her efforts in bringing the lessons of the real world to the classroom, State Farm is proud to present Cindy with the Good Neighbor Award. And to contribute $5,000 to her school, Lewes Middle School, in her name.

STATE FARM INSURANCE COMPANIES
Home Offices: Bloomington, Illinois

Good Neighbor Award

The Good Neighbor Award was developed in cooperation with the National Science Teachers Association (NSTA).

EXHIBIT 5–4

© Benetton Group Spa Italy. Photo: O. Toscani. Layout: Gregorietti Associati. Used by permission.

EXHIBIT 5–4
(concluded)

© Benetton Group Spa Italy. Photo: O. Toscani. Layout: Gregorietti Associati. Used by permission.

EXHIBIT 5–5

"Environmental responsibility fuels our research."

Roberta J. Nichols, Ph.D
Ford Environmental Engineer

At Ford Motor Company, responsibility for the environment goes hand in hand with building quality cars and trucks. That's why we're already building vehicles that meet California's strict emission standards for the late 90's. It's also why we're the first U.S. manufacturer to build a car with CFC-free air conditioning and why we'll soon have a fleet of electric vehicles on the road. At Ford Motor Company, we take our responsibilities seriously.

Ford

Ford • Lincoln • Mercury • Ford Trucks

QUALITY IS JOB 1. IT'S WORKING.

Buckle up–Together we can save lives.
1993 TLEV 1.9L Ford Escort and Mercury Tracer. Available in California

Always insist on genuine Ford Motor Company collision repair parts

6 NO MORE PRESS RELEASES

In the last three chapters of this book, we will look at the core functional components of corporate communications. These "tools for the new era" give the modern communications executive the ability to deal with various constituencies in ways that previous generations of public relations executives never dreamed of. Many of the differences stem from technological advances, others from the changing makeup of the constituencies themselves.

By far the most critical part of any communications department is the media relations function. Its role as disseminator of information to many of a firm's most important constituencies is more important today than it was when Edward Bernays shaped the public relations profession in the United States in the 1930s. Virtually every company from the smallest to the largest has some kind of media relations function, whether a part-time consultant or a department made up of hundreds of professionals.

In this chapter we will look at what media relations professionals do and how best to approach a group of journalists more sophisticated than ever before. We will look at what the media are, how firms should try to communicate with the media through relationship building, and what constitutes a successful media relations program in today's changing environment.

What Are the News Media?

Most people in the United States will have little difficulty answering the question above since the news media are omnipresent in our lives. With the advent of television in the late 1940s and early 1950s, what had once been the domain of the print medium in newspapers increasingly became part of the visual realm through television sets.

The arrival of television forced newspapers to give up headline news since they could not compete with the instantaneous nature of the television medium. Newspapers adapted by taking over the news analysis that used to appear in weekly news magazines like *Time* and *Newsweek*. The news magazines in turn took over the feature writing that used to appear in older monthly magazines like *Look* and *The Saturday Evening Post*, which went out of business for all intents and purposes.

Referred to as "the press" in earlier times, the news media are now a powerful part of our society shaping attitudes on issues as diverse as gun control and hemlines, abortion and corporate pay. Because of their special status in America as a result of the first amendment, which guarantees the right of free speech, the media can almost be considered as another branch of government. They constitute a powerful institution that shapes our lives and our behavior while at the same time reminding us of the freedom we all have in a democratic society.

While most Americans feel very strongly about the rights of a free press to say or print whatever it likes if it is not malicious, business has always had a more antagonistic relationship with the press. This stems in part from the privacy that corporations enjoyed in the early part of this century. Unused to dealing with the news media, most companies simply acted as if they didn't really matter.

What changed the nature of these relationships at most companies was a series of events that included changes in laws requiring public companies to release certain information regularly, a Supreme Court ruling in 1964 that put most public figures on notice to prove malicious intent to win libel cases against the media, more public interest in business (see Chapter 1), and more media interest in business.

These last two events in particular, increased public and media interest, have had the most profound effect on business and its dealings with this institution. Which came first? Although it is hard to determine whether the media created the interest in business or was just reflecting changes in public attitudes, we can say with some assurance that sometime in the 1970s things started to change. Business has become less and less private since then and is now very much a public rather than just a private sector.

Part of what created this change was the realization among people that business could have a tremendous impact on their lives. Incidents like the oil embargo, environmental problems at Love Canal, and questionable advertising on children's television programs all became embroiled in other controversies involving government in the 1970s like Watergate and Vietnam. Suddenly people began to see companies as controlling important parts of their lives and not having to answer to anyone in the way that government did to voters. Special interest groups emerged to deal with this problem and to make business more accountable.

Business, on the other hand was used to the privacy it had maintained for decades and was reluctant to admit that times had changed. Even today, as we near the end of the century, some older businesspeople refuse to accept the importance of communicating through the media and would rather maintain little or no relationship with what they see as an institution that tries to tear down everything they build up. As each industry has found itself the subject of some kind of scrutiny from an interested public and voracious media, such attitudes have changed in most cases to one of healthy antagonism between business and the media.

Before the 1970s, business news was relegated to a few pages in the back part of the newspaper (usually mostly stock quotations), a handful of business magazines, and virtually no coverage at all on national and local television news broadcasts. As public attitudes began to change, however, the business news sections in newspapers began to take off.

The *New York Times* developed "Business Day," a separate section published every day devoted to business issues, in response to increased interests. *The Wall Street Journal* became the number one selling newspaper in the United States around the same time. Business magazines started to become profitable, and more appeared on the scene. And television networks and local affiliates began to devote time to business news.

Today, "Business Day" at the *Times* has hundreds of reporters on the business beat at what many consider to be America's newspaper of record. So many magazines are devoted to business that one has to search hard to find an aspect of business that is not covered thoroughly somewhere at some time in some kind of media outlet. Early on in the 1970s and into the 80s, businesses complained that coverage in the media was often spotty at best and not well thought out. Many of the reporters covering the business beat had little or no background in business and would spend an inordinate amount of time getting up to speed on business topics during interviews with busy executives. This is much less true today as most of the business reporters, particularly those involved in national publications and networks, have business degrees or experience in the industries on which they report.

And business news in the 1990s is actually exciting. I remember seeing the large format *Fortune* magazines in my doctor's office when I was growing up in the 1950s and 60s. The magazine was basically a dull vehicle for companies to express their point of view. *Fortune* was more successful than others because it allowed executives to check its quotes—a practice unknown anywhere other than this one magazine. Today, although the magazine still calls back sources to check information, it has cover stories that appeal to a wide audience. A recent issue, for example, had a picture of the sun in the background and a headline that read: "Why Japan will emerge stronger," a subject that many Americans would be interested in as the Japanese economy adjusted to the aftermath of the burst in its bubble economy of the 1980s. And *Forbes* garners wide attention from a larger audience by publishing salaries of top entertainers, while *Business Week* attracts an audience through its widely read rankings of business schools.

Television coverage of business is equally interesting and often the all-important "lead story" on national news broadcasts. CBS business correspondents can often be seen sitting next to CBS anchorpersons Dan Rather and Connie Chung to cover some aspect of the economy as Americans struggle to understand what is happening both on Main Street and Wall Street.

After more than 10 years of increased coverage on television news, business has become more a part of everyone's life and more understandable to the layperson at the same time. While executives in the past would often blame the low esteem they received from the general public on their ignorance about business, such claims would be laughed at today in the current environment.

Finally, most executives today realize that the media is typically not going to get very excited about the good things that companies do; that is what we all expect from our institutions. Instead, the worse the news is about a company or an individual, the more likely it is to become a major news story that will capture the media's attention, if only briefly. Realizing that it is their own responsibility to get out the good stories about the corporation was business's first step toward becoming adept in relations with the media. In addition, executives needed to learn about the best way to communicate with such a sophisticated set of communicators as print and television reporters.

Building Better Relations with the Media

To build better relationships with members of the media means that someone in the organization must take the time to cultivate relationships with the right people. For most organizations, this is still something relegated to employees in what is often considered a low-power department or given to a public relations firm to handle. Neither approach is usually very effective for a number of reasons.

First, most of the old-style public relations experts rely on a system that simply does not work any longer. That system is to send out press releases to a mass audience and hope that someone will pick up the story and write about it. Why is this system no longer valid? Most reporters in the United States simply do not read press releases. Nor do they open mail from public relations agencies because of the quantity of the mailings they receive. Journalists who write about business for national publications such as *U.S. News & World Report* or *The Wall Street Journal,* can receive hundreds of such releases in one day. The editor of the op-ed page at the *New York Times* told me that they receive so many unsolicited articles by fax each day that they simply cannot respond when people ask if they are going to print the piece or not: "If you have another newspaper that you think will print it and you don't want to wait to hear from us, take it."

When Federal Express first came into being in the early 1980s, many public relations professionals started "FedExing" releases to reporters thinking that this would look more serious and thus get read. While this may have worked for a while, reporters caught on to what was happening and began screening overnight letters for the round file just as they had with regular mail for years. The analogy to what a consumer faces each night as he or she walks into a stack of unread catalogs is most appropriate.

Such catalogs coupled with the enormous amount of third class junk mail can often make it difficult to believe anything that doesn't come through with a first-class postage stamp could possibly have any value.

A public relations newsletter called *The Bulldog Reporter* recently made a stir and even received some media attention when it attacked the sacred institution of press releases, so central to what most public relations firms pride themselves on. Writing in the newsletter, the publisher, James E. Sinkinson, said: "We don't like it when we're called flacks, but as a profession we play right into the image when we spray press releases like machine-gun fire at anything that moves."

Although not always bad, press releases are clearly overused by public relations executives because they are relatively easy to write, even formulaic in terms of composition, and you can distribute them widely to certain segments of the media thanks to sophisticated computer programs that now allow you to target the "right" audience. There are firms that will also provide such services for you.

Media Distribution Services in New York, for example, serves over 2,000 public relations professionals, mails over 3 million releases a month to an average of 300 editors for each release at costs ranging from $150 plus postage for a 1-page release, to $450 plus postage for a 2-page release with a photograph. Public relations agencies charge thousands of dollars for the same kind of service. In-house public relations professionals also create and send out hundreds of such press releases to the same people over and over again for such mundane stories as the promotion of a mid-level executive.

With such wide distribution to an audience that is totally saturated with information, how can anyone expect that this system could possibly work? Yet, public relations firms claim that the system is still quite valid and embrace the similarity to direct mail that I mentioned above. Response rates of 2 percent are considered a success in the direct mail business, so public relations executives now get excited if their release gets picked up by a handful of publications.

Part of the problem is that the measure of success in the business has for years been the amount of "ink" (or coverage) that you get for your client whether you are an in-house professional or an outside consultant. Yet no one has ever stopped to figure out what value a "hit" (as they are called in the business, further continuing the flack connection) in a relatively unimportant publication has in terms of a firm's overall communications strategy. Getting lots of ink, which means lots of articles written about you, may not have any value if you aren't achieving the communication objective you started out with in the first place.

So, organizations should use mass-mailed releases sparingly. I usually advise clients to use this method for stories that they are sure will have a wide audience. And then, the same result can be achieved by placing the story on the Public Relations Newswire or convincing the Associated

Press to put the story out on its wire for you if it is truly a major story that everyone is going to want.

Instead, what companies need to do is find out who the right journalists are for a given story. The reason they do not use this method, however, is that it takes more time to conduct such research, and senior executives outside the corporate communications function may feel a bit ill at ease about pitching a major story to one journalist at a time. But, I am convinced that this is the best approach to use in a field cluttered with information coming from all sorts of technologies that virtually everyone has access to.

Conducting Research for Targeting Media

The way a typical research operation might unfold for a company is as follows. First, senior managers working with the members of the corporate communication department determine what objectives they have for a certain story. Let's assume, for example, that the story is about a major company that is moving into a new, international market.

The objective that managers might have is to create awareness about the move into the new market, while at the same time discussing how the firm has changed its global strategy. Thus, this story is part of something that could be considered a trend at the company rather than a one-shot situation. Given such objectives, the company would begin to search for the right place to pitch the story.

First, the corporate communications professionals would look to their files to find out who covers their industry and company. This is relatively easy for most companies to do since the same reporters typically cover the same beat for a period of time and have established relationships with the company either directly or indirectly. Some of these reporters, typically from print journalism, are definitely going to be interested in the story. If the company is maintaining records properly, it can determine at a glance who is most likely in this group to cover the story and even more so, who is likely to write a "balanced story" (code words for a positive piece) about the situation.

How do companies determine who is going to write a positive piece before rather than after pitching the piece? This is where ongoing research really pays off for a firm. Each time a journalist covers a firm in the industry, the corporate communications professionals need to determine what angle the reporter has taken. Thus, to continue with our example, supposing a look at the records shows that *The Wall Street Journal* reporter who covers your beat wrote a piece recently about a competitor firm moving into a different market as part of its new global strategy. Chances are that this reporter is not going to be interested in writing the same story again about your firm. Thus, you would not pitch the piece to the reporter at all.

If the records are really well documented, the corporate communications executives should be able to determine who among the list of many reporters is due to write such a piece and who is not. In this way, the reporter is not given information that he or she is not interested in, and the communication between your firm and the specific media only occurs when your audience is most likely to be receptive. While this system is not foolproof, it makes far more sense than sending out a story to 300 reporters hoping that four or five may pick it up, with no idea who they are or whether you want the story placed with them or not.

Responding to Media Calls

Another way to build relationships with members of the media is to be responsive to their requests for information. I am amazed at how many companies willingly spend up to hundreds of millions of dollars on advertising, but are unwilling to staff a media relations group with enough personnel to handle incoming calls from the media.

What typically happens is that a call will come in for an interview with the president or CEO for a major story in a national publication. Again, responding to such requests carefully can make a huge difference in how the company appears in the story. Let's say, for example, that the company is changing its image and has gotten negative press over the last couple of years because it hasn't kept up with the times. A call comes in from a reporter at CNN and another call comes in from a reporter at *Forbes*. What should the communications staff do to ensure that both of these requests are met in a timely manner to the best advantage of the company?

Calls should come into a central office that deals with all requests for information from important national media. While this sounds like common sense, often the phone is answered by a central switchboard operator who has no idea which calls from the media are important and which are not. Many an opportunity has been lost because an operator failed to get the right message to someone in the corporate communications department. Be sure that any media requests are automatically routed to a knowledgeable person in the corporate communications department.

Next, the person who takes the call should try to find out what angle the reporter is taking on the story. It takes a bit of investigative work to determine whether the person has a particular point of view that can either help or hurt the company. In our example, the CNN reporter may or may not have a particular point of view, but you can be sure that the *Forbes* reporter does since they pride themselves on taking a particular approach to all stories. Finding out what that approach is before responding to their request is critical. For this example, let's say that the CNN reporter wants to look at your company as part of a trend in the industry to a more upscale positioning among all the major companies. The *Forbes* reporter, on the other hand, seems to imply from the conversation that he sees the company's new approach as less than positive.

The person who is responsible for that telephone call should try to get as much information as possible while giving in return little or no information that is not already common knowledge. The tone of the conversation should be as friendly as possible, and the media relations professional should try to communicate honestly about the possibilities of arranging an interview and so on. At the same time, he or she should find out what kind of deadline the reporter is working under. This is often a point of contention between business and the media. Particularly with senior executives who are accustomed to arranging schedules at their own convenience, a call from the media at an inconvenient time can be an annoyance. But all reporters must meet deadlines. This means that they have to file their stories—whether on television, radio, or in print—by a certain time. These deadlines usually have little flexibility, and knowing in advance what the deadline is allows you to respond within the allotted time. The conversation should end with the media relations professional agreeing to get back to the reporter within the allotted time.

In addition, the media relations staff needs to conduct research to determine what kind of reporter they are dealing with. This is easier to do than most people outside of the communications profession realize. For the CNN reporter, one needs to know who the producer for the piece will be. Then, you can call the head office in Atlanta and actually purchase the producer's last two or three stories. For the *Forbes* reporter, you can use one of the computer databases to find all of the stories that reporter has written for a period of time. In this case, we might like to look back over a two-year period.

What can you learn by looking at previous stories the producer at CNN has filed and earlier stories that the *Forbes* reporter has written? An individual tends to write about things or put together reports in a particular way. Very few reporters change their style from one story to the next. They have found an approach that works for them, a formula if you will, and they tend to stick with formulas that work.

What you will typically find from such an analysis is that the journalist tends to write or present stories with a particular point of view. One such analysis that I performed for a company on a *Forbes* reporter's work showed that he liked to write ''turn-around'' stories. That is, he liked to present the opposite point of view from what everyone else had written about. So, given that the company in our example is trying to make a case for such a turn-around, this reporter would be likely to write the kind of article that would be very helpful for the company despite his negative tone.

Watching the CNN producer's work, however, you could determine how that particular person conducts interviews, how the stories are edited, whether he or she likes to use charts and graphs as part of the story, and so on. Let's say that the producer in our example seems to present balanced interviews, as opposed to antagonistic ones, and likes to use charts and graphs. Again, this seems like it could easily turn out to be a positive story for the company and should be pursued with some vigor.

Each call that comes in, particularly from an important national media organization, deserves this kind of approach. Many of the people I have worked with complain about the amount of time such analysis takes, but the rewards can be tremendous for a company that is trying to get its views out to as wide an audience as possible. Yes, it does take time, but the benefits from handling the interview correctly rather than simply responding off the top of your head can be enormous.

Preparing for the Interview

Once the analysis is complete, the executive who will be interviewed needs to be prepared for the actual meeting with the reporter. If the interview is to be conducted by phone, as is often the case with print reporters, a media relations professional should plan to sit in on the interview. The following approach works best.

First, the executive should be given a short analysis of the reporter or producer's work with examples from the information you have to back up your assertions. For example, if you posit that the *Forbes* reporter likes to write turn-around pieces, show the executive the appropriate passages from past stories. Make sure that the point of view the reporter is going to take is clear to the executive. Also be sure to explain that the agenda for the story is very difficult to change. You typically cannot introduce a new topic into the interview once the reporter has decided to write a particular kind of story.

I once prepared a CEO for an interview with CNN by telling him about the last two or three major stories the producer had filed. He watched them with me, and was able to begin the conversation with the producer by saying how much he liked one of the stories. This immediately started the relationship off in a very positive way and set the tone for the rest of the interview. We also had found out that the producer always used a list of bullet points as part of each story he filed. We came up with a list of points about the company in bullet point form and handed it to him before he left. The story appeared, was very positive, and our list of bullet points was right up there on the television screen to the delight of the CEO, who had worried for days about the interview.

Next, the executive should be given a set of possible questions that the reporter is likely to ask. This can be developed from what you have gleaned in previous conversations with the reporter, from your analysis of the reporter's work, and from what you know to be the critical issues on the subject. If possible, a trial run with the executive to go over answers to possible questions should be arranged.

If you are preparing someone for a television interview, a full dress rehearsal is absolutely essential. The interview should look as if it is totally natural and unrehearsed when it actually occurs, but the executive should be prepared well in advance. This means thinking about what to communicate to the reporter no matter what he or she asks during the interview. While you cannot change the agenda for the interview, you can get certain points across as you bridge from one idea to the next.

In addition to thinking about what to say, however, executives need to think about the most interesting approach to saying it. Using statistics and anecdotes may help bring your ideas alive in an interview. What is interesting, however, often depends on who your ultimate audience is. Many people mistakenly assume that the reporter is their audience. But it is the people who will watch the interview that you are really communicating with. Keep this in mind when trying to determine the best approach for a television interview. (See Chapter 2 for more on communication strategy, especially analyzing constituencies.)

Finally, the executive needs to be prepared to state his or her most important ideas as clearly as possible at the beginning of the interview. In addition, the answers to questions need to be as succinct as possible. Long-winded responses have no place in any media interview. Especially in television where "sound bites" of three or four seconds are the rule rather than the exception, executives need to be trained to get complicated ideas into a compact form that the general public can easily understand.

Maintaining Ongoing Relationships

By far the most critical component in media relations, however, is developing and maintaining a network of contacts with the media. A company cannot simply turn the relationship on and off when a crisis strikes or when it has something about which it would like publicity. Instead, make sure that the company has worked to develop long-term relationships with the "right" journalists for your industry. This usually means meeting with reporters just to build goodwill credibility. The corporate communications director should meet regularly with journalists who cover the industry and should also arrange yearly meetings between key reporters and the CEO. The more private and privileged these sessions are, the better the long-term relationship is likely to be.

Since these meetings with reporters have no particular agenda, they can often be awkward for all but the most skilled communicators. I am amazed at how many organizations hire people to handle media relations who simply do not like to meet and greet people and who have little or no curiosity. These elements are particularly important as companies try to establish long-term relationships with the media.

Often, the meetings occur at lunch or breakfast and should be thought of as a time to share information about what is going on at the company, but with no expectation that a story will necessarily appear anytime soon. In the course of the conversation, the skillful communicator will determine what is most likely to interest the reporter later as a possible story. Without being blatant about it, the communicator can then follow-up at the appropriate time with the information or interviews that the reporter wants.

What often stops media relations professionals short is the problem of getting rebuffed from time to time. I have been turned down for lunch several times by reporters who are particularly busy only to find them very receptive to a long telephone conversation. Of course, as in any relationships, you will find that you simply do not get along with every journalist you come into contact with. This is a problem only if the reporter is the only one covering your beat at an important national media outlet.

One executive that I worked with thought that he simply didn't need to have any sort of relationship with the reporter covering his beat at *The Wall Street Journal*. After almost two years of being left out of nearly every major story on the industry, I persuaded him to try again to establish a relationship with this reporter. She was only too happy to make amends as well since she needed the company's cooperation as much as they needed her.

Building a Successful Media Relations Program

What does it take, then, to create the most successful media relations program possible? First, the organization must be willing to put a minimal amount of resources behind the effort. This doesn't always imply huge outlays of money; an executive's time can be just as valuable.

Jim Koch, brewmaster and president of the company that makes Sam Adams beer, brought his beer into the national limelight through the skillful use of media relations with the help of one outside consultant at a fraction of the cost for a national advertising program. I recently worked with two sisters who started a greeting card company that specialized in gay greeting cards. Just through their own efforts, writing letters, reading the newspapers to find out who the best reporters would be for their message, they were able to get "hits" in both the *New York Times* and *The Wall Street Journal*. In both cases, the media relations effort paid off in sales, which was the ultimate goal.

But for most larger companies, the media relations effort will involve more personnel and often the use of outside counsel. Here is what is needed for the effort at a minimum.

Involve Media Relations Personnel in Strategy

As one public relations executive at a large company put it: "They like to keep us in the dark, like mushrooms, and then they expect us to get positive publicity, usually at the last minute." Instead, companies need to involve someone, preferably the most senior corporate communications executive, in the decision-making process. Once a decision has been made, it is much more difficult to talk management out of it because of potential problems with communications.

The Hooker Chemical case is a good example of that. Although executives were told that buying out homes next to the dump sight was the best thing to do in terms of public relations, they were already convinced by more legalistic approaches presented earlier that this was not a feasible idea. Had the communications professionals been there at the time of the decision to express their point of view, the decision, and the outcome, might have been very different.

Communications professionals who are involved in the decision-making process, also feel more ownership for the ideas that they must present to the media. While the communications point of view will not always win in the discussions that take place at top management meetings, both the other executives involved and the communications experts will know what the pros and cons of each situation are, which may help later on.

Develop In-House Capabilities

While using consultants and large or small public relations firms may be beneficial in some cases, by far the best approach for the long term is to develop an in-house, media relations staff. As we have seen throughout this chapter, there is no magic to what communications professionals do, and the company can save thousands of dollars a month by using staff within the company and investing in the right data bases to conduct research for analyzing the media.

One of the problems that I have found in many companies, however, is that they do not consider media relations to be important enough to hire a real professional. I have found lawyers, secretaries, accountants, and even former securities dealers assigned to the task of handling communications because of the unfortunate assumption that anyone can communicate; therefore, it doesn't matter who you put on this assignment. Although it may not be rocket science, building relations with the media is a skill that some people have been trained for. And, as we discussed earlier, certain personalities are better suited to the task than others.

Also, do not make the mistake of thinking that a former reporter will be the best person for the job. If the reporter were really good at reporting, he or she probably wouldn't be looking to change professions. Such persons are as unlikely to have a network of connections as someone who has experience in a totally different field. Hire professionals from the field who will represent the company in the best light.

Use Outside Counsel Sparingly

Companies should hire outside counsel for advice (as consultants, if you will) in both good times and bad to help out with a really major story and when a crisis hits. Otherwise, what you are typically hiring when you hire a major public relations firm is the time of a recent college graduate who is getting training to one day take the in-house job that you have waiting in your own company.

Another important use for outside firms is to help with the distribution of press releases and to create video news releases. This new form of communication can be very valuable for a company trying to get its message across to a wide audience. What these firms do is put together what looks like a real news story. It is then sent up via satellite for anyone to take down for their nightly news broadcasts. The better firms usually do a finished version of the story with a reporter, and then send "B-role," which is backup tape, so that the local station or network can put together its own story.

Conclusion

As technology develops new mechanisms to disseminate information and communications professionals are able to develop databases through the use of more sophisticated software, the media relations function will continue to evolve away from the old PR "flack" into a professional group that can help the organization get its message out honestly, quickly, and to the right media.

CASE
ADOLPH COORS COMPANY

Shirley Richard returned from lunch one April afternoon in 1982 and found a message on her desk that Allan Maraynes from CBS had phoned while she was out. "God, what's this?" was all she could say as she picked up the phone to discuss the call with her boss, John McCarty, vice president for corporate public affairs. Now in her second year as head of corporate communications for the nation's fifth-largest brewer, Richard was well aware of the Adolph Coors Company's declining popularity—a decline that she partially blamed on an ongoing conflict with organized labor. But the conflict was hardly breaking news, and she was almost afraid to ask why CBS was interested in the company.

Richard found out from her boss that Maraynes was a producer for the network's news program *60 Minutes*. Reporter Mike Wallace had already phoned McCarty to announce plans for a *60 Minutes* report about the company. Program executives at CBS were aware of accusations of unfair employment practices that the AFL–CIO had raised against Coors and wanted to investigate the five-year battle between the brewery and organized labor.

Once McCarty explained the message from Maraynes, Shirley Richard sank into her chair. She had spent the last year working hard to understand organized labor and its nationwide boycott of Coors beer; she was convinced that the company was being treated unfairly. She believed the union represented only a small faction of Coors's otherwise satisfied work force. But Richard also doubted whether the facts could speak for themselves and was wary of the AFL–CIO's ability to win over the media. She was well aware of Mike Wallace's reputation for shrewd investigative reporting

and was reassured to some extent that the program would depict the company fairly.

On the other hand, *60 Minutes* was considered by many corporations as anti-big-business, and Richard had no idea how corporate officials would respond under the pressure of lights, camera, and the reporter's grilling questions. McCarty and Richard met with the two Coors brothers to discuss the network's proposal and to determine whether producer Maraynes should even be allowed to visit the Coors facility. Company president Joe Coors and chairman Bill Coors were skeptical of the prospect of airing the company's "dirty laundry" on national television. But McCarty was interested in the opportunity for Coors to come out into the public spotlight. Richard had already calculated the enormous risks involved in granting interviews with Wallace and filming the Coors plant and employees and knew the Coors brothers' reservations were warranted.

Richard was frustrated by growing support for the boycott and by her own strategies, which had failed to overcome opposition to the company. She believed the interview with CBS could only exacerbate a losing situation. Her own public relations effort had been an attempt to show the company as she believed it stood: good management harassed by disgruntled labor organizers. She was convinced that her job was not an effort to cover up Coors's employment practices. "PR doesn't make you into something you're not," Richard stated. "You can't whitewash."

Shirley Richard debated how the company should handle the proposal from CBS, realizing that the communications strategy could seriously affect the corporation's public image. Any decisions about approaching *60 Minutes* would also have to be approved by company president Joseph Coors and his brother, chairman William Coors. Richard felt uncertain about how much control she would ultimately have over the communications strategy. Joe Coors, an ardent conservative and defender of private enterprise, would undoubtedly resist an open-door policy with the network. At the same time, Shirley Richard wondered if she should convince management of this traditionally closed company to open itself to the scrutiny of a *60 Minutes* investigation or whether the best defense would be a "no comment" approach. But with no comment from Coors, anything organized labor was willing to say on camera would be uncontested.

History of the Adolph Coors Company

The Coors brewery was established in 1880 by Adolph Coors, a Prussian-born immigrant who came to the United States in 1868. Having trained as an apprentice in a Prussian brewery, 22-year-old Adolph Coors became a foreman at the Stenger Brewery in Naperville, Illinois, in late 1869. By 1872, Coors owned his own bottling company in Denver, Colorado. With his knowledge of brewing beer and the financial assistance of Joseph Schueler, Coors established his own brewery in Golden, Colorado. His product was an immediate success. In 1880, Adolph Coors bought out Joseph Schueler and established a tradition of family ownership that was maintained for almost a century.

The company remained vital during Prohibition, switching to production of malted milk. During Prohibition the Coors Company also expanded with the development of new manufacturing operations. A cement manufacturing facility and a porcelain products plant were essential to the company's survival during the 17 years of Prohibition. Its brewing operations flourished again when alcohol was legalized in 1933.

Famous for its exclusive "Rocky Mountain spring water" system of brewing, the Adolph Coors Company soon became something of a legend in the beer industry. The Coors philosophy was one of total independence. A broad spectrum of Coors subsidiaries combined to create a vertically integrated company in which Coors owned and managed every aspect of production: Coors Container Manufacturing plant produced aluminum and glass containers for the beer; Coors Transportation Company included refrigerated trucks to haul the beer to its distribution center as well as vehicles to transport coal to fuel the Golden brewery; Coors Energy Company bought and sold energy and owned the Keenesburg, Colorado, coal mine which was expected to meet the brewery's coal needs through the end of the 20th century; the Golden Recycle Company was responsible for ensuring a supply of raw materials for aluminum can production. By 1980, the recycling plant was capable of producing over 30 million pounds of recycled aluminum a year. Other subsidiaries fully owned by Coors included Coors Food Products Company, Coors Porcelain Company, and American Center for Occupational Health.

The Coors Mystique

A certain mystique surrounding the Golden, Colorado, brewery and its unique unpasteurized product won the beer both fame and fortune. Presidents Eisenhower and Ford shuttled Coors to Washington aboard air force jets. Actors Paul Newman and Clint Eastwood once made it the exclusive beer on their movie sets. Business magazines lauded Coors as "America's cult beer." As Coors expanded its distribution, the mystique appeared irresistible; Coors moved from 12th to 4th place among all brewers between 1965 and 1969 with virtually no advertising or marketing.

Part of the Coors mystique was attributed to its family heritage. For over a century of brewing, company management had remained in the hands of Adolph Coors's direct descendents. Reign passed first to Adolph Coors, Jr., then to his son William Coors. In 1977, Bill Coors turned over the presidency to his younger brother Joseph but continued as chairman and chief executive officer. The company's newest president, Joe Coors, was a well-known backer of right-wing causes such as the John Birch Society; a founder of a conservative think-tank, the Heritage Foundation; and a member of President Ronald Reagan's so-called "Kitchen Cabinet." The family name was closely associated with strong conservatism by consumers, labor, and the industry.

The Coors Company was built on a tradition of family and, even after going public in 1975, remained an organization closed to active public relations. Bill Coors recalled that his father, Adolph Coors II, was a shy man, and throughout its history the company was reluctant to attract any public attention. In 1960, the sensational kidnapping and murder of brother Adolph Coors III focused the public eye on the family and the business, but Coors maintained a strict "no comment" policy.

The Nature of the Brewing Industry

From the mid-1960s through the 1970s and into the 1980s, the brewing industry was characterized by a shrinking number of breweries coupled with a growing volume of production and consumption. In 1963, Standard and Poor's Industry Surveys reported 211 operating breweries. Ten years later that number had dropped to 129, and by 1980 there were only 100 breweries in operation. On the other hand, per capita consumption of beer rose from 15 gallons a year in 1963 to 19.8 gallons in 1973. By 1980, per capita consumption had jumped to 24.3 gallons a year.

Until the mid-1970s beer markets were essentially local and regional, but as the largest breweries expanded so did their share of the market. Combined, the top five brewers in 1974 accounted for 64 percent of domestic beer production, up from 59 percent in 1973. Previously strong local and regional breweries were either bought by larger producers or ceased operations.

A notable exception, however, was the Adolph Coors Company, which dominated the West. The company's 12.3 million barrel shipment volume was distributed only in California, Texas, and 10 other western states until 1976. Coors's share of the California market alone was well over 50 percent in 1976. In fact, the Coors mystique dominated its limited distribution area, capturing at least 35 percent of the market wherever it was sold statewide. The Coors Company ranked fifth in market share throughout the 1970s trailing giants Anheuser-Busch, Joseph Schlitz, Phillip Morris's Miller, and Pabst, all of which had substantially broad distribution areas.

Competition for market share among the top five brewers was intense during the 1970s and led producers to more aggressive attempts to win consumers. According to compilations by Leading National Advertisers, Inc., advertising expenditures for the first nine months of 1979 were up 37 percent from the previous year for Anheuser-Busch, 18 percent for Miller, 14 percent for both Schlitz and Pabst, and 78 percent for Adolph Coors.

Marketing and Distribution at Coors

Industry analysts criticized the Coors Company's sales strategy for stubbornly relying on its product's quality and reputation rather than marketing. But in 1976, the Coors mystique appeared to be losing its appeal to strong competitors. For the first time since Prohibition, Coors could not sell all its beer. The company finally responded to competition by intensifying its marketing and development operations. Between 1976 and 1981, the company attempted to revive sales by adding eight new states to its distribution. In May of 1978, the brewery began to market its first new product in 20 years: Coors Light. In 1979, Coors began the first major advertising campaign in its history to defend itself against aggressive competitors such as Phillip Morris's Miller Brewing Company and Anheuser-Busch. The company's 1981 annual report pictured Coors's newest product—George Killian's Irish Red Ale—along with a newly expanded package variety designed to "keep pace with consumer demand."

The Coors Company went public in 1975, but investors did not fare well as stock prices declined for the rest of the decade. Coors entered the market at 31 but by 1978 had fallen to 16—a loss of about 50 percent for the first public stockholders. Net income, according to the company's annual report, was $51,970,000 in 1981, or $1.48 per share. That figure reflected a 20 percent drop from $64,977,000, or $1.86 per share, in 1980.

Management–Labor Relations at Coors

During pre-Prohibition years, breweries, including Coors, were entirely unionized. In 1914, the first vertically integrated industrial union in the country established itself at Coors. When the country went dry, Coors remained viable through alternative operations, but the workforce still had to be reduced. Coors offered older workers employment but fired younger employees. A strike of union employees resulted and remained in effect until 1933 when Prohibition was repealed. The company, however, continued to operate without a union until 1937 when Adolph Coors, Jr., invited the United Brewery Workers International (UBW) into the Coors Company.

In 1953, the company experienced an abortive strike by the UBW to which a frightened management immediately gave in. In 1955, Coors's organized porcelain workers struck because their wages were less than those of brewery workers. Although the plant continued to operate, all of Coors's unionized workers engaged in a violent strike which lasted

almost four months. The union ultimately lost the battle 117 days after the strike, when workers returned to the plant on company terms.

Negotiations over a new union contract in 1957 ended in a stalemate between labor and management, and workers again decided to strike. For another four months, workers were torn between paternalistic and small-town personal ties to management and the demands of the union. Bill Coors, who was then plant manager, recalled that during the strike, management had wanted to show the union it was not dependent on union workers. Coors hired college students during the summer of 1957 as temporary replacements for the striking brewers. When the students left, the picketers were threatened by management's vow to hire permanent replacements and returned to the plant. The strike was a clear defeat of the union's demands and ultimately left international union leaders with an unresolved bitterness toward Coors. Back in full operation by the fall of 1957, Coors management believed it had won complete control.

By the end of the 1950s, 15 local unions were organized at Coors. Management tolerated the unions, but claimed they had no impact on wages or employment practices. The Coors family firmly believed that good management removed the need for union protection and that management could win workers' loyalty. In 1960, the plant's organized electricians struck but failed to garner the support of other unions, and the plant continued to operate with nonunion electricians hired to replace the strikers. Similar incidents occurred with Coors's other unions. A 1968 strike by building and construction workers ended with Coors breaking up 14 unions. By 1970, Coors's workforce was predominantly nonunion.

A contract dispute between Coors's management and UBW Local 366 erupted in 1976. Workers demanded a 10 percent wage increase and better retirement benefits. After more than a year of negotiations, union officials rejected management's compromise offer, which labor contended would erode workers' rights. In April of 1977, over 94 percent of UBW workers voted to strike. Production at the plant continued at 70 percent of normal capacity, however, and management boldly announced plans to replace striking workers. In defense of the union, AFL–CIO officials declared a nationwide boycott of the beer until a new contract settlement was reached. But within five days of initiating the strike, 39 percent of the union members crossed the picket lines to return to work.

In 1978, Coors management called an election for decertification of UBW Local 366. Because more than a year had passed since the strike began, National Labor Relations regulations restricted striking union members from voting. Only workers remaining at the plant, including "scabs" hired across the picket lines, could vote on whether to maintain the UBW Local. In December of that year, Coors employees voted a resounding 71 percent in favor of decertifying the Local UBW.

Since 1957, the Coors brewery had been a "closed shop," in which workers were required to pay union dues if they were to benefit from union action. But company officials called the 1978 decertification vote a victory for the "open shop," wherein workers could enjoy union benefits without paying dues as members. Union officials, frustrated over the lack of a new contract and the decertification vote, publicly charged Coors with "union busting."

In fact, according to AFL–CIO officials, the UBW was the 20th Coors union decertified since the mid-1960s. Management consistently argued that employees simply rejected union organization because they didn't require it; good management eliminated the need for a union to protect workers. But organized labor maintained that all 20 unions had been "busted" by votes called while members were on strike and scabs were casting the ballots. By the end of the decade, only one union representing a small group of employees remained active at Coors.

Nationwide Boycott

The AFL–CIO was determined not to be defeated by the ousting of the UBW Local from the Golden plant. In defense of the union, AFL–CIO officials declared a nationwide boycott of Coors beer until a new contract settlement could be reached and soon began to claim that their efforts had a significant impact on sales. In fact, 1978 figures reported a 12 percent profit decline for the brewery during fiscal 1977 and predicted that 1978 figures would fall even lower. Corporate officials conceded the boycott was one factor influencing declining sales but refused to admit the drop was consistent or significant.

The defeat of the Coors local brewers' union fueled the boycott fire, but the protest focused on issues beyond the single contract dispute begun in 1977. The other issues of protest related to Coors's hiring practices. Labor leaders claimed that a mandatory polygraph test administered to all prospective employees asked irrelevant and personal questions and violated workers' rights. In addition, the protesters claimed that Coors discriminated against women and ethnic minorities in hiring and promotion. Finally, boycotters argued that Coors periodically conducted searches of employees and their personal property for suspected drug use and that such search and seizure also violated workers' rights. The boycott galvanized organized labor as well as minority interest groups who protested in defense of blacks, Hispanics, women, and gays.

The boycott's actual effect on sales was the subject of dispute. Coors's sales had begun to fall by July 1977, just three months after the boycott was initiated. Some analysts attributed the drop not to protesting consumers, but rather to stepped-up competition from Anheuser-Busch, which had begun to invade Coors's western territories. Despite a decline, Coors remained the number-one seller in 10 of the 14 states in which it was sold. Labor, on the other hand, took credit for a victory at the end of

1977 when Coors's fourth-quarter reports were less than half of sales of the previous year for the same period. Dropping from $17 million in 1976 to $8.4 million in 1977, Coors was faced with a growing challenge. There was no doubt that management took the AFL–CIO protest seriously and began attempts to counter declining sales through more aggressive advertising and public relations.

Federal Lawsuit

The AFL–CIO boycott gained additional legitimacy from the federal government. In 1975, the federal Equal Employment Opportunity Commission had filed a lawsuit against Coors for discrimination in hiring and promotion against blacks, Mexican Americans, and women. The suit charged Coors with violating the 1964 Civil Rights Act and challenged Coors's hiring tests, which the EEOC said were aimed at revealing an applicant's arrest record, economic status, and physical characteristics. The lawsuit stated that the company used "methods of recruitment which served to perpetuate the company's nonminority male workforce."

In May of 1977, one month after the initiation of the AFL–CIO boycott, Coors signed an agreement with the EEOC, vowing that the brewery would not discriminate in hiring. But according to media reports, Coors still refused to admit any past bias toward blacks, Mexican Americans, and women. Coors said it would continue a program begun in 1972 designed to increase the number of women and minorities in all major job classifications. Striking brewery workers refused to sign the agreement, although the Coors's Operating Engineers Union entered into the agreement.

David Sickler and the AFL-CIO

The principal organizer of the AFL-CIO boycott against the Adolph Coors Company was the former president of the Coors's Local

UBW. David Sickler had been employed by Coors for 10 years, acting as a business manager from 1973–1976. Sickler left the plant in 1976 to take a job with the AFL-CIO in Montana. In April of 1977, the AFL–CIO decided to put Sickler in charge of coordinating the national boycott against Coors. Sickler moved to Los Angeles where he also served as director of the Los Angeles organizing committee and the subregional office of the AFL–CIO.

Sickler initially resisted the AFL–CIO's request to put him in charge of organizing the boycott. He believed that his past employment at the company made him too close to the situation to offer a fair position on the issues at stake. But the AFL–CIO felt that Sickler's tenure with Coors made him an ideal choice; according to Sickler, his personal reports of abuse by the company in hiring and employment practices were shared by numerous Coors employees and were the central issues of the boycott.

Sickler contended that when hired by Coors, he had been subjected to questions on a lie detector test regarding his personal life and sexual preference. In addition, he reported the company's practice of searching individuals or entire departments for suspected drug use. Despite corporate officials' insistence that the accusations were false, Sickler was convinced that Coors employees were generally "unhappy, demoralized."

Coors management was determined to fight back against the boycott, and filed a breach of contract suit against the Local 366. The company charged that any boycott was prohibited under contract agreements. Management also made clear to the public its outrage over the boycott, as chairman Bill Coors began to speak out in the national media. In a 1978 interview with *Forbes* magazine, Coors stated about the AFL–CIO: "No lie is too great to tell if it accomplishes their boycott as a monument to immorality and dishonesty." Earlier that year, Bill Coors defended the company against charges of being antiunion. A *New York Times* report on the dispute quoted the CEO as saying: "Our fight is not with Brewery Workers Local 366. Our fight is with organized labor. Three sixty-six is a pawn for the AFL–CIO; that's where they're getting their money."

Corporate Communications at Coors

The 1977 boycott forced company officials to re-examine the area of corporate communications. Because labor leaders set out to "destroy the company," Bill Coors, now chairman and chief executive officer of the company, believed management must relate its side of the story. "There was no lie they wouldn't tell," the CEO recalled. "No one knew about Coors, and we had no choice but to tell the story."

In 1978, John McCarty, a fund-raiser at Pepperdine University, was hired as the vice president for corporate public affairs. McCarty brought to Coors expertise in minority relations and set out to repair the company's damaged reputation among minority groups. McCarty established a staff of corporate communications officers. The division was organized into four branches under McCarty's leadership: corporate communications, community affairs, economics affairs, and legislative affairs.

In response to the boycott and declining sales, McCarty enlisted the expertise of J. Walter Thompson's San Francisco office to help the company improve its corporate image. Coors launched what analysts termed a strong "image building" campaign in 1979, with messages aimed at ethnic minorities, women, union members, and homosexuals. The theme throughout the late 1970s was clearly a response to labor's accusations against the company: "At Coors, people make the difference."

Another component of the new image campaign, according to media reports, was to condition company managers to project charm and humility in dealing with reporters. Coors executives participated in a telecommunications course designed to help them overcome a traditional distrust of the media.

Shirley Richard

Shirley Richard was hired along with McCarty in 1978 to direct the company's legislative affairs branch but was familiar with the Coors Company long before joining its staff. From 1974–1978, Richard worked on the Coors account as a tax manager for Price Waterhouse. One important issue for the Coors account, Richard recalled, was the deductibility of lobbying expenses and charitable donations. As part of her job, Richard became involved in the political arena, helping Coors set up political action committees. When Richard decided to leave Price Waterhouse in 1978, she asked Coors's vice president of finance for a job and was hired to head the legislative affairs department, a position she held until 1981.

Richard recalled her first year with the company as a time when Coors was "coming out of its shell"; Phillip Morris's purchase of Miller Brewing Company meant increased competition for Coors and a demand for more aggressive advertising. In 1975, the company sold its first public stock. The bad publicity from the 1977 strike and its aftermath combined with greater competition led to a serious decline in sales and disappointed shareholders. Clearly, the Coors mystique alone could no longer speak for itself, and an aggressive public relations campaign was unavoidable.

One year before the *60 Minutes* broadcast of the Coors story, Richard became Adolph Coors Company's director of corporate communications. In that position, she managed 25 people, including corporate advertising, internal communications, distribution communications, training programs, and public relations personnel.

Confrontational Journalism

The challenge of CBS's *60 Minutes* to any company under its investigation was formidable. The 14-year-old program was consistently ranked in Neilsen ratings' top 10 programs throughout the 1970s. Media critics offered various explanations for the success of this unique program, which remarkably combined high quality with high ratings. A *New York Times* critic summarized the sentiment of many within the broadcast profession when he called *60 Minutes,* "without question, the most influential news program in the history of the media."

The program had earned its popularity through consistently hard-hitting, investigative reporting. Executive producer Don Hewitt proclaimed *60 Minutes* the "public watchdogs." In his book about the program, Hewitt recalled, "I became more and more convinced that a new type of personal journalism was called for. *CBS Reports, NBC White Papers,* and *ABC Closeups* seemed to me to be the voice of the corporation, and I didn't believe people were any more interested in hearing from a corporation than they were in watching a documentary." Stories revealing insurance executives taking advantage of the poor with overpriced premiums, companies polluting streams and farmlands by irresponsibly dumping, or physicians gleaning profits from unnecessary surgery had all worked to rally public support and faith in CBS as a sort of consumer protection agency.

The program's success in uncovering scandal was due in large part to the aggressive and innovative technique of Mike Wallace. Wallace had been with the program throughout its history and was responsible for shaping much of the *60 Minutes* image. His reporting was always tough, sometimes theatrical, and was commonly referred to within the media as "confrontational journalism." Wallace had a reputation in broadcast circles and among *60*

Minutes viewers for making the sharpest executives and politicians crumble.

But the program was not flawless. Hewitt admitted he had made mistakes, and one of the most glaring cases against *60 Minutes* was a story about the Illinois Power Company. In November of 1979, *60 Minutes* broadcast a story about cost overruns at a Clinton, Illinois, nuclear power plant, a story that included some obtrusive inaccuracies. Illinois Power was not to be victimized by *60 Minutes* and produced a videotape about the program, portraying it as antibusiness and antinuclear. Hewitt admitted that the company's defense had worked. "Five years after Illinois Power took us over the coals for that story, the plant is now seven years behind schedule and more than two and a half billion over budget. Have we reported that? I'm afraid not. You see, their beanball worked."

Allan Maraynes was assigned to produce the Coors segment. His experience with *60 Minutes* was highlighted by some significant clashes with big business. He had produced stories on the Ford Pinto gasoline tank defects, Firestone tires, I. Magnin, and Smith Kline. Maraynes was alerted to the Coors controversy when *60 Minutes* researchers in San Francisco told him they suspected bad things were happening at Coors. The research group told Maraynes that the AFL–CIO was calling Coors a "fascist organization," which sounded to the producer like good material for a story.

Maraynes first flew to California to interview David Sickler. "We said we were setting about to do a story explaining that a fascist state exists at Coors," Maraynes recalled about his conversation with Sickler. "If it's true, we'll do it." Maraynes wanted Sickler to give him as much information about the boycott as he had. Maraynes wanted the angle of the story to be a focus on case histories of the people who had experienced Coors's unfair treatment.

April 1982

With the phone call from Maraynes, all of the pressures from David Sickler, the AFL–CIO, and the boycott were suddenly intensified. Shirley Richard had worked hard in the last year to focus public attention away from the boycott, but now her efforts to project a positive corporate image were threatened. Thinking ahead to the next few months of preparation time, she felt enormous pressure in the face of such potentially damaging public exposure.

Shirley Richard was not naive about Mike Wallace or the power of television news to shape a story and the public's opinion. Richard, along with other Coors executives, believed that the company was not at fault, but that did nothing to guarantee that their story would be accurately portrayed in a *60 Minutes* report. Mike Wallace himself had voiced the reason for a potential subject to fear the program's investigative report. In an interview with *The New York Times,* Wallace stated: "You (the network) have the power to convey any picture you want."

Richard knew that a big corporation's abuse of employees was just the kind of story *60 Minutes* was built on, and she didn't want Coors to be part of enhancing that reputation, especially when she believed organized labor had fabricated the controversy about Coors. Given Mike Wallace's desire to get the story, Shirley Richard guessed the company would automatically be on the defensive.

It was clear that *60 Minutes* was determined to do the story, with or without cooperation from Coors. Richard wondered, however, whether an interview with Mike Wallace would do the company more harm than good. On the other hand, she considered the possibility that the company could somehow secure the offensive and turn the broadcast into a final clarification of Coors's side of the boycott story.

Richard was clearly challenged by an aggressive news team, and she was uncertain about cooperation from the conservative Coors brothers. Even if she could convince them that an open door was the best policy, would corporate officials be able to effectively present the facts supporting Coors's position? The national broadcast would reach millions of beer drinkers, and Richard knew that the *60 Minutes* report could either make or break the future success of Coors beer.

7 A RANDOM WALK DOWN WALL STREET

Finance theorists talk a great deal about something called the "efficient market theory," which suggests that all companies competing in a particular market have the same information available to them. While this theory seems to hold true for large, well-known companies, such as those in the Fortune 500, most experts in investor relations agree that smaller companies, such as those traded over the counter, need to communicate aggressively to get the right information out to the investment community.

As a result, over the last 30 years, the investor relations function within the larger field of corporate communications has become one of the most important for senior management. In a country that strives to maximize shareholder value, the communications effort that accompanies that goal has become of paramount importance.

In this chapter, we look at every aspect of this all-important subfunction. We begin by tracing the evolution of investor relations from a rather minor effort half a century ago to its present role as a sophisticated communications function. Next we turn to a discussion about the environmental factors that have had a particular influence on the investor relations function. Having an understanding of where it came from and what influenced it, we can then talk about the development of an investor relations function within an organization.

The Evolution of Investor Relations as a Function

In this section, we look at how investor relations (IR) has developed over the last 50 years. Despite the enactment of federal securities laws in the 1930s that required continuous disclosure of financial information by public companies, IR played only a minor role until the 1950s.

It wasn't until the 1960s, however, with the founding of the National Investor Relations Institute (NIRI), that IR received any official recognition. Since then, IR has become a critical function, which ensures that the investment community fully understands the financial and strategic position of a company.

Federal Regulations

The U.S. Securities and Exchange Commission (SEC) is the administrative rule-making body enforcing the federal securities laws. The two securities laws that defined disclosure requirements for public companies are the Securities Act of 1933 and the Securities Exchange Act of 1934. Here is what those regulations stipulate:

The Securities Act of 1933

The Securities Act of 1933 requires the registration of all securities publicly offered by a company, and the dissemination of a prospectus to all potential investors. The Securities Act was deemed incomplete for two reasons: (1) disclosure depended on the issuer making a public offering, and (2) there was no provision for updating information.

The Securities Exchange Act of 1934

The Securities Exchange Act of 1934 was then enacted to remedy these problems. It requires all companies listing securities on a national exchange to register the securities with the SEC prior to listing and trading; it also required companies with registered securities under either of the two acts to file annual and quarterly reports with the SEC. These two laws left one remaining disclosure gap. There were companies that were widely traded but had never made a registered public offering and were thus not listed. The Securities Exchange Act of 1934 was amended in 1964 to close this gap.

1964 Amendment to the Securities Exchange Act of 1934

Companies with more than $1 million in total assets (this has since been increased to $3 million) are required to register under the Exchange Act a class of equity securities in which they have at least 500 shareholders of record.

Within the legal boundaries of these three laws, most widely held companies must file annual, quarterly, and other periodic reports. Companies with securities registered under the Exchange Act are also subject to proxy rules requiring the dissemination of a proxy or information statement in connection with the annual meeting, the election of directors, and other shareholder action. Here is what each of these reports must include:

1. *Annual report*—A report that must be distributed to shareholders in connection with the annual meeting at which the board of directors is elected. This is generally an unstructured document, but it must contain standardized financial statements along with other basic information about the company.
2. *Form 10–K*—Reporting companies must also file a 10–K with the SEC within 90 days of their fiscal year-end. Unlike the annual report, this document is highly regulated in terms of content, requiring extensive disclosure of financial condition, business and properties of the issuer.

3. *Form 10–Q*—This is the quarterly report required of reporting companies within 45 days of the end of the first three fiscal quarters. It includes uncertified financial statements for the quarter and the year-to-date period on a comparative basis with the prior year's performance.

4. *Form 8–K*—This report is required only by the occurrence of certain events, and is due within 15 days of such occurrence. These events include acquisitions/dispositions of significant amounts of assets, resignation or dismissal of the certifying accountants, resignation of a director, and changes in control of registration.

5. *Proxy statements*—These statements must be filed with the SEC in connection with the solicitation of proxies for the election of the board of directors, the annual meeting, and other shareholder actions.

In addition to these five reports, which are by far the most important, there are nine other forms of reports that relate to various types of registration under the two acts. All of these reports relate directly to the disclosure of company information for use by analysts, investors, and investment advisers.

In the early part of this century, corporate secrecy was the most important concern for a company. As a result, any kind of disclosure was seen as potentially harmful to the interests of the corporation. With the enactment of federal regulations from the SEC in the 1930s, the paranoid attitude about information, which was common in corporations of the pre-Depression era, changed dramatically.

Specifically, the Securities Exchange Act of 1934 served to raise management's awareness about its responsibility to keep shareholders informed. Despite this responsibility, however, IR did not flourish with the enactment of the two securities regulations. Corporations were only interested in mandatory disclosure, which required little in the way of IR.

Environmental Changes Shaping IR

It took three significant environmental forces to transform IR from just an idea to an active, needed function. These major changes included:

1. More Individual Shareholders For Publicly Held Companies
For individual companies to capitalize on the large cash inflow to the stock market, IR activities were needed to stimulate and attract investor interest.

2. Increased Power of Institutional Investors

Institutional investors followed individual investors' lead and invested their reserves of excess cash, dramatically increasing their share of total equity holdings. The role of institutions has continued to expand since this time, and today, they exert more influence than ever on corporate management. Institutions are an important constituency because their block trading activities can have a tremendous short-term effect on a company's stock price performance. This is particularly true for small to medium sized companies whose share prices are more sensitive to block trading.

3. Growing SEC Interest in Corporate Disclosure

Finally, the SEC became increasingly interested in what companies did and did not tell the investing public. This interest culminated with the previously mentioned 1964 amendment to the Securities Exchange Act of 1934.

As a result of these environmental factors, by the late 1960s with the establishment of the NIRI, the modern investor relations function began to emerge. During the first stage of the development of this function, from the early 1970s until the early 1980s, IR's purpose was to distribute basic financial publications to brokerage firms, securities analysts, and shareholders.

The "bull market" from 1982–1987 forced the IR function to change once again. During this time, the Dow Jones Industrial Average went from the 700s in mid-1982 to a high of 2,722 in the summer of 1987. IR's role expanded with the growth of market participants and trading volume.

The stock market crash in October 1987 catapulted IR into the current stage. One expert, Robert Amen, president of Robert Amen & Associates, a Greenwich, Connecticut, firm specializing in investor and corporate relations, characterizes the environment since the crash as "marked by further institutionalization and globalization of investment markets, the simultaneous shrinking of markets for equities . . . and a short-term transaction oriented stock market fomented by the growth of derivative products."

In the current stage of IR's development, the tactical activities for the function have not changed drastically, but the corporate attitude towards IR as a function has changed. It has gained the respect and attention of senior management, because it has become a critical function in shaping investor attitudes. As Amen puts it, "The pressure is on for [IR] programs to adopt a proactive marketing strategy: to seek new markets and not wait for the phone to ring, to not expect the sell-side to do the job alone."[1]

---

[1] Robert Amen, "How to Whet Investor Appetites in the Institutional, Global Markets of the 1990s," *Cash Flow Magazine,* June 1989.

Part of a more proactive strategy for IR will be meeting the challenges that grow out of the current environment, which will influence the function over the next several years. These forces include the globalization of capital markets, further institutionalization of investment markets, and corporate restructurings (LBOs, recapitalizations, ESOPs, acquisitions, and divestitures). Let's take a closer look at each of these to see how they will affect the IR function.

Globalization of Capital Markets

The global equity market has come about because of the deregulation of financial markets, the appeal of financial assets over fixed assets, and the worldwide participation in the bull market of the 1980s. Foreign markets have also experienced increased privatization, legislation providing tax incentives for equity investments, growth of pension fund assets, and expansion in money supplies.

Increased Power of Institutional Investors

The inflation of the 1970s had caused individuals to flee the stock market, seeking safety in mutual funds instead. By the end of the 1980s, therefore, institutional investors represented 85 percent of all public trading volume. The IR function has to understand these institutions, along with pension funds, which grew from less than a trillion dollars to over $2 trillion during the 1980s.

The 1974 enactment of the Employee Retirement and Income Security Act (ERISA) contributed to the growth of institutional influence because it held pension fund managers responsible for acting in the best interests of their beneficiaries. Institutions that are required to rationalize their investment decisions are therefore going to flex their muscles if portfolio companies are not performing. State and local laws in the 1980s also enabled pension funds to increase the equity allocation in their portfolios. That share rose to 36 percent in 1989 from 22 percent in 1982. By 2000, experts predict that pension fund assets will almost double again to over $3.5 trillion.

Shrinking Market for Equities

Despite the increased power of institutions and the incomprehensible value of pension fund assets, experts see the investment trend moving away from equities as this decade progresses. The factors that have triggered this development include the growth of "derivative products" (e.g. futures and options), the pace of merger and LBO activity in the 1980s, and stock repurchase programs.

The growth in institutional assets, on the one hand, expands the market for equities. But the larger the asset bases become, the more likely it is that some institutions will turn to passive management. This doesn't necessarily shrink the equities market, but it is damning from an IR perspective. Investment decisions for passively managed funds are made by computers, unaffected and unreachable through IR activities.

These trends certainly put the burden on IR to find creative ways to market the company's stock. This is by no means an easy task. IR practitioners must evaluate the investment policies and decisions of existing and prospective institutional investors, and disseminate information in a succinct and timely manner.

Now that we have a clear understanding of how the investor relations function developed and the challenges it faces over the next several years, we can turn our attention to a discussion of how to develop a successful investor relations function as part of a complete corporate communications program.

Developing an Investor Relations Program

According to Thomas Garbett, the concept of investor relations as a separate business function started at General Electric over 40 years ago. The objective for that function, and for the best investor relations functions today, is to ensure that the investment community fully and accurately understands the investment potential of a particular company. This does not mean simply producing and distributing annual and quarterly reports, answering shareholder questions, and sending information to securities analysts. Having traced the evolution of this function, we can see that these activities can be classified as mandatory or traditional. Instead, the best IR programs in today's environment must help investors and analysts understand a company's earnings potential, and how the company plans to reach that potential. As a result, IR really has to assume the role of marketer of a company's stock, which clearly involves much more than the basic activities listed above.

Perhaps the most important aspect of any IR program is its credibility. An IR program cannot tout its company's stock when times are good, for example, and go into hibernation when performance is less than expected. It is the open, candid discussion during the bad times as well as the good that really builds credibility for a company. In hard times, when the company is not performing as well as it should, analysts and investors need to be assured of the steps that management is taking to turn the situation around. Such candor is definitely in the company's best interests. As Garbett says:

> Information reduces risk. The stock market, as a process, arrives at a stock price based upon all known elements relating to the company. some of the

unknown factors add to the price, others subtract. Areas about the company that are unknown usually contribute to the minus side of the price equation.[2]

The job for an investor relations function today, then, is to disseminate this appropriate information on a consistent, timely, and equal basis. Companies must answer four critical questions in the development of a formal IR program:

- What is the current perception?
- Where and how does IR fit into the organization?
- What are the objectives of the IR program?
- What activities are necessary to achieve these objectives?

What Is the Current Perception?

The first step toward developing an IR program is to evaluate the current perceptions of the company in the investment community. A survey of the institutional owners of a stock, analysts who recommend the stock, and analysts who follow the company's competitors should provide information on the prevalent attitudes towards the company.

Management benefits in two ways from this kind of research. The survey conveys that management is concerned about best serving the needs of the company's constituencies, and management stands to gain valuable insights from sophisticated analysts and investors.

Such research does not have to be highly quantitative or extremely expensive. A small qualitative research project is generally viewed as more valuable in this area. The thoughtful opinions of a few people who know the company provide the most useful information to understand where a company stands at the outset. This research should be conducted periodically to monitor the effectiveness of the IR program and to restructure the program as needed.

Where and How Does IR Fit into the Organization?

Most analysts would agree that the most critical element in any IR program is the person who actually manages the function. They want to work with an IR professional who responds quickly to requests for information, is powerful enough in the organization to arrange meetings with the CEO and/or the CFO, who really knows what is going on in the organization through direct contact with senior management, who understands the workings of Wall Street, and who is willing to share both the good news and the bad.

---

[2] Thomas F. Garbett, *How to Build a Corporation's Identity and Project Its Image* (Lexington, Mass.: Lexington Books, 1988), p. 99.

The willingness to share information is obviously something that analysts would want, but it puts the IR professional in a very difficult position. The manager must be able to tread carefully when speaking to analysts and be careful to know what can and cannot be shared legally and ethically. Since this is a strong position to be in, the person in IR must also have the kind of personality that does not take advantage of being in the driver's seat in terms of sharing information.

One company that I worked with had an investor relations professional with years of experience, who was universally despised among the analysts. No matter what this person had to offer, the way in which she shared the information was so unpleasant that analysts would invariably present the information in the most negative light possible. She was delighted with her power position and constantly reminded analysts that she knew much more than she was willing to share and that she was plugged into top management in a way they never could be.

When I shared this assessment of her with the CFO, he was shocked because she was a consummate professional in terms of her technical expertise within the organization, and she was very gracious in her dealings with top managers. Despite that, the analysts finally were able to share their concerns with the CFO and the CEO, and she was put into a position that allowed the company to benefit from her technical ability without putting her into direct contact with analysts. The new person they hired for direct relations with analysts was assessed much more on personality and the ability to get along with other people than simply on financial expertise.

In addition to sharing information and maintaining good relations with the analysts, the connection with senior managers is probably the single most important quality that IR must possess. While the person must have a good relationship with senior management and be an insider in terms of what is really happening, he or she must also be able to use discretion, judgment, and communication skills to communicate what is most appropriate.

One of the biggest problems for this function in terms of the larger scope of corporate communications is that it is so dependent on what goes on in the chief financial officer's domain. Consequently, it is often the last of the subfunctions to come under the direct control of a vice president for corporate communications. The problem with keeping this position under the domain of the finance or treasury department in an organization, however, is that the same person must often deal with the financial press.

As a result, many companies have tried to come up with innovative reporting relationships that essentially require the IR department to be a part of both finance and communications. Too much emphasis on either of the two functions works against the best interests of the company. How this gets resolved at individual companies depends to a great extent on the relative strength of each of the functional areas as well as the importance that the CEO places on IR in terms of either the financial or communication side of the business.

What Are the Objectives of the IR Program?

Once the IR professionals have a clear understanding of how the company is perceived in the investment community and have the cooperation of senior management, the two can work together to set the objectives for the IR program. These objectives will certainly vary depending on the results of the survey, the size of the company, and the format of its existing IR function, if one already exists.

Pamela Jameson, an IR director for Dayton Hudson, stresses that two criteria are critical to the success of any IR program. First, the program must have the commitment of senior management, and second, it must establish credibility with the investment community. Once these criteria are met, Jameson characterizes IR as a proactive marketing function that has five major objectives:

1. *IR must ensure that the stock price is appropriate for the earnings prospects, industry outlook, and the economy.* The difficulty is determining just what is appropriate. An undervalued stock in conjunction with a reactive IR function make a hostile acquirer's job very easy. Simply put, an undervalued company is a great takeover target.
2. *IR must limit stock price volatility.* The growing influence of institutions and the effects of program trading create enough volatility without a lack of information worsening the situation.
3. *IR must understand the current shareholder base as well as what is common to the industry.* This also includes knowing the mix of institutions and individuals. Further, IR should be in regular contact with the major institutional investors to understand their investment objectives.
4. *IR must build or restructure the shareholder base.* This is accomplished by targeting potential shareholders determined to be potential long-term holders.
5. *IR must provide feedback to management regarding investor concerns.* Two-way communication is essential to ensure that shareholders' and analysts' needs are met, and that their concerns are addressed. This is really a benefit to the company because feedback will enable management to gain insight into what existing and prospective investors are thinking about.

Jameson also recommends that if a company does not already have a disclosure policy, one should be established that satisfies all departments affected by it. A disclosure policy will ensure that the information released from the company is consistent and will enable the company to build and maintain credibility.

Other experts on investor relations would probably add two additional objectives for a successful IR program. First, the IR program must try to increase trading volume, especially if the business is a small growing concern. In addition, such companies need to encourage analysts to publish research on the company's stock. Again, this is not usually a problem for larger companies, but often even they need to get analysts to pay attention to information that might go against the current trend.

What Activities Are Necessary to Achieve These Objectives?

So many activities are necessary to reach the objectives we have outlined, but it might be useful to classify these into five major categories.

Developing a Message

Before IR can start communicating, it must have a clearly defined message. The message should include management's philosophy, current conditions in the industry including recent trends, as well as the earnings potential. Basically, IR must communicate the company's strategic vision for future growth. The communications, therefore, should address issues including the expected rate of growth, the reasons why the company expects this growth, and how the company expects to achieve it. The investing public is interested in the long-term financial outlook and not the current year's earnings.

Corporate advertising expert, Thomas Garbett also points out that the IR message must be balanced. Such balanced communications reflect a flexible management team that can perform well in an economic downturn. IR will not pass the test of credibility if everything always looks rosy. Thus, communication from IR should explain problems that must be overcome to achieve goals. By explaining even the internal difficulties that had/have to be overcome to reach their goals, companies can gain credibility. In addition to being candid, forward-looking, and balanced, the message has to be simultaneously crisp and concise—difficult achievements for even the best companies.

Starting with the Basics

Certain activities are crucial to accomplish the objectives just identified. Here are some of the basics for running a successful IR program at any company:

Disseminate information to securities analysts and buy-side institutions in a timely manner. Using a news release for this audience is much more acceptable than for the news media. IR should maintain a current list of the key players in each of those categories. After a significant company event or activity, IR should contact the people on that list by phone to make sure they are aware of the news. Aside from the phone list, there should also be a fax list of a wider population who would be interested in receiving more detailed financial statements after earnings releases, full-text press releases, and so on. These audiences would also be interested in nonfinancial material (e.g., product information, copies of speeches, and employee newsletters and publications of any sort).

Arrange periodic group meetings with analysts and institutional investors. The presentations at these meetings should be brief and to the point. The investment community is concerned about strategy and philosophy as well as financial results. These meetings can be harmful to a company if they are poorly planned. With the wave of Wall Street cutbacks in recent years, an increasing number of companies are competing for the attention of fewer analysts. IR departments have to be both aggressive and effective if they plan to attract favorable attention from this group. These meetings can take the form of field trips to plants, ground breakings, new store openings, or any other facilities. These combination meetings/tours give the attendees a better feel for what the company is about and how it is implementing the strategies it is articulating. I strongly recommend that these presentations and meetings be kept separate from the media. Often companies lump the two constituencies together; I have never seen it work for the analysts, although the media seems to like it very well.

Monitor the effectiveness of the program by periodically canvassing the constituencies for their opinions. In this way, IR can modify its objectives, its message, the information it distributes, and its meetings schedule as needed. It is also a good idea to follow up with key analysts and investors after a major meeting to elicit their reaction to the company's presentation.

Analyzing the Shareholder Base

Virtually everyone involved in this field agrees that IR must spend a significant amount of time understanding not only who owns the company's stock but why. IR professionals should analyze the mix of individual and institutional holders. Depending on the company, this mix may be worth changing.

Data bases that are easily accessible are full of information on institutional stock holdings, turnover rates, and basic portfolio characteristics, which IR can use to identify those institutions that might be interested in the company's stock. IR professionals can focus on managers whose portfolio characteristics closely coincide with their company's price/earnings (P/E) ratio, yield, market capitalization, beta value (which measures risk) and industry classification. IR can then target potential investors who select stocks with characteristics similar to their own. What companies need to avoid is wasting time communicating with those who may not be interested in the company at all. With the growing influence of institutional investors, IR can no longer rely on purchased mailing lists to identify prospective investors.

Marketing to the Buy Side

As I have mentioned several times before in this chapter, institutional investors are the most important constituency for IR. In investment circles, this group is often referred to as the ''buy side.'' These are the decision-makers, the actual shareholders. They include banks, insurance companies, and pension funds. They have their own research staffs who publish opinions within their respective firms. Although they do receive information from Wall Street firms, it is the in-house opinions upon which decisions to buy, sell, or hold are ultimately made.

Having identified those institutions whose investing criteria match the company's characteristics, IR should develop a plan to invite them to invest. Companies must focus on the long term in this regard. The bull market of the 1980s is a major cause for the short-term orientation of the investment community. Everybody wanted a piece of the action, and they wanted it immediately.

Going Global

As we discussed earlier, the world capital markets have essentially become one. IR departments, therefore, should include overseas institutions in their marketing plans. There is less competition for the attention of non-U.S. portfolio and money managers. An international IR program will give the company access to different investing approaches, which tend to be more long-term oriented. Thorough planning and preparation is of course necessary for this effort. In addition to general investor skepticism, language and cultural barriers must also be overcome.

Conclusion

No two IR programs are going to be exactly the same because so much of this effort depends on the kind of company, its industry, size, and so on. Yet, over the last several years, some of the lessons that we have learned from applying basic communication strategy to this effort have helped the field become a more mature professional part of the corporation.

Many other considerations come into the normal activities of IR such as planning and running annual meetings and putting together the actual reports that are necessary today under the law. But the way these particular situations should be approached is no different from any other communication activity. Companies must again make sure to follow a good communication strategy that includes a clear understanding of the company's objectives, thoroughly analyzing all of the important constituencies, structuring an appropriate message for the constituencies, and listening to the feedback that you get when it's all over (see Chapter 2 for more on strategy).

No company can afford to deal with the current investment community without developing an effective investor relations function. The price that you pay for overlooking this advice is far greater than the investment you will make in the personnel that will staff the function. Any other approach is akin to a random walk down Wall Street.

CASE
JEWETT BANK*

Read through the attached financial highlights from Jewett's 1992 annual report. Do you agree or disagree with their overall communication strategy?

Financial Highlights

	1992	1991	1990	Percentage Increase (Decrease)	
				1992 versus 1991	*1991 versus 1990*
For the Year ($ in thousands)					
Net interest income	$2,023,882	$1,771,937	$1,555,701	14.2%	13.9%
Provision for possible losses	263,000	211,000	189,500	24.6	11.3
Other operating income	758,922	686,240	583,195	10.6	17.7
Other operating expenses	2,135,070	1,605,756	1,405,972	33.0	14.2
Income before securities gains (losses)	332,495	443,901	364,654	(25.1)	21.7
Net income	307,483	412,150	354,178	(25.4)	16.4
Per Common Share					
Income before securities gains (losses)	$ 8.47	$ 12.53	$ 10.47	(32.4)%	19.7%
Net income	7.73	11.56	10.15	(33.1)	13.9
Cash dividends declared, annually	3.40	3.10	2.80	9.7	10.7
Cash dividends declared, quarterly	.85	.775	.70	9.7	10.7
Common stockholders' equity	81.42	78.35	70.25	3.9	11.5
Financial Ratios					
Income before securities gains (losses) as a percentage of:					
Average total assets	.43%	.59%	.53%	(27.1)%	11.3%
Average common stockholders' equity	10.7	17.2	15.8	(37.8)	8.9
Cash dividends paid on common stock as a percentage of:					
Income before securities gains (losses) applicable to common stock	40.1	24.7	26.7	62.3	(7.5)
Net income applicable to common stock	43.9	26.8	27.6	63.8	(2.9)
At Year End ($ in millions)					
Interest-bearing deposits placed with banks	$ 7,891	$10,231	$ 8,227	(22.9)%	24.4%
Investment and trading account securities	5,332	4,935	5,456	8.0	(9.5)
Loans	55,156	51,001	46,974	8.1	8.6
Reserve for possible losses	558	541	468	3.1	15.6
Total assets	80,863	77,839	76,190	3.9	2.2
Deposits	56,858	55,300	56,846	2.8	(2.7)
Long-term notes and debentures	1,046	944	985	10.8	(4.2)
Redeemable preferred stock	150	280	280	(46.4)	—
Nonredeemable preferred stock	375	125	125	200.0	—
Common stockholders' equity	2,761	2,593	2,283	6.5	13.6

* This is a fictional case based on information contained in a variety of annual reports. The name of the company, its industry, and characters have all been disguised.

Letter to Stockholders

It is with mixed feelings that we review the performance of the Bank in 1992.

On the one hand, it was a difficult year for Jewett. We absorbed substantial losses—the result of our well-publicized problems relating to Ledyard Government Securities and to loans acquired through the Citizens Bank, S.A. which failed in August.

On the other hand, that we were able to absorb these losses and still achieve a solid performance for the year underscores the fundamental strength of our institution.

As we explained in our letter in the Second Quarterly Report, on May 18, 1992, Ledyard failed to pay accrued coupon interest then due on U.S. government securities it had acquired through Jewett.

We agreed with Ledyard to pay the interest to third-party security lenders and to take over and liquidate the positions acquired by Ledyard. At the same time, we reserved our rights against third parties. In so doing, we sought to minimize Jewett's exposure to claims for consequential damages and to maintain order in the U.S. government securities market. Further, we intended to live up to our reputation as a responsible institution.

As we previously reported, due to the Ledyard situation we sustained a special aftertax loss of $117 million, or $3.49 per common share, in the second quarter. In October, we initiated a suit to recover our losses against Ledyard, certain related entities, and others. Also during the year, we charged off $75 million in housing-related loans acquired through the Citizens Bank. The future value of this portfolio obviously will be affected by conditions prevailing in the housing market. But the $75 million charged off represented our best estimate at year-end 1992 of losses incurred.

When these events came to light, we extensively examined both the internal and external elements involved. In the third quarter, as a result of those examinations, we modified our senior management organization and further strengthened the control and monitoring mechanisms within the Bank.

While legal actions to recover losses are being vigorously pursued and while improvement in our procedures must be ongoing, we believe these events are now behind us.

Capital Strength. One of the prime indicators of a bank's financial strength is the capital available both to maintain the institution's current financial position and to enable it to grow.

In 1992, as a result of a combination of innovative equity issues, the retention of earnings, and our dividend reinvestment plan, Jewett-defined equity increased $487 million, compared with a $369 million increase in 1991.

Using Jewett's definition of capital, the average equity capital to risk assets ratio, a key measure of capital adequacy, increased from 5.0 percent in 1991 to 5.3 percent in 1992, our highest ratio since 1986.

Jewett's ongoing capital planning has positioned us to take advantage of market opportunities as they arise. In a period of economic volatility, this kind of flexibility is extremely important.

Earnings Summary. Jewett's income before securities transactions declined 25 percent to $332 million or $8.47 per common share from the record $444 million or $12.53 per common share in 1991. This decline was primarily the result of the Ledyard and Citizen situations.

We elaborate on Jewett's 1992 performance in the Management's Discussion and Analysis section and in the financial statements. Highlights of that performance included:

- Net interest income on a taxable equivalent basis, the largest component of our pre-tax earnings, was $2.0 billion, up 14 percent from 1991.

- Other operating income rose 11 percent to a record $759 million.

- Offsetting these favorable factors and reflecting, in part, the global economic recession, Jewett's nonperforming loans increased as did our charge-offs. At year-end 1992, nonperforming loans were $1.4 billion, and net charge-offs for the year totaled $230 million.
- Despite a higher level of charge-offs, we were able to absorb our losses without significant changes in the level of the loan loss reserve. At year-end 1992, the reserve of $558 million remained at slightly above 1 percent of loans and lease financings.

In recognition of management's belief in the underlying strength of our balance sheet and capital position and in the earnings capability of the Bank, Jewett's Board of Directors voted at its January 1993 meeting to increase the quarterly dividend on common stock from 85 cents per common share to 87$1/2$ cents, our fifth consecutive year of dividend increases.

The Environment for Our Businesses.　For many of the participants in the world economy, 1992 was indeed a difficult year.

The last few years of limited economic growth and low interest rates have placed considerable strain on corporate balance sheets.

In periods of economic difficulties, Jewett has a responsibility to support its customers around the world. Failure to do so, within the limits dictated by prudence, would be against the long-term interest not only of our customers but also of Jewett and the public at large.

During 1992, we continued and strengthened our commitment to the corporate market both here and abroad. We have fully implemented our global corporate organization to better serve the financial needs of corporate customers around the world.

In our U.S. Area Banking Group, serving middle-sized businesses, we opened regional marketing offices in Atlanta, Boston, and San Francisco. With offices in major financial cen-

ters coast to coast, Jewett is positioned to deliver the services required by emerging growth companies.

A recent example of the innovative manner in which we meet our corporate customers' financial needs is our vendor program agreement with U.S. Telephone. Under this agreement, which is the largest and most significant vendor program offered by Jewett Commercial Corporation, U.S. Telephone will offer its customers the option of Jewett-backed financing to cover the purchase and installation of U.S. Telephone terminals and other equipment. This is a pioneering venture for both Jewett and U.S. Telephone.

Internationally, the world focused considerable attention in 1992 on the problems of developing nations in eastern Europe, especially the much-publicized economic difficulties in Russia.

Clearly the debts carried by some developing nations have grown to substantial levels. Heavy commitments to economic development and a particularly severe global recession have contributed to the present debt problems.

But by and large, we believe these problems are of a temporary nature—temporary liquidity difficulties rather than permanent insolvency problems. And with cooperative efforts, these problems can be overcome.

We are encouraged by the efforts thus far, and, in particular, by the actions of the primary participants in this situation:

- First, there is the leadership of the *International Monetary Fund (IMF)*. Formal agreements between the IMF and its member countries have become keystones of a wider process, involving not only economic policy commitments by the borrower countries but also new credit commitments by commercial banks.
- Second, *central banks*—particularly the U.S. Federal Reserve Bank—are providing reasonable flows of liquidity.

- Third, the world's *major commercial banks*—the principal lenders to developing nations—have accepted their responsibility to work constructively with those nations experiencing liquidity problems and to reschedule repayments of certain outstanding credits.
- Fourth and most important, the *borrowing countries* themselves have shown increasing resolve to take those steps necessary to adjust their individual economies to the realities of the global environment.

We at Jewett will continue to work toward solutions of these problems. One of the historic strengths of Jewett is its international scope and network. The protection and enhancement of Jewett's international earnings capability are critical objectives of management.

And there is a much broader reason for assisting in these solutions. In our interdependent global economy, all nations will suffer if the economic development of other countries is hampered. Certainly, many jobs in the United States are tied to the export of products to these nations.

Reform of the Financial System. The banking system, particularly in the United States, continues to need a major regulatory overhaul.

American banks still are sharply limited in the range of services they are permitted to offer, and, in a few cases, are even prevented from pursuing what were once clearly seen as banking activities.

Because commercial banks have been prevented from providing many of the services which consumers or businesses have indicated they want, nonbank financial institutions, most of which are neither regulated nor insured by government agencies, have stepped into the gap. As a result, the banking system—a major resource for this nation's economic prosperity—is not being fully used.

Regulations also sharply limit the geography of American banking. Thus, although eco-

nomic activity in the United States has long been national in scope, American banking, with some exceptions, continues to end at the state line. The fundamental issue is how to frame a system of banking regulations that recognizes the financial needs and realities of an integrated national economy.

Although 1992 did not bring as much progress as we would have liked on the deregulatory front, there are some positive signs for the year ahead.

President Clinton has urged Congress to examine the Glass-Steagall issue with an eye toward making banks more competitive with the securities industry. And the Secretary of the Treasury, Comptroller of the Currency, and others have spoken out in support of expanded powers and a loosening of geographic restrictions.

At Jewett, we continue to speak out against those competitive imbalances which are not only contrary to the interests of the banking system but to the public interest as well. In testimony before Congress early in 1992, for example, we endorsed the approach of a Treasury Department proposal to expand the range of permissible bank holding company activities to include all financial services, such as the underwriting of municipal revenue bonds and mutual funds.

We continue to prepare Jewett for the broadened powers that we hope will be forthcoming in the years ahead, and, within the limits of present legislation, we are expanding the services Jewett offers.

Early in 1992, for example, we formed Jewett Capital Markets (Holdings), Inc. and subsidiaries as corporate vehicles for our capital markets services. When the laws that govern commercial and investment banking are amended, a Holdings subsidiary—Jewett Capital Markets Corporation—will be positioned to offer new domestic activities. To be ready for that change, we have registered the subsidiary with the Securities and Exchange Commission. The subsidiary is also a member of the National Association of Securities Dealers (NASD), and employees will be qualified as registered representatives, principals, or agents as required by the NASD and state broker-dealer laws. This will enable the subsidiary to operate in all 50 states.

In February 1993, we announced our intention to acquire the New York–based discount brokerage firm of Munter & Company Investment Brokers Inc. to expand our range of services to consumers nationwide. The acquisition would allow us to develop new products and services by integrating brokerage capabilities with our other consumer banking businesses. Munter & Company, a registered broker in all 50 states and the fourth-largest discount broker in the nation, has offices in Chicago; Los Angeles; Washington, D.C.; Pittsburgh; Houston; and Boston.

Challenges in 1993.   Looking ahead, management doesn't expect a buoyant performance for the domestic economy in 1993. Worldwide, economic growth is likely to be weak.

On the plus side, progress continues to be made on the inflation front. The rate of inflation is likely to continue at its current lower levels, and interest rates may continue to trend down.

All this once again means major challenges to Jewett in several key areas:

Asset quality—The implications to Jewett of such an economic scenario are clear. In an overall sense, the challenge of maintaining asset quality in an uncertain and difficult environment is a major one for all our lending units in 1993.

Strategic focus—Over the past several years, we've taken a hard look at certain products and businesses where present or projected returns do not justify continued investment. In light of the rapidly changing economic environment, we plan to accelerate this effort in 1993 as we focus more directly on our core businesses.

Strategic momentum—Related to this is the challenge to continue the momentum of our key strategic programs—for example, our nationwide expansion efforts and major investments in systems.

Optimizing performance—And finally, we must optimize our performance in our lending activities, our fee-based services, our financial management of assets, liabilities, and capital, and in the management of our expenses.

Management Changes.   In terms of management, we gratefully acknowledge the contributions of two of our most senior people who retired from Jewett in recent months.

In December 1992, Vice Chairperson Lauren Argenti retired after 35 years of service. We deeply appreciate Lauren's numerous contributions to this institution, particularly in the establishment of our controller and financial functions, in the areas of credit training and development, and as the Bank's senior officer responsible for coordinating our federal and state government relations.

In February 1993, Vice Chairperson and Chief Financial Officer John Shank announced his decision to take early retirement in order to pursue another career. After a distinguished 30-year career at Jewett, John leaves behind an exceptionally strong team in financial management.

Succeeding John Shank in his position as chief financial officer is Nicholas Shinn, formerly one of our key sector executives. Nick assumes responsibility for the Treasury, Corporate Controller, Financial Planning, Capital Planning and Economics divisions. He also will serve as chairperson of Jewett Capital Markets (Holdings), Inc.

Lindsay Rahmun, executive for the Trust and Global Private Banking divisions, will take on additional responsibilities for Information and Investment Services and Domestic Institutional Banking, succeeding Nick as sector executive for all these areas.

Early in December, we also announced the promotion of Anita Warren to vice chairperson and welcomed her as a member of our Board of Directors. Anita serves as the Bank's chief credit policy officer and is chairperson of the Credit Risk Management Committee.

In another move to strengthen corporate management, Executive Vice President Sam Ash was given responsibility for strategic planning as well as for legal affairs. Sam's duties as general counsel were assumed by Giulio A. DeConti, Jr., formerly a partner in the law firm of James, Harris, and Roberts. Sam Ash continues to spearhead our nationwide expansion efforts.

In addition to Anita Warren, we added four new members to our Board of Directors in 1992. David S. McCallum, president and chief operating officer of Xantak Corporation; Donna Dalise, chairperson of the board and chief executive officer of Outboard Engine Company, Inc.; Ray Boyer, chairperson and chief executive officer of Packard Motor Company; and Marilyn Wyatt, chairperson, president, and chief executive officer of Tasty Cabbage Inc.

In summary then, the financial system does indeed face significant challenges in 1993. However, it is well within the capacity of Jewett to meet the particular challenges presented to us. Our capital base and our earnings capability are strong and so, too, is our management team around the world. We look forward to the year ahead.

Susan Schwarz
Chairperson and Chief Executive Officer

Robert Parker
President and Chief Operating Officer

8   COMMUNICATING INTERNALLY

Many communications experts would say that communicating effectively with employees may be the single most important aspect of corporate communications in the 1990s. Employees can be motivated to work harder for the organization when management communicates with them honestly and regularly; they can be ambassadors of indifference when managers forget that they are the organization's most important asset.

In this chapter, we look at how companies can create strong internal communication programs to go along with the external programs that we have been talking about in the preceding chapters. We start by looking at some of the changes in the environment that have created the need for a stronger internal communications function. Then we look at ways to organize a strong employee communications effort through planning and staffing. Finally, we discuss how to implement the right program for today's environment.

Changes in the Environment Affect Internal Communications

What is so different about today's environment, and how does it affect the way companies communicate internally? As we discussed in Chapter 1, the environment for business has changed dramatically over the last half century. Today's employee is a different person in terms of values and needs than the employee in earlier decades of this century. In addition, the workplace is very different as employees face tighter staffing, longer hours, a greater workload, more emphasis on performance, and in many cases, greater autonomy.

Other changes have taken place in companies that also affect the employees within. First, the overall environment is more competitive than ever before, more global than in the past, and more interdependent on other organizations and government agencies. These changes put greater pressure on employees today and create the need for a more coordinated approach to employee communication.

Many companies, facing pressures from outside the organization make the mistake of taking employees for granted. Just as a parent facing problems outside of the home might neglect his or her children, managers sometimes forget that employees are perhaps the most important constituency of all. Once a company has lost the faith and goodwill of its employees, it faces an uphill battle as it tries to correct its errors and rebuild credibility with the very ones who hold the future of most corporations in their grasp.

Part of the problem at many companies is that senior managers simply do not involve other employees in most of the decision-making process. This tends to make them feel alienated and less willing to accept the changes that managers then impose upon them.

Thus, managers find that a new generation of employees, most of whom are better educated, have higher expectations than their parents did, and want to work more with their heads than their hands, are more likely to want more information about the company they work for than previous generations did.

And, the Japanese have made it obvious to most American managers that getting employees more involved in the process of running the company leads to greater productivity. More than anything else, communication is the key to getting workers to become more productive. That communication must be a two-way process rather than the traditional downward spiral of communication that we still see in most American corporations. More interaction also gives management more credibility with employees, which can be a tremendous asset in both good times and bad.

As a result of these changes in the environment, companies must try to communicate more honestly with employees. Typically, most companies communicate with employees through company newsletters. These vehicles are often some of the most boring reading that employees are likely to encounter either on the job or off. Instead of focusing simply on who got promoted to what position, who won the bowling contest, and other human interest stories, today's newsletters need to focus on the company's plans for the future, its personnel policies and how they affect the individual employee, and the impact that external events are having on the company's performance within the industry.

Imagine if a company newsletter were really interesting for employees to read, if it really told them about the pressures that senior managers are so aware of, if it tried to explain in simple terms what the pressures from competitors mean to the individual employee. How powerful such information could be in helping managers to get employees rallying around a common goal.

Instead, most companies still are fearful of sharing information with employees, even though they are much more educated than their counterparts of an earlier era and have less of an interest in simply climbing the corporate ladder. Enlightened managers, however, know that the more information they provide to employees, the more likely they are to be highly motivated to do a better job, to advance in their positions, and to further the goals of the organization itself.

One company that exemplifies this enlightened attitude to employee relations is Hewlett-Packard. Faced with intense competition in the late

1980s, the company found itself for the first time in its history in a financial bind that could have led to laying off employees in several different areas.

Instead, the company went directly to the employees, explained the pressures that it was facing, and got them to agree to take some leave time without pay rather than having any of its employees go through the terrible experience of losing a job. Such an enlightened approach to a financial problem made the employees more loyal to the company than ever before. It also allowed managers to get employees to understand directly the pressures they were facing rather than trying to solve the problem in the more traditional way.

Much of what we are talking about has to do with creating an atmosphere of respect for all employees within the organization. This can be accomplished in many ways, but the best way to create this atmosphere is through the communication that managers have with employees. Most of this communication should, ideally, come directly from one manager to the next, from supervisor to employee. But as companies grow larger and more complex, this often becomes difficult, which is where the need for an employee communication function arises.

The function can deal with the employee in all stages of his or her development within the firm. Initially, the interest of the employee is probably fairly selfish and focused simply on the job he or she is hired to do. As the employee becomes more comfortable with the job, however, and more a part of the department or group he or she works in, the focus will be more externally oriented toward those around the employee.

Eventually, the locus of interest ultimately focuses on the company itself, however, and what the organization is trying to accomplish within the industry. At each stage of the employee's development, the company has an opportunity to create loyalty and to get more of what one manager describes as the employee's discretionary time—that time that the employee doesn't have to devote to the job but chooses to nonetheless.

Perhaps the best way to begin such an effort is to determine what the current attitudes are about the firm. Just as with external constituencies, communication professionals in employee communications can conduct what is often called a *communication audit* to determine how employees feel about the company. Based on this assessment, the professionals can design the right program for the organization.

In the past, the focus was on keeping employees in the dark about what was really going on in the company and informing them when they needed to know, or when the general public was about to learn about something happening in the organization. Today, however, as a result of the changing environment for business, companies should consider employees as insiders, or as what one consulting firm refers to as "ambassadors of commitment." This puts the burden on senior executives to embrace the role they can play in becoming more involved in employee communications and thinking of it as less a problem for the personnel department but an opportunity for everyone in the firm to work for the greater good of the whole organization.

Organizing the Internal Communication Effort

Now that we have seen how the environment has changed and how it affects the internal communication effort, we need to explore ways for companies to organize the function in such a way that it can support the overall mission of the firm. Let's begin, however, by first describing what the goals for an effective internal communication function should be, then we will look at where the function should report.

Goals for Effective Internal Communications

A Conference Board study of over 200 companies in a wide variety of industries conducted in the late 1980s indicates what top managers see as the key goals for effective employee communications. In order of importance these goals are:

1. To improve morale and foster goodwill between employees and management.
2. To inform employees about internal changes such as a reorganization or staff promotions.
3. To explain compensation and benefit plans such as a new health-care plan or an Employee Assistance Program.
4. To increase employee understanding of the company and its products, organization, ethics, culture, and external environment.
5. To change employee behavior toward becoming more productive, quality oriented, and entrepreneurial.
6. To increase employee understanding of major health/social issues or trends affecting them such as child care or AIDS.
7. To encourage employee participation in community activities.

Perhaps more important than any of these goals, however, is to create the sense that employees are an important asset to the firm. This can only be accomplished if management believes that it is true, and if the communication effort is handled by professionals.

Where Should Internal Communications Report?

In the past, the answer to this question would have inevitably been that the employee communication function should naturally report to the personnel or human resource area since this is where all things related to employees' welfare should rest. Recent surveys we have conducted of major companies have shown, however, that over two thirds of the top corporations in the United States place the responsibility for internal communications in the corporate communications area.

This shows that companies today realize that the internal constituency is not that much different from external ones in terms of the need for sophisticated communications techniques. This is particularly true in terms of the more important print materials that corporate communications departments are more likely to produce as well as the more sophisticated audio-visual communications. But how can companies separate what personnel should produce from what the corporate communications department produces in terms of internal communications that will be mass distributed?

For print materials, the breakdown between what each of the two functions produces may be classified as the difference between what we would think of as an image-oriented vehicle and what we can classify as more narrowly defined publications.

For instance, it makes sense for the corporate communications department to produce the employee newsletter or magazine since this is a more global publication with image-oriented goals. The purpose of this publication is, after all, to create a certain image of the organization in the employee's mind rather than to describe some specific aspect of an employee's job or set of benefits. This publication should also be tied very closely with the overall corporate communication strategy so that the messages that employees are getting are closely allied with the messages that are being distributed to external constituencies.

For instance, if a company is facing increased competition from a foreign competitor, employees are likely to be reading about this phenomenon and the corporation's response in the local or national press. The company should, therefore, try to give employees an idea of how they see the problem and what response they have to meet the challenge in a communication that is designed specifically for employees. This kind of communication about a current event is going to make the employees feel more like insiders.

But printed information about more specialized aspects of employee communications is obviously the purview of the human resources department. For example, the information the company provides for new employees about benefits or payroll procedures should not be generated by corporate communications since they are simply describing an existing policy. If, however, the health benefits are going to change dramatically and be reduced significantly in a given year, the corporate communications function would be far better equipped to communicate such changes to employees than the human resources department because of the sensitive nature of the information.

As for visual communications, the orientation films that companies create are more typically created by human resource professionals while the weekly broadcast from senior management to subsidiaries in outlying areas is more deftly handled by the corporate communications department. Again, the more global the information is, the better equipped the communications department is to handle it rather than the human resources department.

Ideally, then, each of the two departments would have someone in charge of communications to employees. The person in the corporate communications department would obviously report to the vice president in charge of that area while the person in the human resources department would report to his or her respective vice president. But both should have a dotted-line relationship with the vice president in the other area to ensure that the goals of each of the departments are fully met in all communications and to keep the lines of communications open between these two critical functional areas in a firm.

Cooperative activities in a variety of different firms were recently described in a research report from the Conference Board:[1]

• *Keeping employee communications within the jurisdiction of human resources.* At Pfizer Inc., the employee communication unit reports to the Corporate Vice President, Personnel. The location of the function within Personnel has a long history in the company where "internal communication is viewed as one aspect of managing employee relations and building employee commitment," says the Director, Employee Communication.

• *The Coca-Cola company also links employee communications and employee relations.* The Director of these activities reports to the Senior Vice President, Human Resources. However, the employee magazine and some internal memos are produced by a separate communications function. The two groups maintain an informal relationship, talking and interacting frequently, especially about top-management communiqués. Moreover, the Director of Employee Relations and Communications is a member of the editorial board for the employee magazine.

• *At Bell South Corporation, human resources and employee communications "are two different organizations, but work closely together,"* says the Operations Manager, Public Relations. Most joint activities focus on labor relations or benefits. Messages targeted to the entire employee population must go through the communications function. The two groups cooperate to ensure that their portrayal of the company is consistent. One recent communications priority was to promote the firm's newly developed statement of values. Says the public relations executive: "Communications has the responsibility to inform the employees about the values and to encourage their adherence. Human resources has the responsibility to cultivate and maintain a corporate culture that encourages the type of activities that support these values."

---

[1] Kathryn Troy, "Employee Communication: Top Management Priority," Report 919 (New York: The Conference Board, 1988).

These examples show that the two functions can work together quite well in a variety of ways. Even when they have little formal connection, however, these two departments share common goals and tend to collaborate on an ad hoc basis to the greater good of both departments.

Implementing an Effective Internal Communications Program

Once the goals for a program have been established and everyone is clear about where the function should report, the internal communications program is ready to be implemented throughout the organization. In smaller organizations, the function may just be a part of everyone's job because the ideal method of communicating with employees is one on one or in meetings with small groups of employees.

Even in larger organizations, however, this intimacy in the internal communications effort is a good start for building a more formal program. Let's begin this discussion of implementation by looking at how programs grow from the basic one-on-one model to a more formal program using sophisticated technology on a global scale.

Communicate Up and Down

In most larger organizations, the biggest problem companies have is appearing to be faceless organizations with no soul. This impression is exacerbated by lack of input from employees upward to management. Top managers often isolate themselves physically and psychologically from other employees at the peril of effective communications.

A billion-dollar organization I visited recently had a separate dining room for the top 11 officers of the firm. Cocktails were served in a wood-paneled room with elaborate *hors d' oeuvres* for less than a dozen people. The senior managers, all men in their late 50s, were served by four different waiters. Lunch was followed by cigars and cognac in the equivalent of a men's club reading room adjacent to the lunch room.

As the discussion progressed, the vice president of corporate communications outlined two problems that the company needed help with. One was related to the external image of the firm. But the other more critical problem was the lack of communications between top managers and the rest of the employees in the firm. I asked the vice president how often he met informally with anyone other than the 11 top executives of the firm. He claimed that communication was frequent, but the more we discussed the situation, the more obvious it became to me that the senior executives had little or no contact with anyone other than themselves.

And even though the company spent literally millions of dollars on communications, it was much less effective than a regular conversation with people in each of their areas would have been. Further adding to the senior executives' communication problems and sense of isolation was the placement of all 11 offices on the top floor of the company's headquarters building. Since other employees had no reason to see the top executives, the isolation as defined by where the offices were and the lack of any social interaction at daily lunches continued the erosion of communications.

Effective communications with employees, then, which is the basis for any internal communications effort, must start with the way managers interact with other employees day to day. Such interaction is an integral part of management and should be thought of not as an additional burden but as natural interactions with peers.

A nationwide survey of over 5,000 employees in U.S. firms conducted by a major consulting firm showed that the single biggest criticism employees have of companies is that they do not encourage upward as well as downward communication. A minority of employers seek workers' opinions about key issues, according to the survey, and a quarter of those surveyed do not feel free to express their opinions at all.

What is the best approach for communicating with employees? Certainly it must begin with informal discussions between employees and supervisors. Employees must also feel secure enough in their positions to ask questions and offer advice without fear of reprisals from top management. A report written by Kathryn Troy in 1988 put it best:

> To some extent, the desire to be informed about the company first-hand and to participate in the decision-making process in the workplace reflects a basic human need, and is not new. But it also conveys the growing sophistication of the workforce—the better educated baby boom generation is now mature and makes up a large segment of today's workers—the median age of the labor force is about 35 years and is expected to be 38.9 years by the year 2000. "Our employees are very savvy—not only do they know what is happening at headquarters, but they are also aware of worldwide trends and are not afraid to demand more from the company. They will not come to a meeting if their perception is 'this is what management wants to communicate to you;' they want to participate," says an employee communications executive of a consumer products company.[2]

By giving employees the respect they deserve and listening and interacting with them frequently, managers have the basis for an effective internal communications program. But the task for the most senior managers who have great pressures from both within and outside of the corporation is much more difficult.

Communicating in Meetings

To ensure that the employees do have access to senior management, most companies must have regular meetings with fairly large groups. Such

---

[2] Ibid.

large-scale meetings should be held frequently and should be considered opportunities for management to express its opinions and for employees to ask questions in an open forum.

Some companies, such as Anheuser-Busch, stage elaborate mutimedia events at which employees and spouses are invited to attend in the evening. These annual meetings, which usually feature the most senior executives, may only increase the separation between management and employees, however. A better model may be to meet during lunch hours for regular meetings with the smallest groups possible to exchange ideas in the most informal setting possible. I encouraged one CEO to get off the stage and into the audience during such a presentation; communication at these meetings increased dramatically as a result of such a small change.

Topics also should be limited. Rather than trying to tackle everything that is going on at the company, managers should first survey employees to find out what is most important to them. Then a presentation can be built around one or two critical issues that employees have while also stressing something that management wants to share. Too often, management only sets up such meetings when it has an important pronouncement. Such behavior makes the likelihood of relevant discourse virtually impossible.

Some companies also set up meetings with very small groups of employees, say a dozen, to get a random sample of opinion. For example, the Conference Board study cited earlier reports that an insurance company named General American Life randomly selects 12 employees by computer to form an associate's advisory committee that meets with the president to discuss key issues that are important to the company as a whole. The company also has a junior board of directors, which serves for one year, is made up of management level employees, and advises the chairman of the board.

Create Employee-Oriented Publications

While meetings are an important way to communicate with employees, the most common form of interaction on a regular basis is bound to be through the print medium. Unfortunately, a random sample of such publications turns up some of the worst and most boring publications you have ever seen in your life. Why are such publications so boring? How can companies make them more interesting to employees?

The biggest problem companies have in producing publications, such as a monthly magazine or newsletter is that they simply do not get good communicators involved in the process of creating the publications. At many companies, the ''house organ'' as it is known throughout the United States is given to the lowest-level employee in the corporate communications area. At one firm I consulted with that registers sales in the 10s of billions of dollars, the monthly publication was being produced by a former secretary with a high school education and no professional experience in communications.

Companies need to realize that the competition for such publications is not what other companies are producing for their employees, which are likely to be just as bad, but the national and local media that employees are exposed to. Today's employee is a sophisticated consumer of information, better educated, and more interested in seeing something more akin to *USA Today* than a list of bowling scores and pictures of employees with several years of service to the firm. Thus, this is a job that is ideal for former journalists of which there are an abundance looking for a good job with a major corporation. The most senior communication official and the CEO should also take an interest in the development of such publications to ensure that employees are getting the real story about what is happening to the company and the industry in the most interesting presentation possible.

Another way to reach employees more effectively through such publications is to send them to their homes rather than distributing them at the workplace. Although this is obviously more expensive, it helps to make the company a part of the family, something that the employee and his or her spouse will read and feel proud about.

The publications should, above all, be as honest as possible about what is likely to affect the employees. Nothing is going to hurt morale more than having employees find out about a major corporate event from a source other than the corporation. Use the publications to communicate important ideas to employees and release the information to them at the same time that it goes to the national and local media. Again, the goal is to make employees feel that they are insiders, a part of the team, and on the cutting edge of what is happening within the firm and its industry.

The messages that go into these periodicals will vary by industry and company, but managers must try to get the right balance between what employees are most interested in and what they really need to hear from top management. The ideal that they should strive for is to have employees looking forward to the next issue of the company publication in the same what that a university can generate interest in itself through its alumni magazine. In fact, such publications are excellent models in terms of style and tone for company publications.

Other publications will also have to be produced from time to time as important events that directly affect employees come up. As discussed earlier, for example, the health benefits area is one that needs a special set of publications in many organizations as companies need to take back what many employees feel is theirs to keep. As the company gears up for a reduction in health benefits, it may start communicating with employees months before the actual changes take place to set the stage for what would otherwise be a very controversial situation.

Management should also feel free to write memos and letters to employees about internal changes. These written communications should come out frequently enough so that employees do not feel that it is unusual, but not so often that employees stop hearing the important messages that you are trying to communicate. Such communications can be tremendous morale boosters as management can use the format to again make the employee feel like more of an insider.

Finally, publications are most critical in a crisis situation (see Chapter 9 for more on crises). Corporate communications experts should have all distribution channels ready when an emergency strikes or if a critical piece of information is going to be released about the company. For example, if the company is about to be taken over, the employees should know about it before anyone else. Similarly, any significant management changes are best distributed to employees first before going to external constituencies.

Visual Communications

Even though employees are better educated and more sophisticated consumers of information, they are also becoming more visual in their consumption of that information. For example, we saw earlier in this book that most Americans get their news directly from television as opposed to newspapers. As a result, companies today need to develop ways to communicate with employees through this powerful medium.

At the largest companies today you are likely to find elaborate television studios and satellite capabilities. Such sophisticated systems staffed by professionals are the best mechanisms for communicating with employees through visual channels. But even if your company does not have its own studio, outside vendors are also available for getting information out to employees.

Kmart Corporation located in Troy, Michigan, has one of the most sophisticated communication networks in the world. With thousands of stores spread throughout the country, senior management needed to find ways to communicate regularly with store managers. The company built its studio to "meet" regularly with managers all over the country. Each Friday, senior managers, often including the chairman of the board, discuss the most critical issues of the week with store managers all across the country. Phone lines are open to keep the communication going in both directions, and store managers feel much more a part of the corporation as a whole rather than separate entities.

The company also uses the studio to create a monthly video magazine for the store managers that is a bit more slick and similar in style to *Entertainment Tonight*. Teams of "reporters" go out into the field with video cameras to cover company events for the program, which makes it very relevant and quite interesting to everyone in the company. The show is then broadcast to all of the stores; store managers tape the program for viewing by all of the store employees who are interested in seeing what is happening at other stores throughout the country.

Most large corporations have such video magazines available to employees in outlying areas, which is a good way to keep them feeling like they are really a part of a larger organization. Managers should not see expenditures on such communications as frivolous or wasteful but as an investment in the firm, a way to make everyone feel more a part of what is going on. If these productions are well done, they can be tremendous morale boosters as well as a visual history of the company that can used for years to come.

The Company Grapevine

One expert recently wrote that 80 percent of corporate gossip is reliable: "A company grapevine should be considered as much of a communication vehicle as your house organ or employee meetings. It might be even more valuable because it is believed and every smart manager should tap into it." But how do you tap into this incredibly valuable and accurate distribu- accurate distribution system?

Although we have discussed a number of different ways to implement an effective internal communications program, the human factor is still the most critical. Unless managers are really a part of what is going on at the grass roots level in an organization, they simply cannot tap into something as personal as the company grapevine.

Conclusion

Over the last several years, we have all heard about "management by walking around," and other management philosophies that basically say the same thing. Managers need to get out from behind their desks, put down their telephones, and go out and get to know the people who are working for them. No other method works as well and no quick fix will satisfy the basic need for interaction with other people.

With all of the sophisticated technology available to communicate with employees today, such as electronic mail, desktop publishing, and satellite meetings to far-flung places, the most important factor in internal communications begins with the manager who has a responsibility to his or her employees. That responsibility is to listen to what they have to say, and to get to know who they really are as human beings. It's a long way from Upton Sinclair's *Jungle* to the modern American corporation. Today's employees want the high tech and sophisticated communications, but they also want more of you than ever before. Understanding that fact is the key to an effective internal communications program.

CASE
HANOVER SOFTWARE*

Jan Barry, a recent graduate of the Tuck School at Dartmouth was driving home from work in her Q45 listening to more depressing news about layoffs at a major computer firm. She had just left a meeting with her boss, Bob Morse, the vice president of human resources at Hanover Software. "Jan, we are going to have to let some of the old-timers go. I'm hoping that the CEO will buy my plan for a voluntary severance and early retirement package. We should be able to smoke out some of the deadwood in this company as well."

Now a billion dollar operation, Hanover Software had never laid off anyone in the 10 years of its existence. As the director of employee communications, Jan would be responsible for telling employees about the new policy within the next couple of days.

As she looked at the beautiful southern California hills surrounding the freeway, many thoughts were going through her head. How should she frame the issues involved for all employees? Should she get the people in corporate communications involved? Who would be the best person to release the information? What about communications with other Hanover constituencies?

Hanover Software Background

Hanover was started by Madeline Bernstein, a brilliant, young, UCLA graduate, following her graduation from college in 1983. With only $10 thousand in capital borrowed from her father, Bernstein had built the firm up into a billion dollar powerhouse through the development of two successful software products. One was called Passages, a spread sheet used by virtually everyone with an IBM personal computer. The other major product, called Keystone, was a piece of software that Bernstein herself had created especially for the investment banking community.

As the business grew, Bernstein gradually turned the day-to-day operation of Hanover over to professional managers, preferring young MBAs from top eastern business schools. But the original group of employees, mostly men in their mid-50s, still represented the bulk of senior management at Hanover.

By the early 1990s, analysts were predicting that the software industry in general and Hanover in particular was ready for consolidation. Many of Hanover's competitors had trimmed the work force repeatedly since the stock market crash in 1987. But Bernstein felt that keeping all of her employees happy through good times and bad was more important than anything else.

In a speech that Bernstein delivered to all of Hanover's employees in 1991, she outlined the company's philosophy toward employee turnover: "You, the employees of Hanover are the most important asset that we have. Despite the difficult times this company now faces, you have my assurance that I will never ask any of you to leave for economic reasons. This is not General Motors!"

Corporate Communications at Hanover

The company relied on a small staff of public relations professionals to handle its communications efforts. All of the various activities that could be decentralized (such as employee communications, investor relations, etc.) were housed in the appropriate functional areas. This developed naturally as the company grew to become one of the largest software developers in the United States.

The young owner/chairwoman/CEO enjoyed lots of attention from the press as a result of her meteoric rise in the business world and her association with prominent Hollywood celebrities. She relied on an outside consultant, Todd McEwen, to handle her own public relations; he also had a tremendous amount of influence over the communications department at the company itself.

The vice-president of corporate communications, Cary Blandings, was actually one of the several employees who would be affected by the current plan to trim the work force. He had been hired early on as a favor to Bernstein's father. Blandings had spent 25 years at the *Los Angeles Times* before signing on at Hanover. The problems associated with Blandings made the communications effort more difficult for both Jan Barry and the outside counsel advising her through the process.

The VSI and Early Retirement Program

Although the CEO was very much against the two programs that were about to be implemented, she had been convinced by both Morse, the head of human resources, and her board of directors that something had to be done right away or the company itself would be at risk.

The way the programs would work, several senior managers would be told about the generous voluntary severance or early retirement packages and asked to avail themselves of the appropriate plan. Thus, a director who had received less than stellar performance appraisals for two consecutive years would be a prime candidate for voluntary severance while a vice president approaching 60 would be offered the retirement package. Although both of these programs were "voluntary," the supervisors responsible for identifying candidates were urged to get the right people to sign on immediately.

Communicating about the Plans

Barry reported to work the following day and was asked to attend a meeting with her boss, Bob Morse, Bernstein, and Todd McEwen. "Well Jan, how are you going to pull this one off?" joked Bernstein. "Quite honestly, Madeline, given your position on this issue, my feeling is that you need to get involved with the announcement tomorrow," responded Barry.

As the discussion progressed, however, it was obvious to Jan Barry that she was the one that her boss and the head of the company wanted to take the heat. After two hours, Bernstein looked at Jan squarely in the eye and said: "This was not my idea in the first place, but I know that we have no choice but to adopt the voluntary severance packages and early retirement plans for Hanover Software. Unfortunately, I need to leave the country for a conference in Brasilia the day after tomorrow. You and Bob are going to have to run with the ball this time."

Jan looked over at Bob. He was gazing at a drawing on Bernstein's wall. It was a picture of someone poised to lose his head during the French revolution. Somehow the tableau seemed very appropriate to the current situation.

---

* The name of the company, its industry, and characters have all been disguised.

9 WHAT TO DO WHEN IT HITS THE FAN

Unlike many of the other topics covered in this book, everyone can relate to the idea of a crisis. A close relative dies, our car is stolen, even a broken heart become crises in our personal life. Organizations face crises as well. The most widely known corporate crises even become international events: Jack in the Box's tainted meat, Exxon's *Valdez,* Perrier's benzene problem, Morton-Thiokol's Challenger explosion, Tylenol's cyanide-laced pills, Union Carbide's Bhophal tragedy, and Metropolitan Edison's Three Mile Island disaster all became huge media events as well as crises for the companies and people involved.

As recently as 20 years ago, such events would have received some national attention, but would have more likely been confined to the local and regional area where the events actually occurred. Today, however, as a result of changes in technology and the makeup of the media itself, any corporate crisis is bound to be covered within a matter of hours by the national and international media (the Cable News Network, CNN, being the primary source of information worldwide in English). Thus, a more sophisticated media environment has created the need for a more sophisticated response to crises.

In this chapter, we first define what constitutes a crisis. Next we turn to a discussion of several of the most prominent crises during the last decade. Once we know what crises are all about, we look at how organizations prepare. And finally, we offer some approaches for organizations to follow in times of trouble.

What Is a Crisis?

Imagine for a moment that you are sleeping in bed on a warm evening in Southern California. Suddenly, you feel the bed shaking, the light fixtures swaying, and the house wobbling. If you are from California, you know that you are in the middle of an earthquake; if you are from New England, however, you might think that the world is coming to an end. Or perhaps you are on your sailboat out for a leisurely sail on a sunny afternoon. Two hours later you discover that you have been having such a good time that you didn't notice yourself moving farther and farther away from shore into open ocean. In addition, a storm is forming on the horizon and the sun seems mysteriously to be setting a bit early today.

All of us would agree that these are definitely crises for the individuals involved. If the earthquake is "the big one" that we have heard about for the last decade, the devastation could be massive for both the individual involved and many more around her. If the sailor in the second scenario is a novice, the situation could also be devastating to whoever is on the boat.

Such unpredictable, *natural occurrences* constitute a crisis for individuals. But how do crises affect organizations? Organizations also face crises similar to the examples given above, that occur naturally: a hurricane rips through a town leveling the local waste management company's primary facility; the earthquake we imagined earlier turns the three biggest supermarkets in the area into piles of rubble; a ship is battered at sea by a storm and sinks with a load of cargo destined for a foreign market. None of these events can be planned for and all create havoc for the organizations involved.

Human-induced crises have also become as much of a problem as natural disasters for organizations. With technology moving faster than our ability to grasp the possible dangers associated with its development, the potential for disasters that will occur because of human error has increased dramatically as the 20th century draws to a close. Most of the examples mentioned earlier in the chapter, Bhopal, *Exxon Valdez,* and Tylenol were human-induced crises rather than natural disasters. Today, such crises can be bigger than natural disasters in terms of costs to the organization.

In addition, the perception among the general public is more likely to be negative for crises that could have been avoided, such as the *Exxon Valdez* accident, as opposed to one that the organization really had no control over, such as the destruction of supermarkets during an earthquake. In both cases, however, constituencies will look to the organization's response before making a final judgment about reactions to crises. Certainly, some human-induced crises, such as the Tylenol tragedy, have ended up increasing the overall credibility of the organization involved, while organizations involved in natural disasters, such as the mediocre response from insurance companies following the fires in Oakland, California and from the government following Hurricane Andrew in Florida in 1992, have lost credibility.

Thus, to define crisis for organizations today is a bit more complicated than simply saying that they are unpredictable, horrible events. For the purposes of this chapter, a crisis will be defined as follows:

> A *crisis* is a major catastrophe that may occur either naturally or as a result of human error. It can include tangible devastation, such as the destruction of lives or assets, or intangible devastation, such as the loss of an organization's credibility. In the latter case, the loss of credibility may be the result of management's response to tangible devastation or the result of human error.

Part of the problem in terms of dealing with crises is that organizations have tended to avoid any understanding of how vulnerable they are until after a major crisis occurs. This fits in with many of the other concepts that we have talked about throughout this book such as the way many corporations deal reactively with the media and other constituencies. Lack of preparation for potential crises can lead to further crisis, as we have seen, and thus the downward spiral continues to engulf organizations until someone finally realizes that mitigation is necessary to pull out of the crisis. Let's take a closer look at some major crises from the past decade to bring our definition to life.

Crises in the 1980s and 1990s

For my generation, the defining crisis of our time was the assassination of President John F. Kennedy on November 22, 1963. Virtually everyone who was alive at that time can remember what they were doing when the news that President Kennedy was shot was announced. Teenagers in the United States today probably feel the same way about the explosion of the space shuttle Challenger in January of 1986. These events have become etched in the public consciousness for a variety of reasons.

First, people tend to remember and be moved by negative news more than by positive news. Americans in particular seem to have a prurient interest in such negative news. Just take a look at the nightly news broadcasts of the three major networks to see what I mean. You rarely see "good" news pieces because they just don't sell to an audience that has become accustomed to the more dramatic events that come out of the prime time fare on television.

Second, the human tragedy associated with crises pulls at the heartstrings of us all. The death of innocent citizens at the hands of a sniper, a child accidentally buried in the ground, cross-country skiers lost in the Colorado Rockies—such events make people realize how vulnerable we all are and how quickly events can engulf innocent victims.

Finally, crises associated with major corporations stick in the public's mind because of the lack of goodwill associated with many organizations in the first place. A public that was already predisposed to hate big oil could not be completely surprised by what happened to the *Exxon Valdez*. They almost expected it to happen and delighted in the demise of the large conglomerate as much as they took sorrow in what the accident had done to the environment of one of the most pristine coastlines in the country. As we look at other major crises, we will start to see more clearly why these events stick in the American psyche for more than a short period of time.

Johnson & Johnson's Tylenol Recall

More has been written about this event in the press than any other story in the last 30 years with the exception of the Kennedy assassination according to analyst Marion Pinsdorff. The 1982 product tampering crisis for Johnson & Johnson somehow captured the imagination of the American public like no other crisis we have seen in the 80s and 90s. Why?

In late September and early October of 1982, seven people died after taking Tylenol capsules. The capsules had been laced with cyanide by someone who has never been captured. At the time, Tylenol had close to 40 percent of the over-the-counter market for pain relievers; within days, sales had dropped by close to 90 percent. Johnson & Johnson recalled over 22 million bottles soon after the tragedy came to light and began to bring back the franchise almost immediately.

Certainly the irony of something that is supposed to relieve pain turning into a killer was responsible for this event becoming so critical in the pantheon of crises. But many experts on crisis communication, marketing, and psychology have conjectured that Johnson & Johnson's incredible, caring response was more responsible for turning this tragedy into a plus for the company (despite losses exceeding $100 million, Tylenol came back stronger than ever within a matter of years).

What did Johnson & Johnson do? First, they didn't just react to what was happening. Instead, they took the offensive and removed the potentially deadly product from shelves. Second, they leveraged off of the goodwill they had taken years to build among constituencies ranging from doctors to the media and decided to try to save the brand rather than simply coming out with a new identity for the product. And third, they acted like responsible human beings concerned with life rather than simply looking at the incident from a purely legal or financial perspective.

Audi's Instant Acceleration Crisis

Compare the response from Johnson & Johnson with that of Audi America in 1987. Once a rising star in the high-end automobile market, the Audi, a German car known in the early 1980s for its superb engineering, lost ground to competitors following allegations in a *60 Minutes* broadcast that the company's Audi 5000 was accelerating on its own and creating havoc for drivers. The program showed upscale consumers telling horrible stores about their cars plunging through garage doors, careening into swimming pools, and in one case killing a young boy who was opening the garage door for his mother.

The company's response, which seems to have been developed by a combination of lawyers and engineers, was that the cars could not have been responsible for these accidents. Instead, the engineers claimed, in front of 24 million viewers, that drivers were simply putting their foot on the gas pedal instead of the brake! All of the evidence following years of investigation has shown that the engineers were in fact correct. But telling sophisticated, well-educated, upscale customers that in essence they were doing something very stupid did not play well in the court of public opinion.

Sales for all Audi cars dropped off so quickly that the company was forced to offer huge mark downs on the expensive vehicles and to give consumers three years of service for free as part of the deal. A more enlightened approach would have been to admit that something was happening in these cars and that the greatest automobile engineers in the world were studying the problem to ensure that no further accidents would happen. Given that only one product line, the Audi 5000 in its automatic transmission manifestation was involved, they could have recalled the cars, checked them to make sure they were all fine, and given drivers some assurances that the company had their best interests at heart.

In many cases, the notion that the company was not responsible gets lawyers thinking about liability avoidance rather than public opinion. Johnson & Johnson was probably not responsible for the Tylenol tampering just as Audi was probably not responsible for the instant acceleration of its 5000 series, yet the major difference in these two cases was in how the companies responded to external constituencies during a crisis. Johnson & Johnson took responsibility and Audi simply did not.

General Motors versus NBC

More recently, General Motors has been plagued with allegations that a line of its popular pickup trucks were exploding when hit by other vehicles. In early 1993, the company lost a case in Georgia and was forced to pay over $100 million in damages to the parents of a boy who died in such an accident. With hundreds of other suits pending, the company, beset with financial troubles from a host of other problems, went on the offensive when NBC ran a story on its *Dateline* program that showed a GM truck exploding on impact. The pickup trucks exploded, it turns out, because of an explosive device added by the network testers for effect.

GM was able to extract an unusual apology from NBC on the same program after negotiations between lawyers at GM and NBC's parent, General Electric. So, like Johnson & Johnson, the company didn't just sit back and go on the defensive. Smart, right? Wrong. Here is an example of weak communicators conspiring with lawyers and managers to attain what seemed like victory in the court of public opinion during a crisis. A closer look at this case, however shows just the opposite to be true.

First, unlike CBS's *60 Minutes,* NBC's *Dateline* was a fledgling effort with limited popularity—particularly among constituents that GM would be most interested in pursuing. By bringing a legal suit publicly against NBC, GM called more attention to the matter than they would have ever gotten by handling the case behind closed doors. As I mentioned earlier in the book, Americans have very short memories. What most people will take away from this incident is the memory of the exploding truck that we saw over and over again on newscasts for days on end rather than the awkward apology from NBC. Ironically, in the months following the apology, *Dateline* has continued to attract new viewers who first heard about the program thanks to GM.

These are just some of the other *major crises* that organizations faced in the 1980s and 90s:

- Tainted meat served at Jack in the Box restaurant kills two children in 1993.
- FDA attacks Dow Corning's breast implants in 1992.
- Bristol Myers's Sudafed is laced with cyanide and kills two in 1991.
- Benzene-tainted Perrier gets recalled in 1990.
- *Exxon Valdez* spills oil on the Alaska coastline in 1989 (see case on page 185).
- Pan Am jet explodes over Lockerbie, Scotland, in 1988.
- Sandoz Chemical plant accident contaminates Rhine River in 1987.
- Procter & Gamble logo linked to Satan in widespread rumors, 1986.
- Hyatt Regency hotel walkway collapses in Kansas City, 1985.
- Thousands die in explosion at Union Carbide plant in Bhopal, India, 1984.

How to Prepare for Crises

The first step in preparing for a crisis is understanding that any organization, no matter what industry or location, can find itself involved in the kinds of crises that we discussed in the last section. I took the most famous ones from the last 10 years, but those I have left out were just as devastating to the companies involved. Obviously some industries are more crisis-prone than others such as the chemical industry, pharmaceuticals, mining, forest products, and energy-related industries such as oil and gas and electric utilities. But every organization today is at risk.

Take, for example, the explosion that blew out three underground floors of the World Trade Center in New York in late February 1993. Over 50,000 people work in the twin towers and millions pass through the area each week. Only a handful of people were allowed back into the building two days after the blast (chosen by lottery) to gather up important papers and get individual businesses back on track. Large firms, such as the major accounting firm Deloitte & Touche, had moved their operations to another location within a couple of days. Others, however, found themselves virtually out of business until the building was officially opened again over a week later.

Preparation for such an event would help greatly. Unfortunately, many organizations probably have crisis plans for an evacuation from the World Trade Center now that the event has happened, but very few were prepared in advance. Communications managers must prepare management for the worst by using anecdotal information about what has happened to unprepared organizations in earlier crises. We have so many to choose from that managers should be able to find a plethora of crises in each industry from experiences over the last 10 years. Once the groundwork is laid for management to accept the notion that a crisis is a possibility, real preparation should take the following form.

Assess the Risk for Your Organization

As I mentioned earlier, some industries are more prone to crises than others. But how can organizations determine whether they are more or less likely to experience a crisis? First, publicly traded companies are at risk because of the nature of their relationship with a very important constituency, the shareholders. If a major catastrophe hits a company that trades on one of the stock exchanges, the chances of creating a run on the stock are enormous. Such immediate financial consequences can hurt the organization's image as a stable ongoing operation in addition to the crisis they must face.

Privately held companies do not have to worry about shareholders, but they do have to worry about the loss of goodwill, which can have an effect on sales, when a crisis hits. Often the owners of privately held companies become involved in communication during a crisis to lend their own credibility to the organization. So all organizations, public, private, and not-for-profit are at some risk if a crisis actually occurs. Let's see how you can plan for the worst no matter what.

First, the person in charge of corporate communications should call a *brainstorming session* that includes the most senior managers in the organization as well as the areas that are most likely to be affected by a crisis. For example, this would include the head of manufacturing in some cases because of potential for danger in the manufacturing process. It might also include the chief information officer because of the danger to computer systems when accidents happen. In the case of the explosion at the World Trade Center in 1993, most of the organizations were service organizations. After the loss of lives, the loss of critical information was one of the worst outcomes of the explosion.

During the brainstorming session, participants should be allowed a certain amount of time to develop ideas about potential crises. They should be encouraged to be as creative as possible during this stage. The facilitator should allow participants to say whatever they want, no matter how outrageous, to others in the room. This allows participants to come up with ideas without fear of being put down by other members of the brainstorming team.

Once the group has exhausted every possible idea, the facilitator should help the group to determine which of the ideas developed have the most potential to actually occur. It might be useful, for example, to ask the group to assign probabilities to the potential crises so that they can focus on the more likely scenarios rather than wasting time working through solutions to problems that have a very low probability of occurring. But even at this stage, participants must be very careful to determine risk based on normal expectations or what probabilities others have assigned to a crisis. The risk for an oil spill the size of the *Exxon Valdez* occurring was very low according to outside projections. Thus, neither the oil company nor governmental agencies prepared at all for the worst possible accident. Developing a risk assessment is a tricky part of the process.

Once the probability of risk has been assigned to potential crises, organizations need to determine *which constituencies would be most affected by the crisis.* Crisis communication experts spend too little time thinking about this question. Why is it so important? Since some constituencies are more important than others, organizations need to look at risk in terms of its effect on the most important constituents. For example, in the case of GM versus NBC, which we looked at earlier, if the company had looked at the crisis in terms of its effect on constituents they might have handled the problem differently.

Although their attack and subsequent victory against NBC (and its parent, General Electric) may have given them a short-term boost with employees and possibly shareholders, the attack probably hurt them with customers for pickup trucks who became even more aware of the potential problems associated with GM trucks. Certainly their relationship with the media, already one of the worst without doubt, was not helped nor was their relationship with General Electric.

It is very hard to make such determinations when the crisis actually happens because so many other things are going on. But thinking about risk in terms of effect on constituencies in advance helps the organization further refine which potential crises it should spend the most time and money preparing for. Once the ranking of risk is complete, the participants in a brainstorming session should start thinking about what their communication objective will be for each crisis and constituency.

Set Communication Objectives for Potential Crises

Setting communication objectives for potential crises is different than figuring out how to deal with the crisis itself. Clearly, organizations must do both, but typically managers are more likely to focus on what kinds of things they will do during a crisis rather than what they will say and to whom. Often the latter takes on more importance than the former when the crisis involves more intangible things such as the loss of goodwill rather than the loss of lives.

For example, the demise of investment bank Drexel Burnham Lambert in 1989–90 did not result in anyone's death, but communications experts at the firm realized early on that the organization would be hard pressed to continue operations without its star Michael Milken. Thus, while company lawyers worked long hours throughout the crisis to try to cut a deal with the government that would help both Milken and Drexel, they went public with a huge corporate advertising campaign aimed at employees and investors. No mention was ever made about the case against Milken and the firm. Instead the advertisements tried to point out what the "junk bonds" had done for businesses large and small throughout the 1980s.

Unfortunately for Drexel, the government's case and Milken's guilt were more than the firm could stand. But Drexel's corporate communications during its last two years in operation stand as some of the most innovative work that any organization has developed to date. The focus at the firm was on both trying to handle the crisis itself (which failed) and dealing with communications at the same time (which succeeded).

Assign Different Teams to Each Crisis

Another important part of planning for communicating in a crisis is determining in advance who will be on what team for each crisis. Different problems require different kinds of expertise, and planners should consider who is best suited to deal with one crisis versus another. For example, if the crisis is likely to have a financial focus, the chief financial officer may be the best person to lead a team dealing with such a problem. She may also be the best spokesperson when the problem develops. On the other hand, if the problem is more catastrophic, such as the incident involving tainted meat that Jack in the Box faced in 1993, the CEO is probably the best person to put in charge of the team and to serve as head spokesperson for the crisis. Given that the magnitude of the crisis in the second case is greater because of the potential loss of life, anyone other than the CEO will have less credibility with the general public and a media hungry for instant information.

But managers should avoid putting senior-level executives in charge of communications for all crises. Sometimes the person closest to the crisis is the one people want to hear from. For example, the best spokesperson for a multinational company may be someone on site in the country where the problem actually develops rather than a more senior manager from the head office. This has a lot to do with the culture of the nation involved, language differences, and a host of other considerations for multinationals.

Overall, assigning different teams to handle different crises helps the organization to put the best people in charge of handling the crisis and communications. It also allows the organization to get as many people involved as possible. The more involved managers are in planning and participating on a team in a crisis, the better equipped the organization will be to deal with things later on.

Planning for Centralization

Although organizations can deal with corporate communications using either a centralized or decentralized approach for general purposes (as we discussed in Chapter 3), when it comes to crisis, the approach must be completely centralized. This causes difficulty in decentralized organizations, especially if they have not given full consideration to it in the planning phase.

At General Electric, for example, which has a highly decentralized approach to corporate communications, changing to a centralized approach during a crisis will not happen naturally. Planning for centralization can help strip away layers of bureaucracy, keep lines of communications open throughout the organization, and dissipate conflict. Thus, a crisis at NBC, such as their encounter with GM mentioned earlier, should have involved a centralized team to deal with the legal and communications aspects of the problem. Published reports suggest the former involved centralization while the latter did not.

What to Include in a Formal Plan

Every communications consultant will suggest that you develop a detailed plan for use in a crisis. These are formal in the sense that they are typically printed up and passed around to the appropriate managers who may have to sign a statement swearing that they have read and agree to the plan. This allows the organization to ensure that the plan has been acknowledged by the recipient. The last thing you want to happen is for a plant manager to open the plan when a real crisis occurs having never seen it before. In this way, any disagreements can be cleared up before rather than during a crisis.

We looked over crisis plans from over 50 companies for a study that was conducted at the Tuck School and found the following information almost always included.

A List of Who to Notify in an Emergency

This gives the person involved the names and numbers of everyone on the crisis team as well as numbers to call externally such as the fire and police departments.

An Approach to Media Relations

Frank Corrado, an author who heads a firm that deals with crisis communications, suggests that the cardinal rule for all constituencies in a crisis should be "Tell it All, Tell it Fast!" To a certain extent this is true, but one should be extremely careful about applying such a rule too quickly to the media. Perhaps a friendly amendment to Corrado's rule might be to tell as much as you can as soon as possible without jeopardizing the credibility of the organization. If the organization has done a good job of building relations with the media when times are good, reporters will generally be very understanding when something horrible happens. Having a stash of goodwill with the media is what helped Johnson & Johnson during the Tylenol crisis. Generally, the person who has the best relationships with individual reporters is probably the best person to get involved with them during a crisis. By agreeing ahead of time that all inquiries will go to a central location, organizations can avoid looking like they are completely disorganized in a crisis.

A Strategy for Notifying Employees

Employees should be seen as analogous to families in a personal crisis. You wouldn't want a family member to hear about a personal problem from an outsider. Similarly, you do not want employees to find out from the media about something that affects the organization. Take pains to ensure that a plan for employee notification is worked out with human resource managers in advance and included in the overall crisis plan.

A Location to Serve as Crisis Headquarters

Although consultants and experts who have written about crises suggest that companies invest significant amounts of money for a special crisis center, all that companies need to do is identify an area that can easily be converted to such an operation ahead of time. In addition, consideration should be given to gathering the appropriate technology (e.g., fax machines, cellular phones, hookups for media transmissions) as quickly as possible when something bad happens. This headquarters location should be given to all internal and external constituencies that need to know ahead of time. All information ideally should be centralized through this office. Other lines of communication should then flow through the headquarters for the duration of the crisis.

A Description of the Plan

A detailed description of the approach developed during the brainstorming phase should also be included in the document. This would include more than just communication activities and would have the agreement of everyone involved ahead of time. Obviously what to include would depend on how complicated the crisis was thought to be and how much additional information (such as proprietary information) would need to be given to team members in a crisis.

Following the development of the overall plan, all managers should receive some kind of training about what to do when the inevitable happens. Several public relations firms and academic consultants now offer simulated crises that allow managers to test their crisis management skills in experiential exercises. Managers searching for the right training should be sure that the simulation or training session includes a heavy emphasis on communication rather than just the management of the crisis itself.

Communicating during the Crisis

All of the planning that an organization can muster will only partially prepare it for the actual crisis. The true measure of success is how it deals with the problem when it finally comes to pass. If the plan is comprehensive enough, managers will at least start from a strong position. These are the most important steps to follow in terms of communication during a crisis. Every crisis is different, which means that managers must adapt the suggestions below to meet their needs. But crises have enough common elements for us to offer the prescription to all as a starting point.

Step 1: Get Control of the Situation

The first step is for the appropriate manager to get control of the situation as soon as possible. Everyone in the organization should know who should be contacted when something happens, but in large organizations this is unrealistic. Therefore, the corporate communications department can serve as a clearing house initially. The vice president for corporate communications at the head office should know the composition of crisis teams and can turn the situation over to the appropriate manager immediately.

Step 2: Gather as Much Information as Possible

Understanding the problem at hand is the right place for communicators to begin dealing with a crisis. If it is an industrial accident, how serious is it? Were lives lost? Have families already been notified? If the accident involves an unfriendly takeover you need to know the details of the offer. Was it absurdly low? Have any plans been made to repel such an attack?

Many corporations have been criticized for reacting too slowly during a crisis because they were trying desperately to gather information about the incident. If it is going to take longer than a couple of hours to get the right information, communicators should communicate this to the media and other constituencies right away. No one will criticize you for trying to find out what is going on, but managers can face harsh treatment if constituencies think they are stonewalling during a crisis.

Step 3: Set up a Centralized Crisis Management Center

At the same time managers are getting in touch with the right people and gathering information, they should also be making arrangements for creating a crisis center as described earlier in this chapter. This location will serve as the platform for all communications during the crisis. Care should also be given to providing a comfortable location for media to use during the crisis. This would include adequate phone services, fax machines, and so on. All communications about the crisis should come from this one, centralized location.

Step 4: Communicate Early and Often

Say whatever you can as soon as possible. Particularly if the crisis involves threat to lives and property, communicators should try to avoid panic by allaying fears that people will inevitably have about the situation. Employees, the media, and other important constituencies should know that the crisis center will issue updates at regular intervals until further notice.

Step 5: Remember that Business Must Continue

To the managers involved the crisis will most certainly be uppermost in their minds for the duration, but to others, the business must go on despite the crisis. In addition to finding suitable replacements ahead of time for those who are on the crisis team, managers must try to anticipate the effects of the crisis on other aspects of business. For example, if an advertising campaign is underway, should it be stopped during the crisis? Have financial officers stopped trading on the company's stock? Will it be necessary for the organization to move to a temporary location during the crisis? These and other questions related to the ongoing business need to be thought through by managers on and off the crisis team as soon as possible.

Step 6: Make Plans to Avoid Another Crisis Immediately

Rather than resting on one's laurels, corporate communications executives should work with other managers to make sure that they will be better prepared the next time a crisis hits. Organizations that have experienced crises are more likely to believe that such occurrences will happen again. There is no time like the period immediately following a crisis when everyone is motivated to learn from the mistakes you made the first time.

Conclusion

We all know that crises are a normal part of our private lives. Managers must realize that the same is now true for organizations. Unfortunately, the short-term orientation of most managers today prevents them from acknowledging the risk to every organization. An antiterrorist task force for the World Trade Center told the Port Authority eight years before the devastating blast in February 1993 that the center's parking garage was vulnerable to a bomb attack and should be closed to the public (according to press reports following the blast). Ignoring the advice of experts ended up costing people's lives, millions of dollars, and the disruption of hundreds of businesses. Getting senior managers to pay attention may be the most important part of crisis communication before rather than after a crisis develops.

CASE
EXXON U.S.A.

Frank Iarossi, a senior executive for Exxon, was sleeping soundly in his bed in a Houston suburb when the phone jarred him awake in the middle of the night on March 23, 1989. A frantic voice on the other end was the first he would hear about an oil spill that would become one of the worst crises in the history of American business. "Mr. Iarossi, there's been an accident up in Alaska," said the voice on the other end. "Lots of oil was spilled over on Bligh Reef, clean up hasn't even started yet. Someone from Houston is going to have to get out here real fast." As Iarossi put down the phone, a nauseous feeling began to rise up in his stomach. Just how bad was the spill? Who was responsible? And, most important of all, how should the company respond?

Exxon History

In the mid-1800s, a flood in the petroleum market sent the prices from $20 a barrel in 1859 to 10 cents in 1861. John D. Rockefeller saw that the future of the industry depended on orderly production, transportation, and refining practices. Rockefeller started a small oil refinery in Cleveland in 1863, and seven years later formed the Standard Oil Company, incorporated in Ohio. The name Standard represented high, uniform quality. The company grew into a huge complex of refining, pipeline, and marketing organizations. Since states outlawed one company from owning shares of another, Rockefeller and his partners founded the Standard Oil Trust in 1882.

In that same year he formed the Standard Oil Company of New Jersey, a refining and marketing organization, as an operating arm of the trust. This company would bear the name Standard Oil (New Jersey) from 1892 to 1972. In 1911, a court-ordered dissolution broke the oil trust into 34 separate companies. Eight of these companies chose to keep the Standard Oil name. The negative public image of the Standard Oil monopoly remained with its name, and Standard Oil (New Jersey) carried that burden as the largest of the eight companies.

For 60 years following the breakup, salesmen of the Standard Oil Company (NJ) sold their products under trademarks that included Esso, Enco, and Humble, but longed for a single name under which to market their product. Standard Oil (NJ) and its affiliates took a momentous step in 1972 when they gave up their well-known trademarks to become the Exxon Corporation. Although Exxon registered the name in countries across the globe, it continued to retain the Esso trademark outside of the United States because there was no compelling reason to abandon the well-known Esso name abroad.

Leaving the Port of Valdez

As crewmen loaded the *Exxon Valdez* almost to capacity on the evening of March 23, 1989, the ship's captain, Joseph Hazelwood, went ashore with the chief engineer and radio electronics officer. The three men conducted some official business, ran personal errands, and met at a bar in the late afternoon. They played darts with local residents and each purchased one or more rounds of drinks. The radio electronics officer stated that he drank beer while Hazelwood consumed a "clear" beverage, and the chief engineer drank gin and tonic. The chief engineer said that he had three gin and tonics and did not recall how much Hazelwood had.

After about four hours at the bar, they ordered pizzas from a local pizza parlor and each had another drink. The radio electronics officer believes that Hazelwood drank a vodka while they waited for their pizza. The cab driver who drove the group back to the ship claims that no one seemed to be "under the influence of alcohol."

The state employs pilots to navigate vessels out of the Port of Valdez. The pilot who navigated the *Exxon Valdez* on the night of March 23rd stated that he smelled alcohol on the captain's breath upon his return from town, but his behavior and speech seemed unimpaired. The captain left the bridge soon after the ship began its journey and returned an hour and a half later when the pilot disembarked at Rocky Point. The pilot again smelled alcohol on Hazelwood's breath, but saw no signs of impairment.

There were heavy ice floes in both the inbound and outbound traffic lanes on the night of March 23, 1989 as the *Exxon Valdez* attempted to pass through the Valdez Arm. Hazelwood had two choices: he could slow down and navigate the ship through the ice field or navigate around the ice and pass within a half a mile of Bligh Reef. He decided to cross the traffic lanes and avoid the ice. Darkness posed difficulties for navigating through ice and passing near Bligh Reef posed a hazard only if there were either a propulsion or steering malfunction or a navigation error.

As the ship approached the waterway bordered by heavy ice on one side and Bligh Reef on the other side, Hazelwood asked the third mate if he felt comfortable navigating alone. Even though the third mate had performed excessive work and received little sleep in the past 24 hours, he felt comfortable navigating the ship around the ice. Hazelwood reportedly left the bridge to attend to administrative duties.

Hazelwood knew the area well and could have had an accurate mental picture that would have allowed him to visualize the vessel's movements around the reef. It would have taken him 20 minutes to maneuver the vessel safely around the reef, and he would have had 2 hours to finish his other duties before returning to port.

In addition, according to the *Exxon Bridge Organization Manual,* the captain or the chief mate was required to be on the bridge given the dangerous situation. Since the chief mate had worked long hours earlier, it was Hazelwood's obligation to be on the bridge. According to federal regulations, a federal pilot had to be in charge of a vessel's navigation in those waters, and Hazelwood was the only officer on board who possessed the required federal pilotage endorsement.

Background on Joseph Hazelwood

Hazelwood grew up on Long Island, drawn to the sea from an early age. As a teenage member of the Sea Scouts, he distinguished himself for calm and courage by climbing the 50 foot mast of a schooner to haul in a mainsail blown out by a violent storm. He attended New York's Maritime College, an elite and rigorous state school run in the Bronx. People remember him starting to drink there. Later he developed a reputation as a hard drinker among some of his fellow sailors, who also said that he always knew when to stop so his performance would not be seriously impaired.

He was one of a select group of his Maritime College classmates hired by Esso. His first commanding officer Steve Brelsford claimed Hazelwood had a sixth sense about seafaring that enabled him to smell a storm on the horizon or watch the barometer and figure how to out maneuver it.

Exxon, however, issued a 1982–83 review of officer performance on Hazelwood that recommended he be reassigned to shore duty. This appraisal was never signed or forwarded to Exxon headquarters for review.

In 1985 Hazelwood captained the *Exxon Chester* through a freak storm of 30-foot waves and 50-knot winds. The radar and electronics gear went out, and some of the crew were ready to abandon ship. Hazelwood calmed them, rigged a makeshift antenna, and guided the ship back to port.

He was arrested for drunk driving in 1984 in Huntington, New York. Hazelwood entered a rehabilitation program after that on the advice of his Exxon supervisor, Captain Mark Pierce. Hazelwood was put on 90-day leave after the arrest. Company records at Exxon show Hazelwood as "depressed and demoralized . . . that he had been drinking excessively and episodically resulting in familial and vocational dysfunction."

In May of 1985 Exxon administrative manager Ben Graves wrote a memo to Exxon's legal department reporting that Hazelwood had admitted returning to ships in port "in an intoxicated state on several occasions, and that shipmates . . . reported he had violated company alcohol policy on at least several occasions."

By 1988 Hazelwood had resumed heavy drinking and his 20-year marriage was on the rocks. Between 1984–1989, his driver's license was suspended three times for drunk driving violations. The Coast Guard renewed Hazelwood's shipmaster certification without checking his car driving record.

One crewman recalled that two months before the spill, Hazelwood invited him into his cabin "to destroy a bottle." "It's almost like Joe was trying to get caught," said a good friend of Hazelwood's. "He'd close his door, but everyone knew what went on. He would always say that everything was fine, but then why was he drinking? The guy was begging for help, but he kept it all inside."

The Seven Sisters

Seven giant corporations—Exxon, Shell, BP, Gulf, Texaco, Mobil, and Socal (Chevron)—have had a strong hand in the control of the world's oil supply since the early 1900s. Like the classical sisters in ancient mythology, these Seven Sisters, as they were called as early as 1913, seemed to have achieved immortality. They were the first of the global giants. They had larger incomes than many of the small nations in which they operated.

Exxon's 1973 annual report claimed, "Exxon was a multinational corporation at least 50 years before that term was commonly used." The Seven Sisters, led by the two largest, Exxon and Shell, strove to be self-sufficient oil companies whose oil could flow into their tankers through their refineries to their filling stations.

As the unopposed leaders of the oil trade through the 1960s, the Seven Sisters had an image of permanence and stability that "commanded the awe of governments and publics." The 1970s, however, saw a dramatic shift in the balance of power. Unlike the 1960s, demand began to meet and surpass supply. Oil had become the lifeblood of world energy, and surpluses became a thing of the past. Free-world petroleum demand rose from 19 million barrels a day in 1960 to more than 40 million barrels per day in 1970. Wells in the Middle East satisfied two thirds of this increased consumption and led to a dependence on Middle Eastern oil. In addition, the devaluation of the American dollar gave power to the sellers in the Middle East.

The Oil Crisis

The first challenge to the absolute power of the Seven Sisters came from Libya in 1969. At that time, Libya supplied one quarter of Western Europe's oil. As the cheapest oil to transport after the closing of the Suez Canal, Libyan oil was desirable to the profit-hungry corporations. However, Libya received no extra concessions for their cheaper oil. When Colonel Qadaffi came to power in 1969, he threatened to cut back production if prices were not raised. The companies attempted to stand firm on their prices, but eventually Libya forced them to concede to a 30 cent increase in the posted price and a hike in Libya's share of profit from 50 to 55 percent.

The Libyan crisis set off an avalanche among the oil-producing countries and began to shift the balance of power from the buyers to the sellers. It began not only a retreat by the companies, but a seller's campaign to maintain sovereignty and control over their oil resources.

Earlier, in 1960, oil-producing countries in the Middle East had formed the Organization of Petroleum Exporting Countries (OPEC) to help defend their oil interests. However, OPEC had little power in the 1960s with the oil surplus and dominance of the giant oil companies. The Middle East was now, however, in a position to use their "oil weapon" to achieve both economic and political goals. Some politicians believed that they wanted to use oil to restrict American support of Israel. They also thought the Middle Eastern countries hoped to capture the "windfall profits" of the oil companies.

In 1973, war in the Middle East broke out, and OPEC began demanding a 100 percent increase in the price of oil. The oil companies consulted with the governments of the major consuming nations and together rejected the demand as outrageous

The Oil Embargo

OPEC's power rose in the 1970s, and in September 1973, the organization announced an oil embargo as a political move against Israel. Initially, OPEC's embargo cut back oil shipments by 5 percent every month. Only "friendly states" could maintain their levels of buying. After the United States announced a $2.2 billion military aid package for Israel, the Arab states declared an embargo on all oil shipments to the United States. The price of oil quadrupled in just two months and placed

the oil trade in the hands of 11 countries, not seven companies.

The embargo put the Seven Sisters in a challenging position. They had to allocate their oil in a way that would not appear to defy the Arabs' boycott, yet would satisfy their customers throughout the world. And the American companies had to enforce an embargo of their own home country. Some people began to question the true loyalties of the companies.

The dramatic increase in the price of oil shocked the American public. Some people accused the companies of deliberately plotting the oil crisis and joining the Arab cartel to raise the price of oil. A public opinion poll showed that most people placed the blame for the energy crisis on the companies more than the Arabs. The companies seemed to buffer much of the anger that the public would have directed at the Middle East.

At the height of the oil shortage, Exxon announced record-breaking profits. Profits were up 80 percent in 1973 to give Exxon profits that exceeded those of any other corporation up to that time: $2.5 billion. Exxon and other oil companies explained that profits had previously been too low because they needed the profits for the development of future energy resources. For example, Mobil advertised, "We're recycling the money he pays at the pump right back into oil-finding offshore, Alaska, anywhere." However, the companies could not convince the energy-starved public so easily.

At the end of the embargo in 1974, Washington made many attempts to break the oil cartel and bring down the price of oil. The economy was in the midst of a recession and high inflation that could partially be attributed to high energy costs. By 1975, consumers had cut back enough so that supply began to exceed demand again and economists predicted the fall of OPEC. However, the Middle Eastern countries simply cut their production and maintained their fixed prices.

Iran–Iraq War

The outbreak of war between Iran and Iraq in the late 1970s brought further havoc to the oil industry. It initially removed 8 percent of the free world demand for oil from the market and fear drove prices to an all time high. As prices and profits rose, oil companies sank large sums into new development. The frantic pace caused costs to rise out of control throughout the industry. Exxon spent over a billion dollars in 1980 on the Colony Shale Oil Project, which it had to abandon two years later due to the rising costs of the project and the falling price of oil.

High prices forced the public to make deeper cuts in consumption to lower their energy costs and lessen their dependence on the Middle East. Long lines at filling stations, fuel shortages, and angry consumers again plagued the oil industry. An agreement was reached in 1981 that brought prices down and ended the last large rise in oil prices of the 1980s as the laws of supply and demand gained control over prices.

Oil Prices Return To Normal

After 1983, the world saw a dramatic reduction in oil costs primarily due to reduced dependence on Middle Eastern oil. Development in other countries, including the United States, flourished. Many turned to alternative, cheaper sources of energy. In addition, the industrialized nations moved toward conservation and higher efficiency. By 1985, the United States was 32 percent more oil efficient than it had been in 1973. These three trends reduced the demand on OPEC oil by 13 million barrels per day, a fall of 43 percent from 1979 levels.

Oil Shock

In late 1985, a third oil shock hit the world that reduced prices to as low as $6 per barrel from over $30 per barrel. The surplus in demand had created a war for market share among the oil producing countries. In late 1986, the leaders of OPEC ended the low prices. They established a price of $18 per barrel and instituted a quota system to support this price. Although prices fluctuated between $15–$18, this agreement remained solid through the 1980s. These prices reflected pre-1979 levels and therefore wiped out the increases of the early 80s.

Development in Alaska

The interest in Alaskan oil began as early as 1923 when President Warren Harding set up a naval petroleum reserve on the Arctic coast of Alaska. Wildcatters poked around the region and big oil companies began to take a larger interest following the Suez Crisis in the mid-1950s. Many companies sought to relieve their dependence on Middle Eastern oil, but had to give up after drilling many expensive dry holes in the frigid climate of northern Alaska. Exxon began drilling in 1956, but suspended operations just three years later after drilling the most expensive dry hole ever drilled up to that time.

Richfield, a California independent, continued to investigate the Alaska region and Exxon became Richfield's partner through its Humble Oil subsidiary in 1964. Richfield merged with Atlantic refining to become Atlantic Richfield, or ARCO. ARCO and Humble continued to drill expensive dry holes in Alaska and their final, risky attempt was at Prudhoe Bay on the north coast in 1966. Many had their doubts and ARCO's head later stated, "It was more a decision not to cancel a well already scheduled than to go ahead." In 1967, they began drilling the Prudhoe Bay State well, which would be their last attempt in Alaska if it failed.

In December of 1967, they struck oil in the largest oil field ever discovered in North America. Prudhoe Bay would not destroy oil prices, but it would have the potential to slow American dependence on the Middle East and "reduce dramatically the tautness in the global oil balance."

The Big Three on the North Slope were ARCO, Exxon, and BP. Experts suggested that Prudhoe Bay could become the third-largest producing field in the world. The harsh physical environment of Alaska presented their only large obstacle. Technology had to be developed to drill and produce in such a frigid area with such extensive permafrost. The lack of roads and ice-filled waters also presented a transportation problem.

The Pipeline

After much debate, a pipeline seemed to be the best answer. One idea was an 800-mile pipeline south across Alaska to the port of Valdez where the oil could then be shipped through the Prince William Sound to markets in America or abroad. Many suggested building a pipeline across Canada into Chicago, but the idea was discarded for the "all-American route" which would be more secure and could add flexibility. In addition, the Canadian government frowned on the idea and such an extensive pipeline would take longer to build than a trans-Alaska pipeline.

In 1970, the major companies involved in the pipeline construction, including the Exxon Pipeline Company, incorporated the Alaska Pipeline Service after a joint venture the previous year. When the *Exxon Valdez* ran aground, British Petroleum owned 50 percent, Exxon and ARCO owned about 20 percent each, while Amerada Hess, Mobil, Phillips Petroleum, and Unocal all held smaller stakes.

However, the barriers to the trans-Alaskan pipeline were many. In addition to the technological building problems, the oil companies had to contend with Eskimos, Alaska natives, and environmentalists. The 1969 Santa Barbara oil spill energized environmentalists to win a federal court injunction in 1970 that blocked the building of the pipeline. They claimed that the companies were moving too quickly without sufficient understanding and caution.

The oil companies underestimated their opposition and spent $75 million on equipment to build the roads and lay the pipes. That equipment remained frozen on the banks of the Yukon River until the injunction was lifted five years later as an emergency measure after the oil embargo. By 1977, over a million barrels a day were flowing through the pipeline and over the following two years that amount grew to two million barrels, a quarter of America's total crude oil production. By 1977, the total cost of the pipeline system had reached $8 billion.

Running Aground

According to the third mate, the following events led up to the grounding on Bligh Reef. As the ship approached the Busby Island Light, the third mate shifted the steering from automatic pilot to hand steering. He gave orders to the helmsman for a 10-degree right turn of the rudder, which would gradually turn the ship and return it to the traffic lane. He telephoned Hazelwood that the ship had begun to turn and the ship should pass safely through the ice.

After 1.5 minutes, he noticed that the ship had not turned and ordered a 20-degree right turn of the rudder. After another two minutes, he ordered a hard right turn, recognized that the vessel was in danger, and telephoned Hazelwood to say that they were in "serious trouble." At the end of the phone conversation, the third mate felt the vessel contact the bottom.

The Alcohol Problem

The investigating officers who boarded the ship three hours after the accident detected a strong smell of "stale" alcohol on the captain's breath. When questioned about his drinking, Hazelwood responded that he drank two non-alcoholic beers while the vessel was at sea. The officers later found the two empty bottles in the captain's stateroom. The investigating officers requested toxicological testing of the ship's personnel, but had trouble obtaining the proper equipment. When proper equipment was located aboard the ship 10 hours after the accident, urine samples were taken from the third mate, helmsman, and lookout. The captain did not provide a urine sample because he was unable to urinate.

One half hour later, a medical technician boarded the ship to take blood samples. The captain provided the first blood sample and also gave a urine sample. Analysis of the samples found .06 percent ethanol in the captain's blood and .01 percent in the urine. No traces of alcohol were found in samples provided by other crew members.

Assuming that Hazelwood did not consume alcohol after the accident, calculations show that Hazelwood's blood alcohol concentration (BAC) level could have been around .27 percent at the time of the accident. This concentration is higher than when he was arrested for drunk driving in 1988 with a BAC of .19 percent. The arresting officer reported that he smelled strongly of alcohol, had difficulty getting his driver's license out of his wallet, and was unsteady on his feet. In most states, a driver is charged with drunk driving if his BAC is above .1 percent.

An Exxon policy dated March 1987 prohibited the use, possession, distribution, or sale of drugs and alcohol on company premises. Coast Guard regulation states that a person operating a vessel other than a recreational vessel is intoxicated when (1) the person has a BAC of .04 percent or (2) the person is operating any vessel and the effect of the intoxicant(s) on the person's manner, disposition, speech, muscular movement, general appearance, or behavior is apparent by observation.

It also states that a crew member shall not perform or attempt to perform any scheduled duties within four hours of consuming any alcohol. The marine employer is responsible for ensuring compliance with this rule.

Media Coverage of the Oil Industry

In the late 1970s, oil companies were heavy users of corporate advertising. They promoted their virtues with issue ads rather than their product. For example, Texaco ran environmental and energy crisis ads throughout the 1970s. Only Mobil, however, maintained a steady commitment to issue advertising through the 1980s with their frequent advertisements in national magazines and the op-ed pages of major newspapers.

Despite these efforts, in the 1980s, many of the oil giants did not have a strong image with the American public. "Oil companies are held in remarkably low esteem," said James Foster, president and chief executive officer of Brouillard Communications in New York. "People don't know who they are or what they stand for. A shroud of mystery surrounds them, and it translates into a negative perception. . . . Since the embargo days, the oil industry has gone into a shell and has not told their story very well. They consequently had very little reputation or equity to fall back on when they ran into problems. They've become invisible, and it's catching up to them."

Communications at Exxon

Although Exxon was one of the largest corporations in the world at the time of the spill, Exxon USA's office in Houston was equipped with only one man and an answering machine to respond to the crisis on March 23, 1989. Despite this, Frank Iarossi had to come up with a plan for dealing with the crisis in terms of the spill itself and how the company would communicate with several different constituencies.

BIBLIOGRAPHY

Chapter 1

Brown, M. *Laying Waste.* New York: Washington Square Press, 1981.
Burrough, B. and J. Helyar. *Barbarians at the Gate.* New York: Harper & Row, 1990.
Chernow, R. *The House of Morgan.* New York: Atlantic Monthly Press, 1990.
Lewis, M. *Liar's Poker.* New York: W. W. Norton, 1989.
Peters, T. J. and R. H. Waterman. *In Search of Excellence.* New York: Harper & Row, 1982.
Stewart, J. *Den of Thieves.* New York: Simon & Schuster, 1991.
Thomas, G. and M. Morgan-Witts. *The Day the Bubble Burst.* Garden City: Doubleday, 1979.
Wilson, S. *The Man in the Gray Flannel Suit.* New York: Arbor House, 1955.
Wolfe, T. *The Bonfire of the Vanities.* New York: Farrar, Straus & Giroux, 1987.
Yergin, D. *The Prize.* New York: Simon & Schuster, 1990.

Chapter 2

Alinsky, S. *Rules for Radicals.* New York: Vintage Books, 1972.
Aristotle, trans. by J. Freese. *The "Art" of Rhetoric.* Cambridge: Harvard University Press, 1926.
Minto, B. *The Pyramid Principle: Logic in Writing and Thinking,* 2nd ed. London: Minto International, 1978.
Munter, M. *Guide to Managerial Communication,* 3rd ed. Englewood Cliffs: Prentice Hall, 1982.
Porter, M. *Competitive Strategy.* New York: The Free Press, 1980.
Quinn, J. *Strategies for Change.* Homewood: Richard D. Irwin, 1980.

Chapter 3

Bishop R. *Public Relations: A Comprehensive Bibliography.* Ann Arbor: A. G. Leigh-James, 1972.
Center, A. and F. Walsh. *Public Relations Practices,* 2nd ed. Englewood Cliffs: Prentice Hall, 1981.
Corrado, F. *Media for Managers.* Englewood Cliffs: Prentice Hall, 1984.
Hellriegel, D.; J. Slocum; and R. Woodman. *Organizational Behavior,* 6th ed. St. Paul: West Publishing, 1992.
Kotter, J. and J. Heskett. *Corporate Culture and Performance.* New York: The Free Press, 1992.

Lesly, P., editor. *Lesly's Public Relations Handbook,* 3rd ed. Englewood Cliffs: Prentice Hall, 1983.

Martin, J. *Cultures in Organizations.* New York: Oxford University Press, 1992.

Nowlan, S. and D. Shayan. *Leveraging the Impact of Public Affairs.* Philadelphia: HRN, 1984.

Peake, J. *Public Relations in Business.* New York: Harper & Row, 1980.

Reilly, R. *Public Relations in Action.* Englewood Cliffs: Prentice Hall, 1981.

Simon, R. *Public Relations,* 2nd ed. Columbus: Grid Publishing, 1980.

Chapter 4

Argenti, P. "Managing Corporate Identity," *Design Management Journal.* Winter 1991, 52–58.

Argenti, P.; R. Hansen; and S. Neslin. "The Name Game: How Corporate Name Changes Affect Stock Price," *Tuck Today.* Winter 1988.

Forty, A. *Objects of Desire.* New York: Pantheon Books, 1986.

French, J. and B. Raven. "The Bases of Social Power." In *Studies in Social Power,* ed. D. Cartwright. Ann Arbor: University of Michigan Press, 1959.

Garbett, T. *How to Build a Corporation's Identity and Project Its Image.* Lexington: Lexington Books, 1988.

Kotter, J. *Power and Influence.* New York: The Free Press, 1985.

Lorenz, C. *The Design Dimension.* Oxford: Basil Blackwell, 1986.

Olins, W. *Corporate Identity.* London: Thames & Hudson, 1989.

Chapter 5

Alvarez, P. "Corporate Advertising Survey: Magazines, TV Top '90 Media Lists," *Public Relations Journal.* September 1991, 14–19.

Garbett, T. *Corporate Advertising.* New York: McGraw-Hill, 1981.

Garbett, T. "When to Advertise Your Company," *Harvard Business Review.* March-April 1982, 100–106.

Hartigan, M. and P. Finch. "The New Emphasis on Strategy in Corporate Advertising," *Business Marketing.* February 1986, 42–49.

Kelley, D. "Critical Issues for Issue Ads," *Harvard Business Review.* July-August 1982, 80–88.

Kotler, P. *Marketing Management,* 7th ed. Englewood Cliffs: Prentice Hall, 1991.

Rothschild, M. *Marketing Communications.* Lexington: D. C. Heath, 1987.

Schumann, D.; J. Hathcote; and S. West. "Corporate Advertising in America: A Review of Published Studies on Use, Measurement, and Effectiveness," *Journal of Advertising.* September 1991, 35–56.

Winters, L. "The Effect of Brand Advertising on Company Image: Implications for Corporate Advertising," *Journal of Advertising Research.* April-May 1986, 54–59.

Chapter 6

Arlen, M. *The Camera Age: Essays on Television*. New York: Farrar, Straus & Giroux, 1981.

Aronoff, C., editor. *Business and the Media*. Santa Monica: Goodyear Publishing, 1979.

Banks, L. "Taking on the Hostile Media," *Harvard Business Review*. March-April 1978, 125.

Burger, C. "How to Meet the Press," *Harvard Business Review*. July-August 1975, 62–70.

Corrado, F. *Media for Managers*. Englewood Cliffs: Prentice Hall, 1984.

Hewitt, D. *Minute by Minute*. New York: Random House, 1985.

Howard, C. and W. Matthews. *On Deadline: Managing Media Relations*. New York: Longman, 1985.

Munter, M. "How to Conduct a Successful Media Interview," *California Management Review*, Summer 1983, 143–150.

Sandman, P. et al. *Media: An Introductory Analysis of American Mass Communications*, 3rd ed. Englewood Cliffs: Prentice Hall, 1982.

Simons, H. and J. Califano, Jr. *The Media and Business*. New York: Vintage Books, 1979.

Chapter 7

Amen, R. "How to Whet Investor Appetites in the Institutional, Global Markets of the 1990s," *Cash Flow Magazine*. June 1989.

Garbett, T. *How to Build a Corporation's Identity and Project Its Image*. Lexington: Lexington Books, 1988.

Graves, J. *Managing Investor Relations*. Homewood: Dow Jones-Irwin, 1982.

Marcus, B. *Competing for Capital in the '80s: An Investor Relations Approach*. Westport: Quorum Books, 1983.

Roalman, A. *Investor Relations Handbook*. New York: AMACOM, 1974.

Wilson, M. *The Corporate Investor Relations Function*. Ann Arbor: UMI Research Press, 1980.

Chapter 8

Aldrich, H. *Organization and Environments*. Englewood Cliffs: Prentice Hall, 1979.

Gordon, J. *Human Resource Management*. Boston: Allyn & Bacon, 1986.

Jablin, F.; L. Putnam; K. Roberts; and L. Porter. *Handbook of Organizational Communication*. Newbury Park: Sage Publications, 1987.

Pfeffer, J. *Power in Organizations*. Marshfield: Pitman, 1980.

Troy, K. "Employee Communication: Top Management Priority," Report 919. New York: The Conference Board, 1988.

Chapter 9

Barton, L. *Crisis in Organizations: Managing and Communicating in the Heat of Chaos*. Cincinnati: Southwestern Publishing, 1993.

D'Aveni, R. "Crisis and the Content of Managerial Communications: A Study of the Focus of Attention of Top Managers in Surviving and Failing Firms," *Administrative Science Quarterly*. 35, 634–657.

Davidson, A. *In the Wake of the Exxon Valdez*. San Francisco: Sierra Club Books, 1990.

Meyers, G. *When It Hits the Fan—Managing the Nine Crises of Business*. Boston: Houghton Mifflin, 1986.

Mitroff. "Crisis Management: Cutting Through the Confusion," *Sloan Management Review*. Winter 1988.

Pinsdorf, M. *Communicating When Your Company Is Under Siege*. Lexington: Lexington Books, 1987.

Shrivastava, P. *Bhopal: Anatomy of a Crisis*. Cambridge: Ballinger, 1987.